Problem-Solving Strategies for Writing

Linda Flower

Carnegie-Mellon University

Problem- Solving Strategies for Writing

 Harcourt Brace Jovanovich, Inc.

New York / San Diego / Chicago / San Francisco / Atlanta London / Sydney / Toronto

To my father, Oren W. Stevenson,

with appreciation

ISBN: 0-15-571983-1

Library of Congress Catalog Card Number: 80-83460

Printed in the United States of America

Preface

This book, appropriately enough, started as an attempt to solve a problem. I was asked to design a writing program for a group of pragmatists—students who would attend a noncredit course if they felt it would make a difference in the academic and professional writing they were doing outside the course. They expected substantive instruction in *how* to write, not just in how to analyze a piece of writing. I soon realized that their questions were the same ones I wanted to answer for myself: What are the principles that underlie the act of effective writing? What are some of the more intelligent strategies for tackling common writing problems? I also found that my traditional background in literary criticism and rhetorical analysis of the final text simply hadn't told me enough about how good writers actually went about producing the thoughtful and effective prose I admired.

My growing awareness of these gaps in our knowledge led me into two quite different kinds of research. I wanted first of all to translate some of the product-based wisdom of rhetoric and composition into a more process-based approach to writing. Instead of defining what a well-organized essay looks like, I wanted to show how one would go about the process of making it organized. And I wanted to offer my students the best principles that were known on writing for readers in the real world. Such writing, as I conceive it, goes beyond traditional persuasion and means helping readers to comprehend and remember fully what you have to say. This book, then, is a process-based rhetoric: an attempt to look at the traditional topics of invention or discovery, arrangement, and style—as well as audience analysis and persuasion—from the writer's point of view. Many rhetoricians from Aristotle on, and especially the creators of the "new" rhetoric, have looked at their art as a process of discovery, deliberation, and choice. This rhetorical tradition of teaching writing as intellectual discovery has a great deal to offer students. One of the goals of this book, then, was to translate our knowledge of effective written products into a description of the process that could produce them.

Translation, however, was finally not enough. In trying to offer my students (and myself) more than traditional "good advice" about writing, I discovered how little we really know about the thinking process writers go through. And we know even less about the differences in how good and poor writers handle this process. It seemed that the only obvious response to this problem was research on composing itself. John R. Hayes, of Carnegie-Mellon University, had also become interested in this problem. As a cognitive psychologist studying creativity and problem-solving, he too was asking such questions as "What do writers actually do?" and "How can they learn to do it better?" At that time he had just started a book (The Complete Problem Solver) based on a university-wide course he had developed that focused on general problem-solving skills. We were curious: Were there useful connections between writing and other basic thinking processes such as decision-making, learning, and remembering?

Cognitive psychology is, of course, a young field—a reaction, in part, against the assumptions of behaviorism. In the tradition of William James, it is concerned with the process of cognition and, like the field of English, with the nature and process of creative thought. Many of the ideas in this book, then, are the result of my happy and continuing research collaboration with John Hayes and have been influenced by the example of his constantly inquiring mind. Our objective has been to make unconscious actions a little more conscious: to give writers a greater awareness of their own intellectual processes, and therefore the power and possibility of conscious choice.

This book combines traditional rhetorical concerns with current research in composition—in an effort to create a rhetoric of the writing process. This means offering writers a set of principles and strategies for planning discourse, for generating and organizing ideas, and for designing and editing their prose for a reader. More broadly, it means showing writers how their own intellectual processes are an important part of effective writing.

This book is written for people with realistic reasons for writing: students writing themes, term papers, and reports on academic subjects; professionals writing memos and reports as a part of their job; and people in any field who simply have something to say. It is also written for people who want to know *why*. Many approaches to composition offer the student a wealth of practical but largely ad hoc advice on how to compose. I have tried to speak to writers who want to know the principle behind the practice and who, like me, would like to understand more of their own thinking processes.

The first chapter of the book is an overview of the kinds of writing people do. It looks at examples of academic, professional, and personal writing and introduces two major concepts that run throughout the book: writing for the reader and hierarchical organization. The second chapter extends this introduction by describing one of the basic processes that underlies most expository writing: analyzing a problem. It leads the student through the stages of problem analysis, moving from awareness of a problematic situation to a problem definition to a thesis. Many approaches to composition start with the injunction to "find a thesis." In essence, this chapter describes the process of analysis and exploration that can lead to creating such a thesis.

From this point on, the book focuses on the writing process itself. Chapter 3 looks at familiar theories and models of the writing process, such as the inspiration method, and helps the reader to analyze his or her own strategies for writing. The remainder of the book, Chapters 4–12, is organized around a set of steps or major tasks the writer must handle: planning, generating ideas, and organizing ideas; understanding readers and designing with them in mind; and evaluating and editing one's prose. For each step, I have offered the writer a variety of strategies, such as brainstorming and talking to the reader as ways to generate ideas. These steps are summarized at the beginning of Chapter 4. The intent behind this organization is twofold. First, I wished to introduce the writer, in a systematic way, to distinctive parts of the writing process. Often parts of this process, such as planning or designing for a reader, are tasks writers could handle but simply tend to ignore. Second, I have tried to offer a variety of effective strategies and to suggest the power of knowing alternative ways of coping with the problem of writing.

A practical note to instructors: in order to keep the book as concise as possible I have placed many items in the Instructor's Manual, including additional exercises, more detailed assignments, some evaluation sheets both student and instructor can use, a brief introduction to formats for reports, and a discussion of ways to teach heuristic strategies in the classroom. It is rarely enough to tell a person about a new strategy he or she might find useful; the real results come from instructors who can help students actively experience a new way of doing things.

Many people have helped me think about writing strategies, learn how to teach them, and write this book. I appreciate their intelligence, effort, and generosity, and I would like to thank each of them. First of all, a number of instructors have used earlier versions of this book in their courses. Their experience, comments, and friendly demands have helped me revise it far beyond my blithe intentions. I am particularly indebted to Elaine Maimon at Beaver College and Nancy Sommers at New York University for their perceptive comments, and to their enthusiastic graduate students. I also want to thank Carol Berkenkotter at Michigan Technological University, Kris Gutierrez at the University of Colorado, Bill Harms at Dickinson College, Lee Odell at SUNY, Albany, Ellen Knodt at Pennsylvania State University, Beverly Clark at Wheaton College, Stanford Searl at Syracuse University, Mary Alice Herbert at Allegheny County Community College, and Pete Jones, Lois Fowler, and Bob Gangewere at Carnegie-Mellon University.

At Carnegie-Mellon, the interdisciplinary atmosphere and the support of Deans Arnold Weber and Robert Kaplan fostered research into real-world writing. And a grant from the National Institute of Education helped us carry out basic research on cognitive processes in writing.

It was my good fortune that Richard Young was one of the first and final readers of the manuscript. As a critic (and now a colleague at Carnegie-Mellon) he has a habit of raising those substantive questions that keep one awake at night. I deeply appreciate both his own work, which has contributed so much to our profession, and his help to me. I am indebted to W. Ross Winterowd, of the University of Southern California at Los Angeles, for his comments on an early draft of the manuscript. I am also grateful to Peter Zoller, of Wichita State University, and George Miller, of the University of Delaware, for their insight and advice. Later on, Richard Larson somehow found time to give this manuscript a generously detailed and insightful reading. His advice has made a great difference.

At Harcourt Brace Jovanovich I have had the real pleasure of working with Eben Ludlow, to whose publishing insight our field already owes a great deal, and with Bill McLane. They graciously gave me both good ideas and gentle pushes. Working with Susan Eno, my editor, has been an education in itself. She has the rather unnerving combination of persistence, open-mindedness, and always being right. It has been a pleasure to work with her, and she has shown me such imaginative editing and rewriting that I should have included before-and-after paragraphs of this book as examples. Marilyn Marcus' intelligence and style in book design have made points clear where my words failed. And Carolyn Viola-John's copy editing has a thoroughness I admire. Finally, I am grateful to Nancy Kalal for her efficient management of the production of the book.

Of the many friends who have talked wisely to me about writing and have also listened graciously, I especially wish to thank Susan Harris Smith and Philip E. Smith of the University of Pittsburgh for all their skeptical but warm support. And once again, my father, Oren Stevenson, helped set me straight on the practical side of writing. With her inimitable style, Joan Velar has masterminded the preparation of this text through four pilot versions. And Heidi Swarts, my research associate at Carnegie-Mellon, has improved the manuscript wherever she saw fit, giving it an index and the best of its exercises. Finally, and most of all, I want to thank Tim Flower. His own writing and good advice have helped me develop as a writer, but more than that, his love and encouragement are what made it worthwhile.

Linda Flower

Contents

chapter four
Case Study: A Personal Profile 49

chapter five
Planning 57

STEP **1**

STEP **2**

chapter six
Generating Ideas 71

STEP **3**

chapter seven
Organizing Ideas 81

STEP **4**

chapter one

Real-World Writing

This is a book about how to write: how to say what you mean and how to deal with your reader. It is also about writing in the real world and handling the problems people face when they need to write academic papers, persuasive reports, concise memos, and essays that can open a reader's eyes. In writing this book I have imagined you, the reader, as a person who writes to make something happen, whether your audience is a professor, employer, or peer. I have assumed that, whatever your goals are, you are interested in discovering better ways to achieve them.

Your goal as a writer might often be as basic as making your words say what you really mean. Or it might be as complicated as persuading another person to change his or her mind. In either case, your success will depend in part on the skills and writing strategies you bring to the task. So in this book we will focus on three kinds of strategies.

1. The strategies you have for *composing itself.* That is, the techniques you have for getting started, for generating ideas, for organizing them, and for reviewing what you have written. The kind of composing strategies you use has a large impact on how efficiently you write —how long it takes you to produce a page that satisfies you. Even more importantly, these strategies can also determine how well

you explore and use your own knowledge as you write. Some writers have a large repertory of powerful writing strategies on which to draw; other people appear always to be at the mercy of their inspiration.

2. The strategies you have for *adapting your writing to the needs of a reader.* Good writing is intensely functional. It goes beyond mere correctness to meet the needs of the reader. Some of these needs are practical ones. Mr. H. is reading your paper because he needs to know X so he can do Y—and only you can tell him. But many readers are not so highly motivated. They become impatient if they cannot readily comprehend and remember a written text. Writers meet these readers' needs by making their prose easy to read, their points easy to see, and their arguments logically presented. Good writers do not simply express themselves; they plan their writing around a goal they share with a reader and design it to be understood and remembered.

3. The strategies you have for *evaluating and editing* your own writing. Good writers are their own editors. This means they can test their own writing for effectiveness from the reader's point of view. If it doesn't meet that goal, they can draw on editing techniques that bring it closer.

In brief, the goal of this book is to help you gain more control of your own composing process: to become more efficient as a writer and more effective with your readers.

Why take a problem-solving approach to writing?

How do people become good writers? How do they develop the skills of composing, adapting to a reader, and evaluating and editing their own work? The popular mythology of writing gives us two answers. First, it tells us that the ability to write is simply a question of talent. Some people are just born with "a way with words"; others aren't, and that's that. Secondly, the myth says that the process of writing depends on inspiration. If a writer is lucky or talented —or waits long enough —inspiration will come, paragraphs will flow, and the paper will write itself.

Like all myths this one is right about some things. There are real differences among writers, and inspiration, if you can get it, is a fine composing method. However, there are two problems with this myth. One is that it leads capable people to give up too soon. It assumes that people can't really *learn how* to write except for learning rather mechanical skills such as correct use of grammar and punctuation. So, the myth says, if you weren't born with talent or don't feel inspired, there's nothing much you can do. Secondly, in addition to being discouraging, this myth is just plain wrong about what actually happens when people write.

chapter one / Real-World Writing

The first premise of this book is that writing is not simply a game of chance you play with your muse. Writing is a thinking process. To be more specific, it is a problem-solving process. If we were to look at composing as a psychologist might, we would see that it has much in common with other problem-solving processes people use in carrying out a wide range of tasks, whether they are taking an exam, trying to "solve" the energy crisis, making a move in chess, or persuading the bank to make a loan. In order to solve such problems, people draw both on their past knowledge about the subject and on a set of problem-solving strategies. Good problem solvers —such as master chess players, inventors, successful scientists, business managers, or artists —typically have a great deal of knowledge and a large repertory of powerful strategies to use in attacking their problems. Good writers are the same. They are people who have developed better ways of attacking the problem of writing. The goal of this book is to offer you a set of strategies for dealing with writing as a problem you can solve, and in so doing to give you more alternatives and more conscious control over your own writing.

What is real-world writing?

In the real world people write because they want to make something happen. That is why writing strategies are important. However, when people think of "writing" they sometimes equate it with the old-fashioned, "What I did on my summer vacation" themes they may have written in high school. Their writing strategy at that time may have been rather simple: try to use big words, sound important, and concentrate on avoiding grammatical errors. The problem with this strategy, of course, is that it often produces nothing more than hot air. And it doesn't help people do the kind of serious, practical, and idea-packed writing that is expected by college professors and colleagues at work. In real-world writing, correctness is naturally important, but your ideas and your reader are even more important. This book is about the kind of writing people do when they *know* something they want to *communicate* to a *reader* who wants or needs to hear it.

One of the most common yet most demanding kinds of real-world writing people do is expository writing, or writing that analyzes and explains. In college, as well as in business and professions, people do expository writing—also called analytical writing—whenever they want to analyze a complex problem or issue. The result may be a college paper on the Civil War, a company memo on improving quality control, a research report on solar heating, or a feature article on energy consumption. In all these cases the writer has something to say, the reader needs or wants to hear it, and the topic demands clear and logical discussion.

If expository or analytical writing is so common, why is it often so difficult to do, or at least to do well? One reason is that a writer usually faces not one but three major tasks:

1. *Making meaning.* First he or she has to make sense out of complex situations, and do so in words. Intuitive understanding is not enough. A writer must use language to make meaning; that is, to name key issues, to describe their interrelationships, and turn that sense of the whole into concepts expressed in words.
2. *Communicating.* Secondly, a writer has to communicate that understanding so a reader will see what the writer meant. Simply expressing one's ideas is usually not enough. The writer must use language to anticipate and guide the reader.
3. *Persuading.* Finally, a writer often has to move another person not only to understand, but to respond or take some action. The writer's goal is often persuasion as well as explanation.

In the rest of this chapter we are going to look at three real-world writing problems: a practical problem, a college assignment, and a personal reason to write. As you read them, notice how the writers' priorities may differ—sometimes it is more important simply to describe a problem than to persuade a reader. But all the writers are seeking to make meaning, communicate it, and persuade their reader to respond.

A PRACTICAL WRITING PROBLEM

The following chain of events started in December when a staff writer for *City* magazine did a feature article on potholes (see Example 1). She wanted to analyze, from her perspective, why the local roads were in such bad repair despite rising road taxes. This article sparked a worried note from the City/County Commissioners' office to the Department of Roads saying: "What is the trouble? We must respond." So in response, a city transportation engineer was asked to look into the situation, define the problem more thoroughly, and write a report that explained why the local paving was falling apart (see Example 2). This report in turn led a research engineer with the local asphalt supplier to reply with a more technical analysis of the road mix the department was buying and the alternatives it had ignored (see Example 3).

As you will see in the examples, each writer viewed the problem differently and produced a very different-looking piece of prose. But all shared the three goals of making a meaning out of the facts, communicating it, and persuading a reader to do or see something differently.

EXAMPLE 1

THE POTHOLE 500

by May Britton

It starts slowly. Moisture seeps through the pavement to the soil below. A sudden drop in temperature and the ground heaves as it freezes. Later, when the ground thaws and contracts in the warm afternoon sun, the pavement doesn't. A few pockets you can still dodge begin to show up. Then comes the big freeze, the real snow, the salt trucks. The freeze, heave, and thaw cycle begins in earnest, and pretty soon salt water and traffic begin to gnaw and pound small holes into craters.

Potholes Are a Hole in Your Pocket

Last year the state spent $30 million to repair the potholes in its 45,000 miles of roadway—money you paid into the Motor Fund through license and registration fees and gas taxes. $30 million to repair, but what about the hidden costs of *disrepair*? Here's an armchair estimate of what your ticket to the Pothole 500 could cost you this year.

License	$10
Registration	25
Gasoline Tax	40
One bent rim (replace wheel)	20
Front end realigned	15
One pair shock absorbers	60
Broken springs	80
Ruptured tire	50
Lost hubcap	10
Dental filling replaced	40
Combat pay (driving to work)	self-assigned
This year's total:	$350+

Why Are We Paying This?

Two causes stand out: One is courtesy of Mother Nature, the other thanks to the County Department of Transportation. Nature first. As any engineer will tell you, if a road doesn't have proper drainage, it has problems. Rainfall seeps in or subsurface springs "pump up" water through the surface, and the freeze cycle is set in motion. Add a marked increase in traffic on many roads, and craters are on the way.

Our terrain makes drainage as difficult as it is necessary, so the County has wisely devoted some of its maintenance funds to pothole prevention by installing new drainage systems on older roads.

The problem is that this foresight doesn't seem to extend throughout the Department's decision making. The Pine Road resurfacing done this spring laid down a 2-inch surface of asphalt. The New Jersey Turnpike lays down 12½ inches—and has had only minimal repairs in its 26 years of heavy use. Is this a case of penny-wise and pound-foolish?

A second case in point. The approved drill for patching potholes is clean the wound, apply the mix, and if the hole is small, compact it with a mechanical tamper. If a large area is resurfaced, use a 5-ton roller. Then, one wonders, why do we see road crews patting patches into place with thawks of a shovel, or rolling them down with the back wheels of a truck? Why is it the County is just now "looking into" equipment that will heat the mix laid in winter (cold patch) so that it will last as well as summer repairs?

The solution to the technical problems of good roads and dependable repairs lies with the City and County engineers. But all of us, since we're footing the bill in more ways than one, might well ask, "How good is the decision making that's coping with this problem?" Perhaps there should be an answer.

May Britton is a free-lance writer and member of the State Consumers Board.

EXAMPLE 2

MCDR MIDLAND COUNTY DEPARTMENT OF ROADS

6230 Grafton, Midland 03416   Willard Harris, Director

January 20, 198–

The City/County Board of Commissioners
City/County Building
Midland 06102

Attention: Mr. Andrews, Transportation Supervisor

Subject: Special Briefing Report on Road Repair
              Prepared for the February Open Hearing
              of the Board of Commissioners

Attachments: Department of Roads Planning Paper No. 459–B

Gentlemen:

      At your request we have prepared a special report on road
repair for the February Open Hearing. We hope it will allow
you not only to answer questions but to educate the public
about the real costs of good roads.

The Problem: Conditions and Costs
      The underlying problem is that our area is a natural pro-
ducer of potholes. Here, even the best–laid roads are subject
to the extremes of both natural and man–made conditions: a
hilly terrain, constant severe freeze and thaw conditions, un-
stable soil beneath the roadbed, heavy salting due to frequent
road ice, and increasing traffic density.
      The stress placed on our roads is increasing, but the
funds to maintain the roads are not increasing at the same
rate. Our area is not alone in this: the national pothole
average is 49 holes per mile and we now maintain 45,000 miles
of road. This year there were 12,000 potholes reported and the
city made plans to resurface 100 miles of streets. On the
average that means buying 100 pounds of asphalt filler to patch
each pothole. Although our costs for crews and equipment are
subject to only normal inflation, the cost of asphalt is taking
sharp and unpredictable rises because it is a petroleum–based
product.

This combination of limited funds and severe pothole-producing conditions forces a series of trade-offs. Here is a typical problem. One way to keep asphalt from shrinking and cracking under winter conditions is to use a soft asphalt. But at high summer temperatures, cars running over soft asphalt will produce ruts, which create pools of rainwater and encourage hydroplaning and skidding. Using asphalt that is safe in summer can mean potholes in winter.

On top of that, the federal specifications on a number of recently "safety-updated roads" require a skid-resistant surface, which prevents an oily film from scumming the surface during a rain. In order to meet those specifications and qualify for federal monies from the Liquid Fuel Tax, we must switch to a large-particle aggregate. Yet this aggregate, unlike our local smaller stone, must be trucked in at considerably increased cost. Once again, there is often no perfect solution because of the natural conditions, but even when an optimal technical solution exists it is often prohibited by cost.

Department Planning and Recommendations

In the face of this the Department has two current plans: one a short-term plan for reallocating repair money and the other a long-term plan for improving new road building. These are presented in detail in the Department's Planning Paper No. 459-B.

In addition we suggest that the City-County Commission attempt to publicize the problem through newspaper publications, such as the AAA Motorist, which will run in-depth features on local problems. Given the current traffic conditions in our county, we can only improve road maintenance if we increase the budget.

Yours,

Thomas Chen

Thomas Chen
Supervisor

TC/jv
Attach.

EXAMPLE 3

McGinnis ASPHALT Engineering

464 Line Road, Midland 03408

```
TO:        Jean Birch, Director of Sales
FROM:      Michael Rourke, Research Engineer
SUBJECT:   Research Update on County Road Repair
DATE:      January 20, 198-
```

In response to your request for an update, the major problem is still the county road commission itself. Our new sulphur-asphalt mix could probably increase road life in this area by 20%, but the commission has consistently failed to lay test paving. Specifically, this mix:

1. offers a soft mix that also resists rutting
2. resists seepage and prevents stripping
3. provides better bonding, which allows the use of cheap local stone
4. will become cheaper as the cost of petroleum-based competitors increases.

If you could get the county to overcome its inertia and fund initial testing, we could offer improved mixes and the strong possibility of lower costs in the next three years. See the attached report for details.

DIFFERENT FORMATS BUT COMMON PRINCIPLES

These three pieces of writing all look quite different from one another. The feature writer starts with a good "lead," or short, catchy introduction to get the reader's attention; she uses pictures, "takeouts" (the headline in the text), and vivid metaphoric language to direct the reader and make a point. By contrast, the research engineer follows a standard memo format; his first sentence bluntly states the reason for writing, and he punches out the final points he expects the reader to remember in numbered order, using technical terms such as "stripping" that a general reader would not understand.

It is important to know the formal features that belong to different kinds of writing. In Example 1, without a good title and lead your article might go unread. If you saved your best points until last in a news article, the editor might chop them off in order to fit the story to the layout. Or, if you omit an informative subject heading (see Example 3), your memo might be misfiled and never seen again.

In spite of these differences, there are two important features that underlie all these examples. First, they are *designed with their readers in mind.* The feature writer tackled her topic from the point of view of her readers: what are they interested in, what do they need to know, and how can I adapt my research to their concerns? Likewise, her visual layout guides readers by setting up expectations and leading the readers along. Both of the report writers are working in an organization in which other people must *use* their writing: the City/County Commissioners will use the first report at next month's open hearing of the Commission; the McGinnis sales director will use Michael Rourke's memo to sell the county on a new idea. As you can see, the headings, references to other reports, and numbered points are designed to let readers find just what they need to know, and find it quickly. Although the features of format may differ, the logic behind each format is the logic of meeting the readers' needs.

A second feature these pieces of writing share is an underlying hierarchical organization. That is, they are organized around a top-level issue or ideas that is then broken down in the paper into its parts. These parts may be subissues, supporting details, steps, causes, or key points —anything that helps the writer to organize his or her ideas. It helps to visualize a hierarchical structure as an upside-down tree, as in Figure 1-1. A good example of such a hierarchy would be a university. The university as a whole is at the top of this hier-

FIGURE **1-1**   *The basic form of a hierarchy with a tree for a university partly filled in*

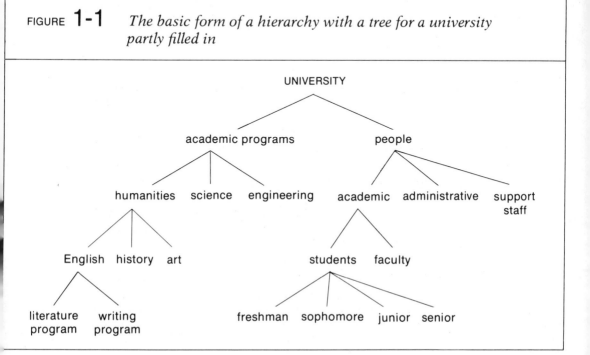

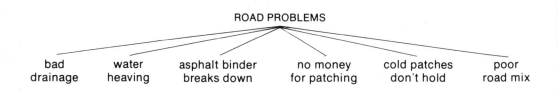

FIGURE **1-2** *A flat, undeveloped hierarchy*

ROAD PROBLEMS

| bad drainage | water heaving | asphalt binder breaks down | no money for patching | cold patches don't hold | poor road mix |

archy—not because it is more important than the programs or the people who make it up, but because it is more inclusive.

The best way to think of a hierarchy is as a large system with a number of working parts. For example, a system or organization such as a university has a number of rather independent subsystems, such as the English department or the sophomore class, within its hierarchy. In the same way a piece of writing has a number of working parts, such as an introduction, body, and conclusion. Each paragraph within these sections is another subsystem—a functional, working part of the whole.

Some hierarchies are logical or highly conventional ones, such as the division of students into freshmen, sophomores, juniors, and seniors. However, the more interesting hierarchies are the ones people create themselves. Ask the next three people you see how they would categorize the different people at your college, and you will see them creating their own hierarchical organizations of experience.

What happens when we apply this notion of hierarchical structures to writing? First, we notice that some kinds of writing have a very flat hierarchy, or none at all. For example, a narrative can use a simple chronological structure. "First this happened, then this happened, and then finally. . . ." Or imagine the pothole magazine article if it had been written as a rather rambling, stream-of-consciousness description of things the writer had observed. The paper would be organized like a grocery list, with each paragraph describing a new problem. This would produce a very flat tree and an unfocused paper (see Figure 1-2).

A list can give a lot of information, but it doesn't always reveal the logical relationship between ideas, such as the fact that bad drainage can *cause* water heaving. In order to turn this type of list into a tree and well-organized report, the writer has to group the facts and create a set of organizing ideas with an underlying hier-

FIGURE **1-3**   *Two different hierarchical organizations of information on the pothole problem*

(a) The feature writer's tree

THE ROAD PROBLEM FOR CONSUMERS

definition of problem — causes — solution

potholes — cost to consumer — nature — county work — better technology — better decisions

(b) The transportation department writer's tree

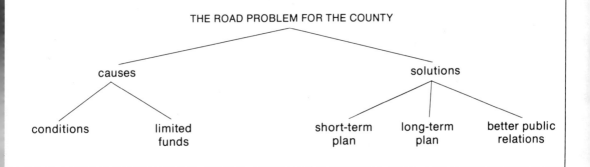

THE ROAD PROBLEM FOR THE COUNTY

causes — solutions

conditions — limited funds — short-term plan — long-term plan — better public relations

archical organization. For example, the feature writer in Example 1 turned her information into a structure like the one shown in Figure 1-3a, while the county report writer (Example 2) set up the structure in Figure 1-3b. Each saw the problem differently, but each used a hierarchical organization to express ideas. And each grouped his or her facts into logical categories such as problems/causes/solutions.

To sum up, then, although different kinds of analytical writing have different formal features, they share two things. They are designed with a reader in mind and they have an underlying hierarchical organization that gives the reader (1) a top-level organizing idea and (2) a logical presentation of the idea's subparts. A good piece of expository writing will let the reader see the tree (the underlying hierarchy of ideas) that lies behind the words.

A COLLEGE WRITING PROBLEM

Now compare the professional writing problem we have just seen to a typical college assignment that asks the writer to understand and analyze some complex situation, such as, "Discuss the rise of the middle class" or "Analyze the probable effects of thermal pollution on a fresh water pond." You will see that many of the writer's problems and goals are the same.

Sometimes college assignments are very explicit about the real-world demands they are making: they help the writer to see a purpose behind the assignment and to identify a real audience that needs to know. For example, it is easy to see the real-world writing problem within this assignment:

> Many students come to college thinking that textbooks all say the same thing and that all textbook writers agree on what should be taught and how to teach it. Do you think this is so? Find three different introductory textbooks on the same subject, whether it is psychology, statistics, composition, or history. Read the prefaces to learn more about the writers' assumptions and then compare the books. Look especially at what they include, what they consider important, and what they say on a few key topics. Then write an analysis of these textbooks and how they differ, with the goal of helping an entering freshman.

Sometimes, however, college assignments are not very explicit and it is harder to see their purpose, as in this one: "Analyze the impact of Darwin's theory of evolution on his time. Three pages." That means that you as a student must mentally rewrite the assignment as a real-world writing problem, filling in the unwritten assumptions the instructor makes but doesn't state. Here is how a student might think out the problem:

> Everyone knows that Darwin's theory of evolution is important. But from the wording of this assignment —"impact on his time"—I'd better focus on the specific effects Darwin had on his contemporaries. This professor, in her role as an instructor, will naturally expect me to use the method of historical analysis she's been teaching in this class in answering the question. So I'll need to define Darwin's key ideas, then sift through the relevant information in the assigned books and articles.
> The professor would also expect me to show I can do some other important things a historian does: make connections between my major points and generate some conclusions and ideas of my own. She'll expect me not only to offer my own interpretation of the facts but to convince her that it is a well-supported and reasonable way to view this historical event.

The following portion of a paper is a response to the assignment of comparing textbooks that was cited on page 12. In it, the student has combined a traditional analysis of three different texts with a real-world purpose of communicating her discoveries and responses to students who will use the text. We will look at the first paragraph, in which the writer defines the problem, and the second paragraph, which sets out her first point of comparison.

Analyzing Your Own Textbook

Are you in the introductory statistics course and in trouble? For many students those phrases mean the same thing. Do you sometimes feel the problem is that you just can't understand <u>statistics</u>? It may be that you just can't understand your statistics <u>textbook</u>. This paper is an analysis of three different first-year statistics textbooks, and as it will show, each book makes radically different assumptions about what you already know and why you want to learn statistics. So if you have trouble understanding the principles behind a chapter, you may find another textbook (and there are a number in the library) that will make the principles clear.

The most important difference among the textbook writers I studied is what they assume about their audience. My first text, by Dowland, assumes you not only know calculus but can understand it well enough to help make statistics clear. Dowland says he is writing for students in math and science, but do many science majors have the background he expects? In contrast, the textbook by Weinberg is called <u>Statistics: An Intuitive Approach</u> because the authors present each new chapter in terms of the basic, intuitive principle of the average or the balance point between two groups of data.

As you can see from even this short excerpt, the writer has organized her paper around the question or problem raised in the assignment. Instead of merely describing the books, she has tried to use her analysis to answer the reader's question. Furthermore, she has given us a hierarchical structure in which her major, top-level ideas are clearly stated. See Figure 1-4.

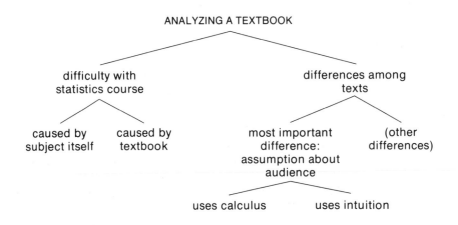

FIGURE **1-4**   *Tree of beginning two paragraphs*

ANALYZING A TEXTBOOK

difficulty with
statistics course

differences among
texts

caused by
subject itself

caused by
textbook

most important
difference:
assumption about
audience

(other
differences)

uses calculus   uses intuition

A PERSONAL REASON TO WRITE

Our final example of real-world writing has much in common
with professional and college writing problems; the only difference
is that the writer's priorities are different. The excerpt below comes
from an article published in a college paper. The author, Tim Cimino,
wrote this essay directly for publication —he wanted to say something to other students and he wanted to argue some of them around
to a new point of view. Yet one feels that this essay, coming at the
end of his senior year, was also written for Tim himself in an attempt
to capture in words part of what he had learned in those four years.
By writing about it, he turned a body of complicated feelings and
conflicting ideas into a meaningful stand.

As Tim described it, "I wanted to make some sort of statement
before I left. I wanted to leave them with something." Tim had done
very little writing in college, but when he decided to turn his ideas
into an article, he spent nearly the whole semester working on it,
going through eight drafts. And as he worked an interesting thing
happened. His initial plan had been to describe "connection" and
"detachment" as merely devices in technical problem-solving; then
he began to see ways of applying the concepts to actually changing
one's own life. As he put it, he saw how to "take problem-solving one
step further."

As you read through Tim's essay (Example 4), look for the underlying hierarchical structure. The heading for the essay states that it is about how academic problem-solving is related to our everyday lives. If that is the most inclusive, top-level idea, how do each of the paragraphs fit into the writer's hierarchical organization? Is it easy to see Tim's underlying structure?

As you read the essay, also look for all the ways in which the author has thought about his audience—the college students reading the paper—and tried to adapt his writing to them. For example, notice how the first paragraph is designed to capture their attention with a dramatic first sentence and show them that they too are people with problems who will find this article relevant. It is clear that Tim Cimino is not simply expressing his ideas in this essay but also trying to persuade the students to see things his way. How does he do that? Treat each paragraph as a functional part of his developing argument and try to figure out how it is working. What is he trying to do to and for his readers?

EXAMPLE 4

Tim Cimino, Senior, Chemistry, discusses academic "problem-solving" and its relation to our everyday lives.

VIEWS

One thing I like about desperate people is that they make such good listeners. Suggest to someone that they might benefit if they changed their ways and they will often get indignant or critical. That is, unless they're having troubles. People who have a problem on their hands are ready to change because it's so painful not to; they're receptive to new ways of dealing with problems because they've run out of ideas themselves.

Whatever problem we're facing, be it a faltering relationship, loneliness, or some other crisis, it is open to some of the same methods we use for solving academic problems: breaking it down into bite-size pieces; research, whether it be by talking to people, reading books, or doing experiments; and solution by analogy to other problems we've known. And of course we use reasoning, both deductive and inductive.

Yet our day-to-day problems are usually more complex than the ones we get in school. There are no ready-made formulas, nor are there wise professors to tell us just exactly what the problem is. Often, there is no specific deadline, though the problem may steadily worsen. Sometimes, there is not enough time to develop a plan of action before it becomes necessary to act. Or by the time we arrive at a solution, the problem has changed so much that the solution no longer works (relationships are like this). So, while we may apply traditional methods to these kinds of problems, we need something more.

Solving a problem can be divided into two stages: a problem break-down stage

(continued)

EXAMPLE 4 (*continued*)

(analysis) and a plan build-up stage (synthesis). Unfortunately, many people rush through their analysis; they make the wrong assumptions, jump to conclusions, neglect some alternatives, or even act before they've given the problem any thought at all. Even before they have begun to plan, they have failed. What they need is a systematic analysis—something like the sway of a cobra before it strikes—one that allows them to spot the problem, find their balance, and gauge the distance to the target.

This withdrawal or detachment is important for several reasons. The first is that we need to completely define and understand the problem. Sometimes, only by *standing back* to take in all its dimensions and implications can we *approach* the problem properly. We should look at it from different perspectives (in 2000 years, will it still matter?) and from different viewpoints (maybe other people's, maybe God's).

Detaching allows us also to relax; to examine the problem, rephrase its questions, and toy with different ideas. More importantly, it is the prelude to creative insights and inspiration. One theory holds that while we rest, our subconscious is churning away, producing new thoughts or recalling forgotten memories which are then leaked to our conscious minds as insight or intuition. Resting, mentally as well as physically, lets us prepare for the plans we finally decide to carry out.

This withdrawal may also be a time of looking inward at ourselves. Unlike academic problems, our day-to-day problems (and their solutions) are somewhat dependent on our personalities. Thus, we must look at ourselves *honestly* (our desires, needs, abilities, and feelings) to see how they partially determine the problem and its solution. We should also be aware of the forces that act on us, in order to decide whether to accept them, resist them, or redirect them. Furthermore, we should realize that our emotions don't come directly from the situation, but from the aspects of the situation that we dwell on. It is through our attitudes that external events are translated into internal emotions. Thus, it is not always the situation that needs to be remedied; sometimes just changing our attitudes is enough. Just by having the right state of mind, we can have some control over how a problem affects us.

But detachment becomes escape if we don't return to the problem. At some point we lose more than we gain by delaying. When we feel the moment's right, it's time to connect, to carry out whatever decision we've made. In connecting, we deal directly with the problem. We make a wave and then ride it. This is the passion—spontaneous, whole-hearted, forceful, pure.

Up to this point, nothing is really new; in one way or another, everyone does about the same thing—they think about a problem, then they think up an answer to it. Yet, by detaching *again,* after having connected, we can evaluate our action and reanalyze the situation. By constantly skipping back and forth between detachment and connection, we can avoid getting lost in thought or (the other extreme) caught up in emotion. Like a guided missile, in which successive in-flight corrections bring it right into the target, the constant reworking and reviewing of the situation is a way in which we may attain a *dynamic* balance, one capable of dealing with our dynamic problems. Beyond this, and most importantly, we arrive at a potential mechanism for enriching and changing our lives. In this way, by meeting (or making) and solving problems, we accept the challenge to be more human and the chance to become more alive.

SOURCE: Tim Cimino, in the *Tartan*, April 24, 1979 (Carnegie-Mellon University).

CONCLUSION

In this chapter we have looked at writing by a variety of people: college students, professional writers, and individuals who need to write in connection with their jobs. As real-world writers, all of these people had three basic tasks: they had to *make meaning* out of a situation as they saw it; they had to find the best way to *communicate that meaning* to someone else; and finally, in different ways, they wanted to *persuade* another person to see or act in a different way. The style and format that each writer chose varied considerably. However, each of these papers relied on an underlying hierarchical structure to communicate its message to the reader. The essence of such real-world writing, then, is simple: it involves a writer who has something to say and a reader who needs or wants to know. Good writing is writing that fulfills a mutual contract and meets the needs of both the writer and the reader.

Projects and Exercises

1 Collect some examples of expository or persuasive writing that you admire. Show how the writer has thought about the reader and describe the underlying hierarchical structure of the piece of writing.

2 Find an example of two people writing on the same topic, as in movie reviews, book reviews, or essays on a controversial subject. Discuss how two writers, looking at the same information, created different meanings and why.

3 Find additional examples of the kinds of writing discussed in this chapter (a student paper, a feature article, a report, a memo, and an editorial). Then try to define some of the earmarks of each kind of prose. Describe the essential features of two of these so that someone else who had never seen a memo, for example, could write one.

4 What kind of writing do people in your major or your field of interest do? Get in touch with someone in your field —a teacher, historian, engineer, social worker, scientist, or whatever —and ask the person to give you examples of every kind of writing he or she does and to tell you who reads it. Even people you don't know will probably be happy to help. Discuss what seems special about the kind of writing you will be doing soon.

If You Would Like to Read More

If you would like to know more about real-world writing—writing designed to meet the needs of the reader—see:

Boetinger, H. M. *Moving Mountains or the Art and Craft of Letting Others See Things Your Way*. New York: Macmillian, 1969. ■ This is a lively strategy book on "selling" your ideas in the practical world of business. See especially Chapter 2 on putting ideas in a persuasive context.

Britton, James, et al. *The Development of Writing Abilities (11–18)*. London: Macmillan, 1975. ■ If you would like to know more about how the real-world demands of the reader function in student writing, this is an excellent and imaginative study of writing in British schools.

Harmon, Margaret, ed. *Working with Words: Careers for Writers*. New York: Barnes and Noble Books, 1977. ■ If you like to write, this book describes a variety of careers that could use your skill, from financial writing and technical editing to writing scripts for television.

chapter two

Writing About Problems

Why write? One of the most basic reasons for writing, which students, academic writers, journalists, and business people share, is to discuss and deal with problems. This chapter will explain how to go about analyzing a problem, then show you one way to express your thinking in a written problem analysis, and finally, show how you can use the process of problem analysis to develop the thesis of an expository or persuasive paper.

What are problems and why do people analyze them? Often, a problem is a situation that occurs when you are at point A but you want to be someplace else, at point B, and there is an obstacle in your way. Solving a problem is figuring out how to get from where you are to where you want to be. But many times the most important part of the problem-solving process is defining the problem itself and deciding what your goal, or point B, really is. Faced with the difficult problem of choosing a college major, for example, you can only make a "good" decision when you decide what goals you expect that choice to realize.

Solving problems is also a major part of many jobs. If you have ever been a group leader, teacher, or coach, you have probably been in a situation in which something—which was as yet undefined—

wasn't going as well as it should. And it was your job to understand or define that problem and solve it—to move the situation from point A to a new, better point B.

There are two important things to remember about problems:

1. A problem is only a problem *for someone;* it is not an impersonal situation waiting for a solution. A problem only exists when someone feels a conflict or dissonance. The conflict may be between his present situation and his goals, desires, or expectations—or it may be between his own attitudes. For example, having to choose a career or major would only be a problem if you also felt that:

- Your family expected you to be an engineer and join the firm
- You were good in math and knew engineering would be easy for you
- But you had just discovered how much more you liked social sciences and working with children
- You weren't sure whether you should use your time at college to get a liberal education or for preprofessional training
- You wondered if it would be foolish to give up job security and money for doing something you enjoy now.

As you can see, this problem exists because of your conflicting attitudes and goals. If you changed your attitude (decided that you really didn't care about planning a career at this point), you could eliminate the problem by choosing social sciences, and thereby eliminate the conflict. The decision would no longer be a problem for you, although it might be one for your parents because of their own desires. Analyzing a problem, then, is understanding the *conflict* that turns a situation into a problem for *someone.*

2. The critical issue or key conflict at the heart of a problem is often hard to see. For example, why isn't your club working up to its potential? What is the conflict that underlies the situation? Do its members have multiple goals that don't mesh? Or take a famous problem raised in Shakespeare's *Hamlet,* namely, why does Hamlet delay? For years people have tried to define the social and psychological conflicts within Hamlet that prevent him from revenging his father's death. We can ask a similar question about Shakespeare himself: what broad human problems in his own mind was Shakespeare trying to dramatize when he wrote the play? Finally, what problems does *Hamlet* raise for us as readers; what unresolved issues does it create in our own minds? The play *Hamlet,* then, really involves a set of problems and conflicts existing in the minds of Shakespeare the author, Hamlet the character, and each of us as readers.

In literature, history, science, or education, much of the writing people do is an attempt to put their finger on the key issues in a situation involving a conflict. They write to define and help solve a problem. Whether you are a historian studying urban decay, or a hospital administrator writing a proposal to reorganize county clinics, or a student in either field, you will often depend on the skill of problem analysis. In this chapter we will look at a six-step process you can use to analyze problems and to communicate your understanding to a reader.

Six steps in analyzing a problem

Problem analysis is a form of detective work. It is the act of discovering key issues in a problem that often lie hidden under the noisy details of the situation. The process of analysis begins when people encounter what is called a felt difficulty. That is, you feel something doesn't fit, you feel a conflict. Sometimes that conflict is obvious: two people disagree, or you discover that you yourself hold two contradictory ideas on a subject such as marriage. Many times both sides of a conflict will have merit, as in the federally required testing of new drugs for long-term dangers, which prevents their immediate use by those who would benefit. At other times the conflict will be harder to see: for example, you may feel that there is some as yet unspecified "organizational problem" at the place you work or in an organization to which you belong.

The question in all of these cases is, "What exactly is the problem?" In trying to answer that question an analyst would normally do the following six things:

1. DEFINE THE CONFLICT OR KEY ISSUE

A problem analyst's first job is to discover the critical conflict or key issue that lies at the heart of any felt difficulty. In trying to understand a problem, bear in mind the difference between defining a problem (finding a conflict) and merely stating a topic or describing a situation such as "pollution." Although everyone might agree that pollution is harmful and unpleasant, there was a time when it was seen not as a problem but as a sign of industrial prosperity. Problems are only problems for someone. Pollution is only a problem when people want clean air but drive cars that pollute, or when society wants both a clean environment and maximum industrial productivity.

An even clearer example is the much publicized "energy problem." Energy per se is not a problem; it is a topic. Even the dwindling supply of fossil fuel is only a situation. However, when we juxtapose this supply against the American tradition of high consumption at low cost, we have begun to isolate a problem. We have found one of the central conflicts that create a problem.

We often like to think of a conflict in terms of good versus evil, but in most human organizations it is a conflict between two goods (a high standard of living and a beautiful environment) or between the legitimate needs of two groups (the farmer versus the food consumer). This is what makes real problems so hard to solve.

2. PLACE THE PROBLEM IN A LARGER CONTEXT

As we have seen, the first step in problem analysis is to zoom in on a problem for a close-up look at its critical issues. The second step is to pull back for a broader view. Now you must try to see the problem in a larger context and fit it into a category of similar problems.

Sometimes the larger problem will seem obvious or implicit: for example, making a good career decision. But it is always important to look at the big picture, not just the immediate conflict. For example, is the "energy problem" a technological problem (production can't meet demand) or a social and economic problem (our wasteful consumption endangers our balance of trade)? The context you choose—and you may see more than one—will have an enormous impact on the solutions you propose. For example, should we treat energy as a technological problem and pump money into developing solar energy for the year 2020, or tackle the social problem and start rationing gasoline tomorrow?

Another way to step back and put your problem in perspective is to look for a larger concern you and your reader share. For example, the student whose paper compared statistics textbooks (p. 13) saw a conflict between what students needed and what textbooks offered and placed this problem in the context of trying to get through a statistics course. If she had been writing to a group of teachers, she might have defined the problem in terms of effective teaching. Either way, her approach would be to step back and put the textbook problem in a broader perspective.

In a sense, students do the same thing when they step back to get perspective on an assignment an instructor has made. They may ask themselves "Why was I assigned this paper?" or "What is the point behind this lab experiment?" or "What is the larger issue or question my work should address?"

3. MAKE YOUR PROBLEM DEFINITION MORE OPERATIONAL

Steps 1 and 2 help you create a two-level definition that defines a conflict or key issue and puts it in its larger context. If your goal is to understand a complex phenomenon, such as a Shakespearean play, these are the crucial steps.

But perhaps your problem is a pragmatic one: someone needs to act, or you wish to persuade them to act. Here you can improve your analysis by making your definition more *operational*. An operational problem definition is more useful than an abstract one and often suggests possible courses of action or the features of a good solution. For example, you could make an abstract definition—such as "The problem is that Americans need to lower their energy consumption"—more operational by saying, "The problem is, how can we lower consumption by increasing fuel prices, without at the same time putting an unacceptable burden on the poor?"

Sometimes an operational problem definition contains details that work as miniature plans for tackling the problem. Let's compare different ways a smoker could define his problem.

1. My problem is cigarettes. (overly abstract problem definition; no identification of conflict or key issue)
2. My problem is that I want to cut down on smoking but just can't do it. (more specific problem definition with identification of conflict)
3. My real problem is how to stop smoking at parties or when I'm out with friends. (more operational definition)
4. My real problem is how to break a long-standing habit of smoking around my friends without feeling left out or unsociable. (an operational definition that suggests a number of places to act)

In defining your problem, try to make the conflict and context as operational as you can.

Here is an example of an operational, two-level problem definition written as an introduction to a paper on creativity.

Context for larger problem	According to Brewster Ghiselin (*The Creative Process*), "One might suppose that it is easy to detect creative talent and to recognize creative work. But the
Critical conflict or key issue	difficulties are considerable." Because every creative act in some way violates an established order, it is likely to appear eccentric, if not patently unreasona-
More operational definition of the conflict (added as example)	ble, to most people. How, for example, could anyone be sure Freud's insights into the human mind weren't motivated—like the bizarre "insights" of his patients—by hidden psychological forces? And how could his contemporaries judge the validity of such startling and novel explanations of behavior? The ca-
Preview of purpose of the paper	reers of Sigmund Freud and Karl Marx show us how society deals with this problem of recognizing creative work.

Note: In the series of boxes in this chapter, guidelines will be given for turning the ideas you generated through problem analysis into written form.

The format of a written problem analysis follows the thinking process in a number of ways. The format treated here, which we will call the basic problem analysis, is widely used in business and organizational communication (see examples on pp. 5–7). In addition, the elements of a basic problem analysis are the core of most research papers, essays, and reports, although the elements are often rearranged and subordinated to a thesis.

WRITING A PROBLEM ANALYSIS

State your operational, two-level problem definition at the beginning

In writing a basic problem analysis, give your reader a clear, two-level definition of the problem somewhere near the beginning of your paper. In a short, one- or two-page paper, most readers will expect you to define the problem (on both levels) in the very first paragraph. Come immediately to the point so your reader will know the key issue. This is also the place to reveal the purpose or point of your paper. Stating this directly at the beginning isn't always easy to do, but your reader will be looking for it.

In many cases you will want to present the larger context or shared problem first, as a way of orienting the reader or catching his attention with a subject you and he care about. Then state the key conflict of issue that is at the heart of your problem.

---

4. EXPLORE THE PARTS OF THE PROBLEM

Once the problem is defined you need to explore the various subissues or subproblems within it. This helps you break a complex problem down into manageable parts. For example, a smoker might decide that the major subissues within the problem of stopping smoking are "health," "costs," "strength of habit," "social pressure," and so on. In isolating subproblems the analyst needs to see how they fit into the hierarchy as parts of the larger problem.

WRITING A PROBLEM ANALYSIS

Isolate and define the major subissues or subproblems within the problem

Make the overall hierarchical structure of your discussion clear.*
Once you have told the reader what the problem is, you will need to
discuss it in more detail. However, instead of simply describing the
situation, organize your discussion and your paragraphs around a
set of subissues or subproblems within your problem. In other
words, you should be able to name the major issues your analysis
will address and the reader should be able to see which issue each
paragraph or set of paragraphs is talking about.

In a short paper, you might use this organization:

First paragraph: TWO-LEVEL PROBLEM DEFINITION

Body of paper: Issue   Issue   Issue

Final paragraph: CONCLUSION

Notice how by defining a problem and a set of subissues or
subproblems, you have created a hierarchical organization of ideas.
Your problem definition is the top-level, most inclusive statement.
The discussion and subproblems or subissues grow out of it, and
your conclusion at the end will work like a new top-level idea in that
it will respond to the entire discussion. Make sure your reader sees
this hierarchical organization of your ideas.

5. GENERATE ALTERNATIVE SOLUTIONS

On the basis of your problem definition and exploration of its
parts, try to find major alternative ways to solve the problem. You
will only know your solution really is the best solution if you consider
other good ones. The chief weakness of most problem-solvers is that
they leap too quickly to a solution. Upon seeing the first strong alternative they breathe a sigh of relief, say "this is it," and look no
further. However, your conclusion will only look strong to your readers if they know you have considered and rejected with reason other
logical solutions.

---

* See Chapter 7 for a further discussion of hierarchical organization.

6. COME TO A WELL-SUPPORTED CONCLUSION

A problem analyst cannot work in a vacuum; he or she must eventually make a decision among the alternatives (or evaluate the information that has emerged) and must come to a conclusion. This may be a proposed solution, a hypothesis, or at least a new understanding of the problem.

A well-supported conclusion depends on the writer's recognition of two things: the assumptions behind the problem analysis and, in some cases, the implications that will arise from the writer's position. These must often be expressed in the final written paper because they give the reader a basis on which to evaluate and use the analysis.

Sometimes the outcome of a problem analysis is a hypothesis — an interpretation of a complex body of information. An analyst must recognize the *assumptions* which underlie that hypothesis or be the victim of their limits. If, for example, you assumed that cigarettes only harm pack-a-day smokers, or that Americans would subvert any gas rationing scheme, as they did during World War II, these key assumptions would have a great impact on the conclusion you reach and should be stated for your reader.

When your conclusion is a proposed solution to a problem, view both the solution and the problem as parts of an ongoing process. Real problems rarely go away; current solutions are often only a temporary fix. Your conclusion stands on a precarious boundary between a problem clamoring for a solution, and the *implications* and consequences of that solution stretching out into the future. A solution with unrecognized implications may only be a new problem in the making. Your job as an analyst is to alert your reader to those implications that he or she must foresee if your solution is to have a real and beneficial impact. For example, giving up smoking can lead to an increase in eating and frequently cause withdrawal symptoms. Prepare your reader to deal with these implications.

WRITING A PROBLEM ANALYSIS

**Tie your conclusion to the problem
and to the foregoing analysis**

**When appropriate, show that you recognize alternatives,
assumptions, and implications**

Your conclusion will be a new idea, but one that takes account of all the discussion that has gone before. Make sure your conclusion isn't simply a package plan you tack onto the end. It should be

---

directly related to the problem *as you defined it*—and you should make that connection clear to the reader. Show how your conclusion deals with the problem and with the subissues or subproblems you defined.

A second way to support your analysis is to show the reader you have considered alternatives and have recognized some of the assumptions and implications of your position. However, you may not have the space or desire to spell out all of them. A good rule of thumb is that you, the writer, should be able to discuss them all, but mention only those that might be important for your reader. Since assumptions underlie the entire analysis process, you sometimes may wish to deal with them at the beginning of the paper.

Evaluating your final written problem analysis

Sometimes people have an intuitive understanding of a problem and arrive at a well-supported solution, hypothesis, or new view of the problem. But in actually sitting down to write the paper, they may let intuition take over and lose sight of the reader's probable reactions. It is one thing to understand a problem intuitively and well. However, if you want your understanding to make any difference, you must be able to communicate it to someone else. Having a good or even the "best" solution to a problem only matters if your analysis convinces someone else. A written analysis, unlike an intuitive one, demands both conceptual clarity as a thinker and rhetorical skill as a writer.

Use the checklist below to evaluate your written analysis. How well have you handled each of the seven important features a reader will expect?

THE PROBLEM DEFINITION
1. Is there a shared problem or larger context?
2. Is the central conflict or key issue defined?
3. Is the problem definition operational?

THE OVERALL STRUCTURE
1. Are specific subissues or subproblems clearly defined?
2. Is the overall hierarchical structure of the discussion clear?

THE CONCLUSION
1. Is the conclusion based on alternatives, with your assumptions stated (if appropriate) and the implications of your solution recognized?
2. Is the solution clearly tied to the problem defined initially and to the bulk of your discussion?

Often, consulting such a checklist can help you see weaknesses or missing portions of your basic problem analysis. Here is a first draft of a problem analysis written by a student who had worked for two summers at a firm called Timmerman Landscape Company:

Where is the problem?   Timmerman Landscape is a local nursery that has recently moved into doing landscaping. They have a year-round staff of around ten people, but in the summer they hire a lot of summer help to meet peak summer workloads. Most of the summer help are college students. There is a waiting list for these jobs because the pay is good and the work is outdoors but not as heavy as construction

Subproblem   work. Or at least it shouldn't be. But because many new summer workers don't know how to move large trees, the best ways to handle the equipment, handle the trucks, or

Is this the key issue or conflict?   the large plants, or dig holes, their job is much harder. But Timmerman does little to help summer employees in these areas.

Subproblem   One problem is that unloading large trees and shrubs can be difficult, even dangerous if you don't know how to position the truck and use the planks. And positioning large plants in the hole is very time-consuming if you don't know how to gauge depth and position before unload-

Subproblem?   ing. Word-of-mouth publicity is very important to Timmerman, but when neighbors come over to ask summer help about the names of plants, conditions they like, or care they need, the new workers usually have no idea, or make a blind guess.

Subproblem?
Conclusion— not tied to problem definition; doesn't recognize alternatives and implications   By my second summer, I had learned a lot about plants and realized that many, even expensive, trees and shrubs were damaged by incorrect rough handling and incorrect planting—in holes too shallow, too close to a house, with air left around the roots. In conclusion, I think Timmerman should develop a handbook for new employees that would be used as part of a brief orientation program for new summer workers.

In analyzing his draft, the writer realized that his problem definition was too long in coming and did not convey the conflict underlying the problem, nor was it very operational. He found that his subproblems were not organized hierarchically; one even appeared before the problem definition. He also decided that his conclusion seemed "tacked on": it did not clearly proceed from what had come before or recognize the alternatives and implications of his proposed solution. Here is his revision:

Larger problem

Timmerman Landscape is a local nursery that has recently moved into doing landscaping. In the summer they need to hire extra help--many of them college students--to

Operational problem definition including identification of conflict

meet peak workloads during that season. Most summer workers like the job because the pay is good and the work is outdoors, but problems arise because Timmerman, in order to save money, spends no time on training them in procedures and techniques that would make them more efficient.

Subproblem

This lack of training affects both the students themselves and Timmerman's profitability. The work is hard for summer employees if they don't know the best ways to move large trees, handle the equipment and trucks, handle large plants, or dig holes. It can even be dangerous, if someone is unloading large trees and shrubs and doesn't know how to position the truck and use the planks.

Subproblem

Further, the lack of training causes reduced productivity, plant damage, and loss of business for Timmerman. Untrained workers waste a lot of time: for example, positioning a large plant in a hole is very time-consuming if you don't know how to gauge depth and position before un-

Subproblem

loading. Many trees and shrubs, including expensive ones, are damaged by incorrect rough handling or incorrect

Subproblem

planting--in holes too shallow or too close to a house, or with air left around the roots. Finally, Timmerman depends on word-of-mouth publicity, but when neighbors come over to ask summer help about the names of plants, conditions they like, or care they need, the new workers usually have no idea, or make a blind guess.

Recognition of alternatives

Apparently Timmerman cannot afford to have its regular help spend much time training summer workers. I think

Conclusion

the best solution is for Timmerman to develop a handbook for new employees that would be used as part of a brief

Recognition of implications; conclusion tied to problem definition

orientation program for summer workers. While this would involve some time and expense, it is a one-time project that could help both the nursery and the new summer workers.

Pitfalls in problem analysis

In trying to write a good analysis, people may encounter difficulty in any of the three major areas: problem definition, structure, or conclusion. Here are some examples of typical pitfalls to watch out for in your own writing.

THE DEFINITION PITFALL

Instead of defining a problem, the writer in Example 1 is simply discussing his topic and describing a situation. He is telling us what he observed, instead of presenting key issues and concepts.

EXAMPLE 1:   Of the three textbooks I surveyed, Brace's offers the most detailed coverage of modern history —1340 pages to carry every day. Howard's book is easier to read and half the length. Unlike most history books, it is organized around topics rather than strict chronology. Levine's is the oldest and is outdated on some recent topics. Each book has unique features.

THE STRUCTURE PITFALL

The writer of Example 2 has given us a useful top-level idea: the book fails to provide background. However, the rest of the paragraph is simply a list of facts, all of which seem equally important but unrelated. The writer needs to reorganize this list into two or three major subproblems, such as the book's lack of social, biographical, and literary contexts, and then use the facts to support her organizing ideas.

EXAMPLE 2:   The poems in this anthology are harder to understand and remember because the book doesn't provide any context for them. There are no footnotes to say when a poem was written and only a sentence or two about the author. Many poems refer to historical events or unfamiliar customs that most students wouldn't know about. If you wonder about why the poem was written, or why it was written the way it was, the anthology offers no help. Although it has a large number of sonnets, it never mentions the nature of sonnets, what kinds of people wrote them, or when.

THE CONCLUSION PITFALL

The writer of Example 3 started with a well-defined problem: The current French text is not organized for easy review, even though that is a necessary part of learning the material. But her conclusion shows two common pitfalls. First, the solution is a prepackaged, unrelated assertion that does not address the problem she defined. Secondly, it is the kind of conclusion that "can't go wrong." As with a statement supporting Mom and apple pie, no one will probably disagree with it, but then no one will bother to listen either.

> EXAMPLE 3: In conclusion, students need to be able to learn at their own pace, and still cover the material required by the course. For many students this will involve not only more time spent studying, but more chance to speak and use French in the classroom.

From topic to problem to thesis

In this chapter we have been discussing the art of problem analysis — the art of thinking through a complex situation. You may now be asking: How does problem analysis help in writing a typical college paper in which you must state and support a thesis? To answer this question, let us look at how writers typically work their way from having a topic, to defining a problem, to finding a thesis.

It is important to recognize the difference between a topic, a problem, and a thesis. In the textbook assignment discussed on pp. 12–13, the topic was "textbooks and the differences among them." A topic simply names a field, a body of knowledge, or a situation (e.g., textbooks differ). Given only a topic, you could simply write a description of different textbooks. But what would you choose to say, how would you order it, and why would you be writing (other than to turn in the paper on time)?

By contrast, when you define a problem *within* the topic, you are identifying a key issue or conflict that you and your reader care about. For example, in writing about textbooks you might define the problem as: "Textbooks often don't meet students' needs." A problem analysis is, by definition, an exploration of a problematic situation. As a result of such an analysis, you might conclude that textbook writers are making the wrong assumptions and thereby making their books hard to use; that textbooks should build on the students' existing skills; or that the current statistics course is a failure. It is at this point that you have a thesis.

A *thesis* can be defined as an assertion about a topic that you believe to be true and that you intend to support and explain in your paper. If we could follow the thinking process of a writer, we would see that it often follows this path from topic to problem to thesis. Faced with a topic or situation, the writer first looks for a felt difficulty that seems worth thinking about. This leads to a clearer definition of the problem or conflict, which leads to an analysis of that problem, which ends up with some form of conclusion. The conclusion, in turn, becomes a thesis the writer is willing to support. If you know a topic extremely well, you may already have a thesis and know what you want to say. You have already done your analysis. However, most college assignments, such as "Discuss the background of the Chinese revolution," are sufficiently broad or challenging that they call for fresh analysis.

Notice how the following examples of a starting thesis all draw on the problem analysis that went before. At times, as in the first two examples, a writer may decide to use his problem definition as his thesis—he wishes to support the fact that a problem currently exists.

Theses that assert that a problem exists:

- The textbook in our course is causing real difficulty for many students.
- The continued fruitless search for the "missing link" in man's evolution suggests that the theory of slow, steady evolution needs to be reconsidered.

Theses that assert a hypothesis or new understanding of the problem:

- Students are failing to grasp the basic principles in our course because the textbook tries to build on knowledge most students don't have.
- The relatively sudden and widespread appearance of early man eliminates the possibility that men evolved by the time-consuming mechanism of competition and survival of the fittest.

Theses that assert a solution to a problem:

- Instructors of large, required courses should consider pretesting their texts with a representative group of students.
- In order to unlock the mysteries of man's development, we should explore the genetic factors that govern two key features of man: the rapid growth of the brain and the slow process of maturation.

To sum up, analyzing problems is an important part of thinking through a topic or a situation. It is a way of discovering the critical issues that often motivate real-world writing. As a thinking procedure, problem analysis basically involves three processes: defining the problem, analyzing its parts, and coming to a conclusion. Many situations, especially in business, call for a written problem analysis that simply follows this format. However, expository writing, such as an essay, is usually organized around a thesis you wish to support and explain. Problem analysis is often the first step in developing that thesis, and though its basic parts may be rearranged, the elements of definition, analysis, and conclusion are important components of most expository and persuasive papers.

Projects and Exercises

1 *An educational problem.* As assistant to the Dean of Humanities, you have been asked to study the "writing problem" that today's students are said to have. The dean wants to get some idea of whether students at your college are indeed having trouble writing and, if so, what the problem is. Your task is to assess the problem by examining it from the *student's* point of view. Interview a representative group of students for your study and write a one-page analysis of the writing problem students face, as you see it after talking to them.

2 *A literary problem.* In the play *A Midsummer Night's Dream*, Shakespeare's characters seem to be arguments for two sides of a question. Clearly the domineering fathers, who want to force their children into marriage at the beginning of the play, are undesirable people, and yet they are also associated with law and a stable social order. This is important because while the world of the fairies is beautiful and poetic (just the opposite of the world of the dogmatic fathers), it also leads to madness, to malicious and spiteful fights between the King and Queen of the Fairies, and to lovers acting in cruel and irrational ways toward each other. Take a further look at this conflict in the play and in human nature: write a paper that analyzes the problem. Obviously this kind of problem does not demand a solution or recommendation. Your job as a writer is to understand this problem in all its complexity and to express your understanding as effectively as you can.

3 *A personal problem.* Michael B. is a college sophomore who commutes to school. He feels he is missing much of the experience of college by living at home with his parents and seeing primarily high school friends who didn't go to college. He wants to live on campus next year but knows that if he does that, he will have to ask for the money from his father who feels Michael should be working instead of going to college, and saving money rather than spending it. The conflict has left Michael unable to act. Can you analyze this problem and offer useful suggestions?

4 *A professional problem.* Jim Grayson and Tom Brand both work for the Ford Motor Company in Chicago. One is a spot welder on the assembly line, the other a plant manager. In his book *Working*, Studs Terkel interviewed both men, asking them to talk about their jobs, and turned up some interesting contradictions.* You have been hired as a trouble-shooter and consultant by Ford with the long-range goal of satisfying the needs of both the employees and management. These interviews, on pp. 164–68 and 171–81 of the book, are your raw data. Analyze them and write a one-page problem analysis to

---

* Studs Terkel, *Working* (New York: Pantheon, 1972).

the vice president in charge of production. No one expects the problem to be a simple one; at the same time, your reader needs to be able to act on the recommendations you give her.

Alternatively, you could read the interview with Steve Carmichael, also in *Working* (pp. 341–43), and write your own analysis of this situation in a one- to two-page report to the district superintendent, who needs to act on this personnel problem.

5   *Your own problem.* Generally the most fruitful problems to analyze are your own. Think of a problematic situation in which you find yourself right now. Remember a problem is only a problem when someone feels caught between two sides of a question. Examine the key conflict in your situation and write an analysis of the problem, giving alternatives, assumptions, and implications.

If You Would Like to Read More

If you would like to know more about problem analysis and designing your written analysis for a professional audience, see:

Mathes, J. C., and Dwight Stevenson. *Designing Technical Reports: Writing for Audiences in Organizations.* Indianapolis: Bobbs-Merrill, 1976. ■   This book shows how to use problem analysis to write effective technical reports within an organization. It gives an excellent introduction to professional writing in all kinds of organizations.

Young, Richard, Alton Becker, and Kenneth Pike. *Rhetoric: Discovery and Change.* New York: Harcourt Brace Jovanovich, 1970. ■   The authors of this important book in rhetoric explore the entire process of problem analysis and inquiry. They analyze what it means to think about problems through the act of writing, and in doing so they lay the groundwork for a modern theory of rhetoric.

chapter three
Understanding Your Own Writing Process

This chapter will look at two practical problems, the problem of getting started and the problem of getting stopped, or temporary writer's block. If you have trouble getting started, if you depend heavily on inspiration or the threat of deadlines to motivate you, or if the idea of having to write makes you anxious and you try to avoid it, this chapter should be of some help to you.

Getting started

Nearly everybody has trouble getting started. Some people procrastinate as far from pen and paper as possible; others sit and stare at a blank page. Getting started is a common problem because it is not simply a question of ability (good writers have difficulty) or of knowledge about the subject (experts with a lot to say have trouble too). Getting started is often a strategy problem directly related to how you tackle the task.

Let us look at the thinking process of a writer trying to begin a paper. What are some of the strategies and goals this writer seems to have? How well do they work?

TRANSCRIPT OF A WRITER THINKING ALOUD

Trial and error

My name is Jo Banta. I'm trying to write a paper on writer's block. In today's world . . . for today's student, writer's block is a matter of great concern . . . of universal concern. In today's high-pressure education, writer's block is a question that plagues many students. . . . In today's high-pressure education. . . . In the high-pressure education of today, writer's block is a problem of great, of universal concern that plagues. . . . In high-pressure education, writer's block is a matter of almost universal concern. . . . In high-pressure education of today, one problem that plagues many students is. . . . This is a problem because. . . . Writer's block is a problem because. . . . Due to the phenomenon of writer's block. . . . Because of its omnipresence, many writers fail to

Perfect-draft block

hand in assignments on time and thereby lose, . . . and they thereby receive, . . . they get lower grades. Because of the omnipresence, because of writer's block . . . oh what the hell do I know about writer's block. I think I'm having it! How can I write about writer's block when I'm in the middle of it!! What an awful assignment. Wonder what dinner will be tonight. Boy, that window's dirty.

O.K., writer's block. . . .

Waiting for inspiration

Writer's block . . . maybe something will come. Just think about it a while. . . . Although many people fail to recognize it . . . Although. . . .

Words looking for an idea

Although what!? I don't know! Oh well. . . . Although many people don't know, don't recognize it, one of the most important determinants of students' grades is . . . is . . . what? O.K. Try again. . . . Not only is writer's block one of the most important, but . . . but . . . but. This is

Brainstorming

crazy. I'm getting nowhere writing sentences. . . . Let's see, what do I really know about writer's block? Sometimes I get it when I don't know what I'm talking about. Maybe because I don't have anything to say yet. But sometimes I get it when I do know a lot, when there's a lot of pressure, and I've got to turn a paper out, and I want it to be really good, and sound like I've got things covered. . . . All right, writer's block is a universal . . . universal problem for students when under conditions of pressure . . . a universal situation in which students placed under

WIRMI

pressure . . . a universal situation in which students placed under pressures of today's university . . . oh, here I go again . . . what I really mean is . . . writer's block is a problem for students who have good ideas but can't express them because of . . . o.k., what are my choices . . . because of the

Notation

$\left\{\begin{array}{l}\textit{environment}\\\textit{educational pressure}\\\textit{pressure of time and grades}\\\textit{limits of time and the pressure of grades}\end{array}\right.$

Satisficing

That's not perfect, but I'll just bracket it as a problem and go on. It's always easier to make those decisions as an editor instead of when you're generating. O.K., now I haven't done much brainstorming yet, so let's see if I can map out what I do know and what I'll want to think about. It's time to brainstorm. What is a block?

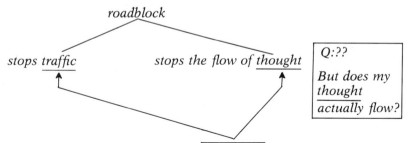

Does writer's block stop something from coming out?
That assumes that the "something" is already there.

Is it? That's a distinction I might play with. How about writer's blank?

WEAK STRATEGIES

The above transcription of a writer's thoughts demonstrates four composing strategies that often cause trouble for writers.

A trial and error approach to producing sentences / One of the first things we notice in this transcript is the almost random way the writer keeps trying to combine words and phrases in the hope that one version will finally sound acceptable. In working out her first major thought, she is trying out six alternative phrasings:

in today's world	*a matter of*
for today's student	*a question that*
in today's high-pressure education	*a problem of*

These trial and error stabs at producing sentences often produce only confusion, because in trying to juggle so many alternatives and keep them all in mind at once, the writer is likely to overload her short-term memory. The capacity of human short-term memory — what we might call our conscious attention span —is rather limited. That is why people often fail at such tasks as trying to listen to two conversations and think of something to say at the same time. Because we can only consider a few separate elements at one time (some say the limit is seven elements, plus or minus two), we are unable to simultaneously consider all the alternative versions of a sentence and make an efficient choice. So we keep reviewing the options. This writer's performance is also characteristic of trial and error in that she often loses track of her search and continues to reproduce previously rejected versions.

A trial and error strategy is not only confusing, it's slow. Say our writer had continued to hammer away at this one sentence alone, juggling its mere two sets of alternatives. There are at least 104 possible combinations and grammatical transformations—including passive, negative, declarative, interrogative, and so forth—that she might conceivably have had to try! Clearly, one of the first strategies a writer needs is a way to narrow this enormous field of options, of all the possible things one could say, down to a set of things one would want to say.

A perfect-draft strategy / Here the writer starts at the beginning and writes a perfected final draft in one slow, laborious pass-through. Looking at the first paragraph as a whole, we see that instead of planning, jotting notes, or defining her goals, the writer has started out by trying to produce a perfect set of sentences. She is trying to generate her ideas and language in the flowing sequence of a finished text. The form of the final product is dictating the form of her mental process.

As inefficient as this strategy is, many people depend on it—spending hours trying to perfect their first paragraph or first page. Once they have sweated out that first paragraph the rest of the paper does indeed come more easily. But why? It is because, in the act of writing those introductory sentences, they have also been planning the point and organization of the entire paper. As if planning one's ideas wasn't hard enough, these writers are also trying to produce perfect sentences, create just the right tone, and make smooth connections between all their points. All of these things must eventually be done, but a perfect-draft strategy tries to do all of them at once. By jumping into producing finished prose before deciding what they want to say, such writers are unlikely to do either task well. They give themselves their own writer's block.

Waiting for inspiration / Some writers wait until they see the whole piece clearly in their mind or until words and sentences start "flowing" and they know just what they want to say. This is a chancy but well-known strategy that will be discussed in more detail shortly.

Words looking for an idea / The writer is still focusing her attention on producing sentences. In the second paragraph the expressions "Although. . . . ," "is . . . ," and "Not only . . . , but . . ." sound promising, until the writer discovers she has no ideas to fill in the slots. She has let the momentum of language itself direct composition and lead her down the garden path.

POWERFUL STRATEGIES

One of the advantages of this simulated transcript is that our writer can suddenly turn very obliging and clever. Once she realizes that the perfect-draft approach isn't working, she switches tactics and demonstrates a set of more powerful strategies that do work. Here are a few:

Brainstorming / Instead of producing perfect sentences, the writer concentrates on her ideas, jotting down thoughts in whatever order they come to her.

Using WIRMI / WIRMI is a strategy for getting yourself to make a clear and concise statement of your point, whenever you find yourself bogged down in trying to perfect a sentence. Simply say to yourself, *What I Really Mean Is* . . . and switch from writing prose to "talking to yourself." Just say what you think, then perfect the prose later.

Using notation techniques / In trying to write a sentence or get an idea clear, it often helps to get it down on paper so you can work with it visually, not just in your head. For example, it helps to write alternative phrasings under one another, or to use more exotic displays of relationships—flow charts, trees, brackets, boxes, arrows, and so forth. If you don't write down fragments and phrases as they come to you, you are likely either to lose them or to find yourself reproducing them over and over. But to take maximum advantage of your notations and visual displays, you must also leave room to rewrite and make changes on your draft. That means skipping lines and leaving generous margins. Your goal here is to ease the load on your limited short-term memory and let yourself write and edit rather than juggle alternatives in your head.

Satisficing / When you are writing a first draft it is often useful to accept an adequate, but imperfect, expression or idea in order to get on with more important problems. People have coined a rather odd but very useful word for this notion, which is "to satisfice." Problem-solvers satisfice, as it is called, when they take the first acceptable solution or alternative instead of searching for the very best one. People satisfice every day (to the relief of grocers) when they take the first acceptable peach at the fruit stall instead of rummaging through the entire bin for the very best one. And writers satisfice when they decide to write now and revise later. Things that are impossible to solve in the middle of composing often become simple when you are editing. So satisficing on a first draft can let you make the best use of your time.

Getting stopped and writing under pressure

Most of us write under pressure, whether it's the pressure of deadlines, grades, critical readers, or our own expectations. Some amount of pressure is a good source of motivation. But when worry or the desire to perform well is too great, it creates an additional task of coping with anxiety. When it comes to writing, some people are automatically so anxious that they can't get started, or they avoid the prospect at all costs by looking for courses and jobs that don't require writing.

These are the extreme cases. For most of us, getting stopped or having writer's block is a temporary condition. It comes at the end of a train of thought when we suddenly find ourselves unsure of what to do next, or when words refuse to fall into sentences and we are left stranded in midphrase.

The causes of writer's block vary. Although external forces such as a deadline often create pressure, it is internal forces that produce anxiety and writer's block. In other words, writer's block is an obstacle that writers throw in their own path. Two ways they commonly do this are by having an overly critical Internal Editor or by depending on an inefficient composing method.

People who write well or who wish they did are often their own worst enemy. Their success or failure in the past leads them to set extraordinarily high expectations: "this paper (which really means 'I,' the writer) must be brilliant, creative, original, or beyond criticism." High standards are a good idea (many writers could improve their performance substantially if they bothered or dared to reread and revise). But *unrealistic* expectations often produce nothing more than anxiety.

Here then is the problem. A writer who demands good results can demand them at the wrong time. He or she often sets up a highly critical Internal Editor who pounces on every scrap as it's written, rejecting the writer's half-formed thoughts because they are disorganized or don't sound like a polished piece of writing. Unfortunately, few papers, even good ones, emerge from the writer's mind in their full glory and polished form. Instead they come out in bits and pieces, in stray thoughts that later become important, and in tentative, disorganized sentences. When such unrealistic expectations set up a severe internal critic, this watchdog stops the thinking process before it starts, and the writer ends up with a series of false starts and crumpled, rejected drafts.

Why do writers do this to themselves? What leads them to expect their thoughts to flow out in polished, finished prose? The answer often lies in the assumptions they make about their composing process.

Alternative composing methods

Let us look at the advantages and limitations of three major approaches to writing: the perfect-draft, inspiration, and problem-solving approaches.

THE PERFECT-DRAFT APPROACH

As noted earlier, this method, which attempts to produce a paper in one pass-through, can be efficient if it works. But if your ideas are not fully formed and you need to concentrate on purpose, content, or organization, it makes little sense to try to juggle the demands of polished prose at the same time.

THE INSPIRATION METHOD

When we feel inspired, writing seems easy and exciting. The words seem to flow unbidden and the first draft is the final one. Unfortunately, muses are notoriously unreliable, and this makes inspiration a very poor choice as a standard composing method. Yet, many people assume that it is the *only* method open to them if they want to produce a really good piece of writing. The perfect-draft approach and steady work can always turn out words on a page, but good writing comes when, and only when, the writer finally gets his or her "inspiration." Or so the myth goes.

One of the best descriptions of the myth of inspiration comes from poet Samuel Taylor Coleridge's account of how he came to compose his famous, mysterious poem *Kubla Khan*. You may think that the creative process of a major poet has little to do with normal expository writing, but, in fact, the exploits of heros and artists are often the source of popular myths that tell us how the experience *should* be.

In his account Coleridge says that he had been reading a book called *Purchas's Pilgrimages*, a fabulous account of the marvels seen on seventeenth-century voyages of exploration. He had been taking opium, which he tells us was, of course, prescribed by his doctor. When he woke up, he began his poem with these words:

> In Xanadu did Kubla Khan
> A stately pleasure-dome decree:
> Where Alph, the sacred river, ran
> Through caverns measureless to man
> Down to a sunless sea.

Writing about this experience, and referring to himself in the third person, Coleridge says:

> ...he fell asleep in his chair at the moment that he was reading the following sentence, or words of the same substance, in *Purchas's Pilgrimage*: "Here the Khan Kubla commanded a palace to be built and a stately garden thereunto. And thus ten miles of fertile ground were inclosed with a wall."

(1) The Author continued for about three hours in a profound sleep, at least of the external senses, during which time he has the most vivid confi-

(2) dence, that he could not have composed less than from two to three hundred lines: if that indeed can be called composition in which all the images rose up before him as things, with a parallel production of the

(3) correspondent expressions, without any sensation or consciousness of effort. On awaking he appeared to himself to have a distinct recollection of the whole, and taking his pen, ink, and paper, instantly and eagerly wrote down the lines that are here preserved. At this moment he was unfortunately called out by a person on business from Porlock, and detained by him above an hour, and on his return to his room, found, to his no small surprise and mortification, that though he still retained some vague and dim recollection of the general purport of the vision,

(4) yet with the exception of some eight or ten scattered lines and images, all the rest had passed away like the images on the surface of a stream into which a stone has been cast, but, alas! without the after restoration of the latter!

Coleridge's account of his experience contains four major elements of the myth of inspiration. This myth becomes a problem when people see it as a description of how the writing process *should* work. In the myth:

1. The vision comes to the writer in sleep. In other words, there is no conscious effort, no preparation, or planning, no thinking.

2. The writer's inspiration or vision comes complete and fully assembled. He does not simply have an intuition or an idea that must then be developed; the state of inspiration reveals a "whole" product, in this case two or three hundred lines that we can assume will not have to be revised.

3. The act of composition itself is not the time-consuming task of testing and modifying alternatives. Instead, the author merely re-members and preserves the content of the dream or vision. This is appropriate because inspiration is often seen as a gift from the gods. Naturally you wouldn't expect such a gift to come only half-written. Moses received the Ten Commandments written on tablets of stone. Athena, the Greek goddess of wisdom, science, and the arts, and an appropriate emblem for creative thought, was said to have sprung fully armed from the head of Zeus. These elements which make up the myth of inspiration are old and well established.

4. The final element of this myth is the most critical one for us. Because the stuff of inspiration is, in a sense, a gift from the gods that appears without conscious effort, it cannot be duplicated or re-peated. Once interrupted by a gentleman from Porlock, the vision will be lost forever. Like that proverbial "bolt from the blue," our ideas come from outside, instead of from our own efforts to assemble our knowledge into new insights.

These elements of the myth of inspiration suggest that writers are passive recipients of visions and that the creative process is a mixture of waiting and luck. Fortunately that's just not true. Although the myth describes the way it often *feels* to create something, it isn't particularly accurate about what actually happens. The magic of inspiration is the magic of a mind hard at work. For example, literary sleuth John Livingston Lowes has shown how the images of *Kubla Khan* had their source in Coleridge's wide reading. Coleridge's combination and translation of these images were unique —a creative act —but the raw material of the creative process was the knowledge stored in his own mind.

If the myth of inspiration is neither a particularly accurate nor helpful model for the creative process, is there a better one that can also include the subjective experience of inspiration we've all felt? In *The Art of Thought* (1926), Graham Wallas showed that inspiration, or "illumination," is merely the third stage in a four-stage creative process:

1. *Preparation* is the first stage. "Chance," Pasteur said, "favors the prepared mind." This is a mind that has read, thought, and worked on the problem. Sometimes this stage can last for years.

2. *Incubation* is a second, little understood stage. No one knows quite what happens or why, but in periods of rest when the problem is not being actively considered, new combinations are formed, new ideas generated.

3. *Illumination*, the third stage, is simply the result of the previous two, but it is the stage that gets all the press. This may be a dramatic moment, or alternatively a quiet one, when preparation and thought pay off and you see your solution, an image of what you want to do. Unfortunately, most illuminations don't spring from the mind as fully armed Athenas or as completely written texts. What we usually "see" is only a plan or a sketch of what the solution might be. This leads to the next step.

4. *Verification* is the working out of the solution. For writers this is often the complex and lengthy process of making language say exactly what they want it to say, and making sure it says it to readers as well as to themselves. Any approach to composing, then, should recognize all four of these processes, not just the moment of illumination.

A PROBLEM-SOLVING APPROACH TO COMPOSING

A problem-solving approach to writing differs from the perfect-draft and inspiration methods in two ways. It stresses a goal-directed kind of thinking, and it often draws on a variety of strategies (also known as *heuristics*) to achieve its end.

It may seem odd to think of writing as a "problem" with a "solution" since we often apply those terms to situations where a precise solution *procedure* is already known, as it is in algebra. A problem, however, is simply any situation in which you are at point A and need to find some way to get to your goal, point B. Problem-solving is the act of getting there, of achieving goals.

What sort of problem-solving approaches do you use when you write? Generally speaking, writers have three alternative ways to proceed. They can use rules, trial and error, or heuristics.

Using rules / Rules tell you exactly what to do when. If you know the time and the rate, you can compute distance by using the rule $T \times R = D$. In grade school many of us learned rules for writing: state your topic; make three main points about it; develop each point in three separate paragraphs, each of which has a topic sentence; then write a conclusion, and you're done.

The virtue of rules is that they are explicit; anybody can follow them. Their weakness is that they are simple-minded and are inadequate for more complex problems such as solving our energy crisis, fixing a car that won't start, or writing a report on either of these.

Using trial and error / People like to use trial and error because it seems like a comfortable way to proceed. You don't have to plan or study the problem; you just start writing and see how it turns out. When the problem is small (e.g., writing a note to leave on the refrigerator) or the problem-solver is lucky, trial and error is efficient. But as we saw in the transcript on pages 36–37, this haphazard method can waste a lot of time if there are too many alternatives.

If your car wouldn't start and you began a systematic trial and error search of its 6,000 parts, you would on the average have twiddled 3,000 screws, plugs, and wires before you found the trouble. Proceeding without a plan can be easy, but expensive in terms of time.

Using heuristics / Heuristics —that is, efficient strategies or discovery procedures —are the heart of problem-solving. Some of them are nothing more than small rules of thumb that say "try this first" and cut down the number of alternatives you must consider. They reduce the size of the problem. For example, in a typical chess game there are 10^{120} possible moves to make but only 10^{16} microseconds in a century in which to make them. So experts rely on a heuristic procedure such as "try to control the center with your pawn" instead of considering all the possible alternative moves.

Heuristics —or strategies, as I will be calling them —have another important feature. They are powerful; that is, they have a high probability of succeeding. For example, a good heuristic procedure for diagnosing a dead car is: first check the gas, then the battery, then the ignition. A powerful heuristic writers often use is "just try to jot down things without organizing them yet." The problem-solving strategies we will be looking at in this book are simply a set of heuristics or techniques that good writers rely on. Some of these strategies are as old as Aristotle's methods of forming comparisons. Some, such as brainstorming, come from the study of creative thinking done by scientists, inventors, and problem-solvers in industry. And some come from recent studies of the thinking processes of writers themselves. In each of these cases, I have tried to translate a heuristic procedure that experts use into a practical strategy writers can learn.

Although heuristic procedures are powerful, they do not come with a guarantee. For example, many good tennis players rely on the following strategy: try to make a hard, deep shot in order to get a soft return from your opponent, so you can then run up to the net and put the ball away. Unfortunately, as you are charging the net, your opponent might just hit a passing shot that goes right by you. Unlike a rule, which will always produce a "correct" answer if followed, a heuristic procedure is only a high-probability way to proceed, so a writer needs to know a variety of alternative techniques. However, for a complex problem like writing, heuristics are the most dependable and most creative way to go.

One of the chief differences between good and poor writers, and good and poor problem-solvers in general, is the repertory of strategies or heuristics on which they draw. Good writers not only have a large repertory of powerful strategies, but they have sufficient self-awareness of their own process to draw on these alternative techniques as they need them. They guide their own creative process, in other words. Although motivation, talent, or experience can strongly affect that process, it is a process writers *can* understand and change. The purpose of this book is to make the intuitive problem-solving process that good writers use more explicit and available to the rest of us.

Let us close this chapter, then, by applying a basic problem-solving principle to the problem of writing under pressure.

Practical suggestions for coping with pressure

When you have trouble with getting started or with getting stopped, the cause may lie in the strategy you have chosen. If you can't eliminate external pressure you can cope with it by changing your own writing method. The key is a basic problem-solving principle: break the large, complex problem of writing down into a set of smaller subproblems that you can concentrate on one at a time.

First, instead of sitting down to produce a paper in its entirety, give yourself a subgoal or separate task such as brainstorming or writing an individual page or paragraph on a topic you are already clear about. It often helps to separate these tasks in time: tell yourself, "All I have to do this morning is jot down my ideas and make a rough plan for the paper. I don't have to do any writing unless I want to."

By concentrating on a manageable subtask, and only a subtask, you often do it better, and ironically, when the pressure is off, you may find that the writing is no longer so hard to do. By setting up a limited and achievable subgoal, you can seduce yourself into starting to write.

A second way to reduce pressure and create manageable subgoals is to use a "write and revise" method. Plan your writing so you can write a reasonably efficient first draft and satisfice on those places that would slow you down. If you don't know how to spell a word, don't give it a second thought. Just write it down and keep on going. Should you use a colon or semicolon here? If you aren't sure, figure it out later. Make this first draft as coherent and as clear as you can; where you need to stop and think about your meaning, do so. But don't get sidetracked into perfecting your prose. Instead, count on revision to be a major second step in your writing process. Give yourself the freedom to just write a working draft.

There are good reasons to do this. First of all, the fact that it is only a rough draft reduces the extra, internal pressure that causes anxiety and writer's block. Secondly, a two-step process of writing and revising is a smart way to use your time. Many local problems that seem insurmountable when you are in the midst of composing are problems because you are still deciding where you want to go next. If you keep the larger picture in mind while writing, minor problems will fall into place when you later edit and revise.

As a general rule, if you find your writing process becoming inefficient or unproductive, that is a signal that you need to switch tactics and tackle the problem in a new way. The following chapters on steps and strategies in writing will offer you some concrete, alternative ways to proceed.

Projects and Exercises

1 *A self-appraisal of your own writing process.* The following self-analysis asks you to do three things: first, to look at your own writing process as objectively as a musician, dancer, or athlete would look at his or her performance. What strategies do you typically rely on and how well do they usually work? Secondly, spend some time collecting data on yourself. What do you really do when trying to write? And finally, how does that compare to your image of what a good writer would do? Jot down your answers on a separate sheet.

A. What are the last four things you have written (excluding short notes), and who read them? We will refer to your writing here as a "paper," but it could have been a college composition, letter, memo, announcement, proposal, or report. (In the questions that follow, whenever you find it difficult to decide what is typical for you, refer back to these four events as your norm.)

B. In general, how do you feel about writing?

   rather enjoy it   neutral   dislike it

C. Do you find it easy to write papers that say what you wanted them to say? In practical terms, is writing a relatively efficient process for you in which your time is in proportion to your intentions?

D. How many hours did you spend writing (drafting, writing, revising) the last three papers you did? Give number of hours and number of pages written (excluding appendices). Is this normal?

E. Do you generally try to write a piece in one sitting from the beginning, or do you work on sections separately and at various times?

F. Do you generally end up having to do the actual writing of papers under pressure —that is, under a tight time constraint?

G. When you think of having to write a paper, what are the main things that come to mind for you?

H. Are any of these problems ones you frequently have?
   1. Getting started:
        Getting the whole paper ordered in your head before you write.
        Getting a beginning paragraph.
        Getting a first sentence.
        Sitting down to write.
        Turning on the flow of creative ideas.
   2. Organizing what you know into a paper:
        Finding a main idea or thesis that fits in all the things you have
           to say.
        Turning an outline or sketch into a fleshed-out, proper paper with
           sentences and paragraphs.
        Turning lots of good ideas into an outline.
        Writing a formal paper when you know you could explain it easily
           if you could just talk to the person.
   3. Writing for an audience:
        Knowing what your reader really wants.
        Finding that readers miss the important things you thought were
           clearly stated.
        Finding that, upon rereading your writing, you don't understand
           it in the same way you did when you wrote it.
   4. Controlling the circumstances under which you write:
        Trying to concentrate with noise and activity around you (the TV,
           stereo, friends, family).
        Writing when you feel tired or sleepy instead of during the most
           alert part of your day.
        Being inadequately prepared (you haven't had time to think the
           problem through before you start to compose).
        Having no time (or less than a day) to let the paper sit between
           writing and editing it.

I. Do you have any rituals that help you get in the mood to write? Many people depend on private rituals that help them to get started and maintain their concentration as they write. The rituals can vary from mere sharpened pencils to special rooms, desks, or times of day set aside for writing. Some people set subgoals and give themselves rewards when they achieve them. Do you have any private rituals that help you get in a frame of mind to write? If so, jot them down.

J. Once you have completed questions A–I, read over your responses. Try to define as perceptively as you can three major problems you have in writing. Make your definitions as specific as possible. Now develop a practical plan for dealing with each of your problems the next time they come up.

2 Use the next paper or report you have to write as an opportunity to do a case study of your own writing process. Note down how you spend your time and keep track of how your ideas and your paper develop. Then, looking back, write a retrospective analysis of your own composing process. Decide what was most interesting about your "case" and write a paper emphasizing what you discovered about your writing process.

If You Want to Read More

If you want to know more about problem-solving, creativity, and ways to explore your own writing process, see:

Elbow, Peter. *Writing Without Teachers*. London: Oxford, 1973. ▪ This short and readable book has helped many people get over their worries about writing.

Hayes, John R. *Cognitive Psychology: Thinking and Creating*. Homewood, Ill.: Dorsey Press, 1978. ▪ This highly readable book traces the history of modern psychology and how it has attempted to understand the mysterious processes of creative thinking. The book covers the major approaches, from introspection to computer simulation, and concludes with current research in cognitive psychology.

————. *The Complete Problem Solver*. Philadelphia: Franklin Institute Press, in press. ▪ This fascinating introduction to the art of problem-solving puts theory and research to practical application. It discusses effective strategies for a wide range of intellectual and practical tasks, from planning to remembering information to decision-making and creative thinking.

Koestler, Arthur. *The Act of Creation*. New York: Dell, 1967. ▪ This classic combines a theory of creativity with hundreds of historical sketches and examples of both scientific and artistic creativity.

chapter four
Case Study: A Personal Profile

I n the following chapters we will be looking at nine steps in the
composing process and at a variety of strategies for taking these
steps.

PLANNING

> Step 1: Explore the Rhetorical Problem
> Step 2: Make a Plan

GENERATING IDEAS IN WORDS

> Step 3: Use Creative Thinking
> Step 4: Organize Your Ideas

DESIGNING FOR A READER

> Step 5: Know the Needs of Your Reader
> Step 6: Transform Writer-Based Prose into Reader-Based Prose

EDITING FOR EFFECTIVENESS

> Step 7: Review Your Paper and Your Purpose
> Step 8: Test and Edit Your Writing
> Step 9: Edit for Connections and Coherence

Each of these nine steps represents a task you as a writer will
need to do. However, these steps are unusual: unlike stair steps that
march straight from A to B, each of these steps may need to be taken
over and over in the process of writing. A simple-minded model of

FIGURE **4-1**   *A simple-minded model of the composing process*

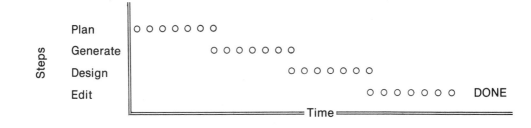

the composing process might pretend that writing was a neat, or-
derly, straightforward set of steps like those in Figure 4-1.

By contrast, the normal process of a writer is not a linear march
forward; it is recursive. That is, writers constantly return to earlier
steps such as planning in order to carry out later ones. For example,
Figure 4-2 shows a more realistic graph of what a writer was doing
over a ten-minute period. In the circled area the writer was editing
a passage he had just written when he realized that there was a gap
in his argument. So he stopped editing, popped back up to the planning step, generated some new ideas, organized them with the reader
in mind, and then reedited the whole passage and moved on, planning what he wanted to do next.

The following chapters, then, will describe nine major steps in
the writing process, but the order in which you take the steps will
depend on the stage you are in and how your writing develops. Presented along with each step will be a set of different strategies that
will help you take those steps, such as strategies to help you plan
more effectively, generate better ideas, or edit for certain specific
effects. These strategies, based on the effective strategies good writers

FIGURE **4-2**   *Model of a normal composing process*

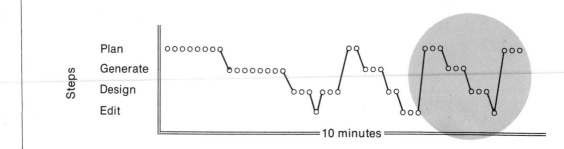

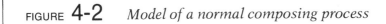

use, can help you increase your repertory of problem-solving skills for writing.

It is important to remember that these strategies are not rules or sure-fire formulas for writing. Instead they are simply an organized description of some of the things good writers normally do when they write. Many may be effective strategies you already use but didn't have a name for. Just to make this point more vivid, let us look at a case study of a real writer in action who uses many of the strategies we will discuss.

Case study of Joan

This short case study describes the experience of a real college student, Joan, with a writing problem: developing a personal essay for a scholarship application. The process of writing went on for nearly two weeks, from the time she started thinking about the essay until it was mailed. In this process she used a number of the writing strategies that will be discussed in the next few chapters. However, as you will see, she often used them without knowing that she was doing so, or in response to someone else's questions. This case study will let you see how individual techniques, such as brainstorming or making analogies, are often an instinctive part of the writing process. The only difference is that as a problem-solver one has the power of conscious choice.

Joan is a junior in engineering at a large university. She is doing well in her courses, but her real career goal is medical engineering — she wants to combine research and working with people. The year in London would give her a first-hand experience of what medical research is really like before she has to specialize. But she can't afford to go to London on her own.

On day one her writing process starts with the decision to write her application. She has a strong desire to go to London and a good school record to back her up, but beyond that she doesn't know what to say. As a result, her writing process begins with a four-day wait for inspiration which doesn't come. On day five, with her deadline approaching, she sits down after dinner with the empty form, a pad of paper, and the TV, to write something anyway. By 12:30 a.m. there is nothing left to watch and she spends an hour and a half on the first draft.

In the hard light of the next morning the draft sounds alternately pompous ("I feel my achievements in scholastic and extracurricular activities will demonstrate my ability to take advantage of an educational opportunity of this sort. . . .") or it sounds young and naive ("The idea of spending a year at the University of London fulfills some of my oldest dreams. It is the kind of experience I most want. . . ."). The section on her courses and past activities was easier to write and sounded all right but was mostly a list and, she felt, rather dull. Whenever she thought of faculty members of a British university reading this humdrum essay, she felt depressed. There was no way of guessing what they were looking for.

At this point her writing plan had two main goals: mention all the achievements she could think of and make sure there were no errors in the essay. The first important change in her strategy came about on day six quite by chance when she stopped by to ask a professor to write a recommendation for her. Although Professor Harris wanted to write a good letter, she knew nothing about medical engineering or the school. She read Joan's first draft and began pressing Joan for information. Joan later said, "It was like being grilled; she was asking me all these questions I couldn't answer. And yet I kept thinking: How can I be applying to this place if I can't answer them?" Here is how their conversation went. The notes in italics refer to strategies you will find discussed in later chapters.

HARRIS: ·A great idea. Wish I could be in London too. But now tell me, why do you want to go to this particular place rather than some other city? *(Setting goals)*

JOAN: Well, it's a great opportunity. And I've never been to England, and I'd just like to get out on my own. . . . Well, I guess they wouldn't care about that. Well, . . . it's a very good place to study medical research. . . . I don't know, . . . if you ask me point blank. Anyone would want to go.

HARRIS: Well I sympathize, especially with being on your own, but that hardly seems like a compelling reason for them to put up $5000 for you to study in London. So there's no particular reason. . . .

JOAN: Oh, but wait a minute. You don't see, there is. . . . You see, I want to prepare myself for a rather new field. There aren't many medical engineers yet. And it's important for people with an engineering background to understand what the real problems in medicine are —to really be up to date in medical research and know where technology can help. What's more, this will help me figure out where to specialize after I graduate. Unlike American schools, the British use a tutorial system that could be tailored to my special interests. And this is the perfect time in my career to do it. You see, I've taken all these courses in preparation. . . . *(Brainstorming)*

Maybe I should put some of this in the essay. I didn't know about the scholarship until a week ago, but I've been preparing myself in a sense for something like this for three years. People think my course schedule is crazy —physiology next to fluid mechanics. But you have to know those things to design an artificial heart.

O.K. now. I guess I do have some sort of answer. I want to go because it would be the best place —I could explain why —to prepare myself for a career in medical technology. This is also the time when I most need to make the bridge to medical research, before I decide where to specialize. *(Stating in a nutshell)*

HARRIS: Sounds good. But if you don't mind my asking, why would they want *you* specifically? *(Simulating a reader's response)* What I want to do in my letter is support, wherever I can, the arguments you are making in your application.

JOAN: This is awful. There will be hundreds of people applying —and lots of people have good grades. I'm not even in medicine. I don't know why anyone would want to give money away anyway, especially to me.

HARRIS: Well, how about looking at it as an investment rather than a gift? What kind of an investment would you be likely to make? *(Thinking by analogy)*

JOAN: Well, if you put it that way, I guess I might really pay off. For one thing, I'm really committed to this. I can show it, too, with my courses and my summer job in the Chicago lab, and I've just finished a first-aid course. I really do care about people; I'm good at engineering, and I've been preparing for this special career for a long time. I guess it also matters that I work hard, not just in classes but on independent projects too. That would matter a lot for this particular year. *(Brainstorming)*

HARRIS: I'm getting convinced. Maybe if you could just say some of *this* in the application? Somehow all this is more persuasive than your first-draft generalizations, which I'm afraid made me feel, "ho hum, I've heard this before."

JOAN: Yes, except. . . . Well, I just realized that the real problem here is to convince them that they want to give this scholarship to somebody in engineering instead of medicine. I've got to show them that it's good for undergraduates like me to spend a year in a medical research school. *(Setting goals and subgoals for writing)* That's the real thing. Maybe if your letter could somehow show that I really can bridge that gap between technology and human concerns. Maybe you could mention the project I did. *(Creating a more operational definition of a goal)*

If it's O.K., I'd like to do another draft of this and bring it in on Wednesday. *(Setting a subgoal)* That'll still give me a few more days to sit on it before the deadline. *(Incubation)*

When Joan set out to write the final version, her plan and priorities had changed significantly. First, she had a better idea of what she wanted the essay to accomplish for her. And in this draft, that's all she chose to worry about; polishing could come later. In other words, she broke the large problem of "write this essay" down into a set of more manageable tasks. *(Setting subgoals)* Since her father had asked a friend in the medical school to look over her draft, she tried writing it with him in mind, trying to anticipate his questions, such as, "Do you know enough about medicine yet to benefit from a medical research program?" *(Talking to your reader)*

According to Joan, this is the first time she had thought this much about her reader, and she was surprised to find out how well the approach worked. In the next two chapters we will pick up the rest of Joan's writing process, using some of her notes to illustrate writing strategies. The final version of her application follows. Notice how she has tried to use the ideas we saw her generating.

NATIONAL INSTITUTE OF HEALTH

INTERNSHIP PROGRAM

PERSONAL ESSAY:

My Purpose in Applying

I am applying for the University of London Internship Program in biomedical research because it would give me first-hand experience in medical research operations and the chance to learn scientific, communication, and personal skills not routinely encountered during an undergraduate education. Furthermore, it is a unique opportunity to combine my interests in engineering and biological research and prepare me for a career in medical engineering. The following is a brief description of my education, experiences, and interests that contribute to my ability to take full advantage of this internship.

Academic Studies

As a result of my strong interest in science and math, I am presently completing a degree in engineering. However, I am doing this as part of a self-designed interdisciplinary program that combines engineering and medicine. This has enabled me to pursue my interests in the biological sciences and to gain analytical and problem-solving skills. In addition to studying chemistry, biology, physiology, and basic engineering sciences, such as thermodynamics and mechanics, I have elected engineering courses related to the biological sciences. For example, I am presently studying the electrical biophysics of muscle, nerve, and synapse and am taking a chemical engineering course in the dynamics of biological systems. This knowledge of both biology and engineering would aid me in understanding the scientific theories and techniques employed in biomedical engineering research.

Goals and Practical Experience

As a biomedical researcher, I would fulfill my goal of a career that will help other people while at the same time be challenging scientifically. I had exposure to research while doing a biochemical assay for a neuropsychopharmocologist at ----- Clinic in Chicago. Besides learning the scientific procedures and techniques that are used, I learned how to deal with some of the practical and organizational problems encountered in research. I saw how the lack of equipment and funds often calls for real cooperation between departments and careful planning of one's own project. The experience also helped me develop more of the patience research requires and recognize the enormous amounts of time, paperwork, and careful steps required for testing a hypothesis that is only one very small but necessary part of the overall project.

But besides knowing some of the frustrations, I also know that many medical advancements, such as the cardiac pacemaker, artificial limbs, and cures for diseases, exist and benefit many people because of the efforts of researchers. Therefore I would like to pursue my interest in research by participating in the NIH Internship Program. The exposure to many diverse projects, designed to better understand and improve the body's functioning, would help me to decide which areas of biomedical engineering to pursue. For example, I would be interested in projects emphasizing chemical, electrical, or mechanical knowledge; work performed on a cellular or macroscopic level; and work concerned with the design of machines and products or the discovery of new processes within the body.

Qualities and Skills

Although my academic program has been of central importance, it has not been of single importance. I feel I have learned many nonacademic skills and qualities necessary for research by participation outside of the classroom. My skills in organization and communication have been enhanced by planning programs, keeping records, writing letters, and working with people as an officer of Tau Beta Pi, the National Engineering Honor Society. I have gained leadership skills as a supervisor of a swim club, learned how to handle staff problems and emergency situations, and learned the importance of maintaining accurate and current financial records. I had to analyze problem situations, search for alternatives, make the best decision possible, and then accept and defend it until it was necessary to change. I feel I have learned self-discipline, motivation, and the value of goal-setting by participating for ten years on competitive swimming and basketball teams.

Summary

A scholarship to the NIH Internship Program would give me both new scientific knowledge and practical insight into biomedical research. In addition it would give me the opportunity, at the best time in my academic program, to wisely plan a career in medical technology. I feel that with this scholarship I could help engineering make a significant contribution to the field of medical research.

Projects and Exercises

1   You have decided to apply for a job, summer internship, or scholarship in your field of interest. As part of your application you have been asked to write a one- to two-page statement of your background *as it is related to* your career objectives, your interests, and your abilities. Since the reader will also have a copy of your résumé with the dates and facts, this statement, or personal profile, is to be your analysis of the meaning of those facts. Select a specific audience for this essay and write a profile that shows how your abilities fit the audience's needs.

   You may wish to work on this assignment (and the following one) as you read the next three chapters. Therefore, for help in *planning* your paper, see Chapter 5; for help in *generating ideas*, see Chapter 6; and for help in *organizing ideas*, see Chapter 7.

2   Many people have trouble adjusting to the first year of college. For some it is a sudden change from the familiar world of high school. For others, it is a return to school after working or raising a family. Analyze this problematic situation and write a paper on "Getting Through the Freshman Year" at your college. Use your own experience to help an incoming freshman understand more about the problems he or she will face—not just to tell your own story. Plan on your paper being used at the Peer Help Center or being included in the Freshman Orientation Materials given to entering students.

chapter five
Planning

STEP **Explore the Rhetorical Problem**

Decide how you are going to represent this rhetorical problem to yourself.

STRATEGY: Define your purpose, reader, and projected self

STEP **Make a Plan**

Sketch out an initial plan to guide your thinking. As you compose, return to this plan, changing and developing it as you go along.

STRATEGY 1: Make your goal operational

STRATEGY 2: Sketch out a plan

STRATEGY 3: Reveal your plan to the reader

If good writers and problem-solvers have a secret power, it is planning. Trial and error can often generate useful results, but if you rely solely on this method you are taking blind luck as your guide. Problem-solvers rely on plans. The twenty minutes you spend planning can save you hours in writing; good planning, as we shall see, can also have a dramatic effect on the quality of your paper. In this chapter we will look at two steps in planning: exploring the rhetorical problem and drawing up a plan to solve it.

STEP  **Explore the Rhetorical Problem**

A rhetorical situation or rhetorical problem is like a rather large, uncharted territory that contains you, your reader, your ideas, and your purpose. The first thing you as a writer need to do is to explore this territory. You need to know the lay of the land before you start building roads or writing prose.

Exploring a problem before you solve it seems like such an obvious thing to do that it hardly appears worth mentioning. The fact is, however, that one major difference between good and poor writers is in how they explore or view their rhetorical problem. People only solve the problem that they *picture* to themselves. Sometimes there is a dramatic difference between reality—the problem out there in the world—and the image of it that we have developed ourselves. Your chance of success often rests on the mental sketch of the problem that you create.

For example, compare the problem definitions of two athletes who were asked to write an article on running for their college paper. One defined the problem in the simplest way possible:

Write down whatever I can think of about running and physical fitness.

The other gave herself a very different problem:

Since I'm writing to college students who always feel pressed for time, my job will be to show them that I share their attitude yet at the same time indicate why they might want to take up running for pleasure. My problem is to convince them that it will reduce tension and perhaps even increase their alertness in studying.

Naturally, it is hard to write a sophisticated paper if you have only given yourself a vague or simple-minded problem to solve.

STRATEGY: Define your purpose, reader, and projected self

Whenever you are planning to write something, first explore the problem by developing a clear image of three things: your purpose, your reader, and your projected self.

The purpose or goal / First, just what do you intend to accomplish with this paper? What effect do you expect to have? In setting your goals, focus on your reader. In a few words, try to describe what you want to happen —what do you want your reader to feel, or think, or perhaps even do after reading your paper?

Secondly, if you could see the finished paper in your mind's eye, what would it be like —a witty essay, a well-organized theme, a carefully documented review of research? How long should it be and how should it be organized? The more you know about your goal, the better chance you have of achieving it.

Planning toward a goal is one of the most powerful of all problem-solving techniques because it lets you cut large problems down to manageable size. In fact, one common cause of writer's block is trying to work under the shadow of a goal that is too big, too abstract, or just too difficult to handle. When you write a paper, you are choosing among an immense number of possible things you could say —all of which could be "correct." Making a choice can be an enormous problem if you focus all of your attention on the *topic* (on what you know). But if you shift your attention to your *goals* (what you want to do with what you know), the choice can become much easier.

Compare these two plans:

Topic-Based Plan	*Goal-Based Plan*

I'm going to write a paper on the psychological effects of noise.
 	
    One effect is. . . .
    Another effect is. . . .
    Effect #101 is. . . .
	I'm going to show my readers (who are college students and professors) how noise can affect their mood and productivity. Then I'll use the research I've found to suggest things people can do to cope with noise.
	
	    That means I'll want to start with a vivid demonstration of how noise actually affects us, then survey the history of the study of noise. . . .

One problem with traditional outlines is that they are often merely topic-based plans, or arrangements of information, unrelated to the writer's goals. Figuring out your goals is obviously more difficult than just naming or outlining a topic (e.g., "I'm writing about noise"). But of the two procedures, it's the one that will actually help you write. Outlines, especially premature ones, are often dominated by the structure of the available information (all the things that could be said about noise), whereas a goal-based plan is governed by the writer (what *you* want or need to say to explain a new idea, stimulate your reader, or perhaps change his or her mind). Frequently, an outline is a list of the topics you might want to cover in your paper, whereas a goal-based plan is an expression of what you want to do by writing.

In most job-related writing, figuring out the purpose of a given piece of writing is crucial. Here is a typical problem someone might encounter on his or her first job. The person's supervisor requests a concise memo on how the remodeling of a new service center is progressing. But the new employee views this request as "Tell me everything you know about the remodeling." So he dredges up all the information he can find, including a long explanation about why the carpenters were late, and takes a week instead of a day to write it.

Although the writer did a thorough job, he lost sight of the memo's purpose. The supervisor asked for a report because he needed to *learn* something: was the remodeling going on schedule, and were they able to enlarge the storage space? Knowing that, he could decide when to start hiring the new staff and how much stock to order. He didn't need to know the trials and tribulations of keeping things on schedule; he needed a concise report that would let him act.

Often the function or purpose of a given kind of writing is reflected in the format of the writing. For example, a chemist's lab report, called a patent notebook, has to let another chemist accurately duplicate the experiment; document the point at which any new compound was actually discovered, in case a legal question arises; and convince a lab supervisor that this set of experiments is well thought-out and worth doing. Likewise, the format of most academic papers is based on the goal of presenting and supporting a new analysis or new ideas. Generally, previous work is reviewed giving credibility and significance to the writer's conclusion or thesis.

The reader / Who is going to read the paper, and what do you know about that reader that matters? For example, will a colleague who must *use* your report need the same things as a professor? The supervisor who reads the service center remodeling memo is a busy person who wants to act on the report. He will be looking for the key information he needs and for potential problems he might want to anticipate. A professor, on the other hand, will have different expectations, some of which are stated in the assignment and some of which are common to academic writing in general. Both people have reasons for reading, and you'll want to design your writing with those needs in mind.

Later, in Chapter 9, we will look at specific techniques for analyzing the knowledge, attitudes, and needs of your audience.

The writer's projected self / Who are you as the writer? What is your own role, voice, or persona? Do you want to sound enthusiastic and specific, or grand and rather vague? Are you the voice of certainty or trying to take an experimental stance? Think of your writing as a form of talking face to face. What relationship do you intend to establish with your reader: student to professor, friend to friend, or expert to expert? Remember, writing is like a conversation; it is impossible not to project *some* version of yourself and set up some relationship with the reader. Have you thought about what you want that relationship to be?

At this point your representation of the rhetorical problem will only be a sketch. You will fill in the details as you compose and perhaps even change the sketch. But remember, you will only solve the problem *you* give to yourself to solve, so make your picture of that problem as thorough and imaginative as you can.

STEP **Make a Plan**

Once you have a sense of where you want to go, a plan states how you intend to get there, and lets you test alternative courses of action. One of the virtues of a plan is that it is cheaper to build than the real solution would be. Therefore, architects start with blueprints rather than concrete, and writers plan a twenty-page paper before they write. As an inexpensive representation of your solution, a plan lets you test and discard ideas as you work. So a good plan needs to be detailed enough to test, but *cheap enough to throw away*.

For most writers a good plan is a sketch, not an elaborate outline. A detailed, formal outline is not only hard to throw away; it usually reflects what you knew before writing and leaves no place for using what you learn as you work. In this section we will look at three particular strategies that will help you build good plans, and at examples of the many different forms planning can take.

STRATEGY 1: Make your goals operational

Let's suppose you have set up a goal: "I'm going to write a letter of application requesting a summer job." However, you realize that merely stating your request probably isn't enough; you need to make your goals more specific, that is, more operational. For example, a more operational goal would be: "I'll try to arouse the reader's interest enough so that he or she will read my résumé, will remember at least two things about me, and will then ask me for an interview." Note that once you have established this set of subgoals or steps in accomplishing your overall goal, every paragraph in the letter you write will have a function. You will expect it to affect your reader in some specific ways, not just list the facts about you.

Goals that aren't operational are often highly abstract, such as: "I want to discuss team sports," "I'd like to impress my reader," "My aim is to do well in this course." They don't give you a clue about *how* to do it. Operational goals are more concrete and specify a set of separate subgoals you can achieve along the way. For example, compare these two goal statements, one abstract, the other with a set of operational subgoals.

1. I intend to become rich and famous.
2. I intend to study probability and statistics so I can get rich quickly in Las Vegas, then study writing and become famous by writing a best seller on how I did it.

We can apply this same process to writing. Let us suppose you were going to write a paper on the role of nonverbal communication in classrooms. Your overall goal might be persuasion: "convince the reader to see things my way." You might then define this more operationally as "I'll try to forcefully argue both sides of this controversy in order to show the reader that I have pinpointed the crucial issues and also to pave the way for my own ideas." For this particular paper you might then set up a number of subgoals such as:

- Define nonverbal communication.
- Use examples to show how it works in the classroom (perhaps putting this section at the beginning for dramatic effect).
- Review the conflicting studies on whether or not a teacher's nonverbal communication can affect students' I.Q. or achievement scores.

- Argue for your position, supporting it with your own observations of the specific ways children respond to nonverbal communication in the classroom (describe Head Start experiences).

STRATEGY 2: Sketch out a plan

The plans writers make vary from mental notes, to informal sketches done on the backs of old envelopes, to well-developed written plans and proposals. In looking at the examples that follow, remember that a good plan contains both topic information (as in an outline) and goals for using that information.

Figure 5-1 shows a plan sketched out by a college student who wanted to get a summer job as a legislative aide. Instead of merely listing his courses and extracurricular activities ("I want to describe things I've done"), he established a goal ("I want to convince the

FIGURE **5-1** *Goal-based plan for a letter of application*

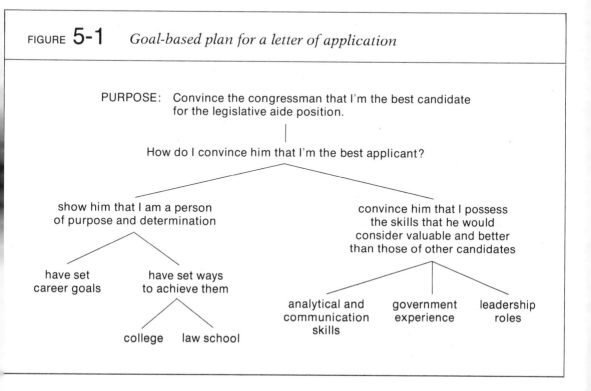

PURPOSE: Convince the congressman that I'm the best candidate for the legislative aide position.

How do I convince him that I'm the best applicant?

show him that I am a person of purpose and determination

convince him that I possess the skills that he would consider valuable and better than those of other candidates

have set career goals

have set ways to achieve them

college   law school

analytical and communication skills

government experience

leadership roles

congressman I'm the best candidate") and then made the goal operational by exploring *how* he could convince the congressman. Notice how he then used the facts about himself to create the effect he wanted to have. In his final letter of application, he began by showing how his desire to be a legislative aide was part of a larger career plan and how he had chosen his college and his courses in light of that career.

Now consider a typical college writing problem. You are a history student with this assignment: "Analyze some aspect of the recent opening of China to the West, discussing how Westerners interpret this event. The class will then select two papers for submission to the college paper." Here are the thought processes of a writer trying to come up with a plan:

Well, some of the things I've read on this subject have led me to believe the discussions about China in the popular press are often based on stereotypes and old assumptions. I might try to make my readers question their own attitudes toward and images of China. I could show how some of our assumptions are based on stereotypes about emigrants and the role they played in the United States in the nineteenth century, not on knowledge about the Chinese in China today. If I want to convince my readers that the popular press is biased, I'd have to document what I'm saying and maybe show the historical basis of those stereotypes.

Before I get too far into this, I'd better review the other things written on the subject and find out what the key issues are as the experts see them. That could mean a fair amount of research, but I think I need this kind of background if I'm to have much credibility. Plus I might find some good quotes to support my points.

Since this is for the newspaper, I'll also have to make the introduction sort of jazzy to pull the reader in right away. Maybe I could start off with a vignette of a Chinese as Americans imagine him and a vignette of a typical Chinese as he actually is. Or maybe I'll come up with some other idea when I'm doing my research. All I know for sure now is that I want to expose the press bias if one exists. When I've done some more reading I'll have a better idea of where I'm going with this.

There are two important things to notice here. First, at this stage the writer is not worried about specifying the content of the paper in detail. Although she isn't even sure yet what all the "major issues" are, she does know she wants to dig them out and discuss them (or allude to them) in her paper. Secondly, her plan is sketchy and flexible—it could easily change when she reads more—but it is firmly focused on her three major goals of capturing attention, establishing support and credibility, and convincing the reader that a press bias exists.

As you can see from this example, plans are a way of playing around with your ideas and considering things you might do. Sometimes, when you are trying to juggle many options and ideas in your head, it helps to express them visually on paper, whether you use flow charts, diagrams, trees (as in Figure 5–1), or just doodles and connecting lines. Figure 5–2 shows a plan sketched out by a writer

FIGURE **5-2** *Preliminary sketch for a magazine article*

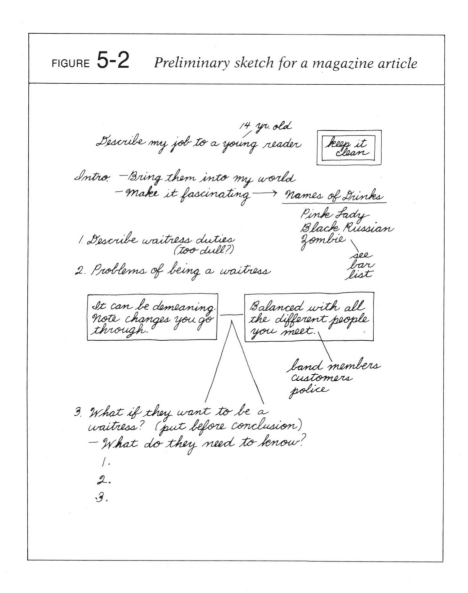

as she began an article for *Seventeen* magazine on her job as a cocktail waitress. Notice how her plan combines both goals and content and how it visually indicates the structure of her ideas, revealing main points, supporting details, and a balance between the pros and cons of the job. Although the plan is very rough, you can see how the writer uses it to adapt her knowledge about the job to the needs and interests of her reader. This sketch is not just a simple printout or outline of the *information* she has stored about this job. It is the beginning of a plan for what to do with that information as a writer. A good plan contains both content and goals for using that content.

Whether you write a formal outline complete with roman numerals and two points under every subpoint, or jot down notes on the back of a grocery list, the important thing is to start by making a plan instead of polished prose. A good plan is detailed enough to argue with, but, unlike a labored-over first paragraph, it's cheap enough to throw away.

WHEN ADVANCE PLANNING DOESN'T WORK FOR YOU

Building a plan around the goals you have established is the most efficient way to go about writing. But sometimes this ideal situation is impossible: you don't know yet what you want to say or how you want your reader to respond. If, for example, you were asked to "write a paper on the effects of urban living as you see them," you might have only the vaguest idea of what you could do with the topic. For some writers the best course of action in this situation is simply to start writing—not to produce a finished text but to discover what they might have to say about the topic. This technique, called brainstorming, is discussed in the next chapter. For many writers, writing itself is a way of planning and discovering one's goals.

STRATEGY 3: Reveal your plan to the reader

Having a good plan makes a paper easier to write. It also makes it easier for a reader to read, particularly if you indicate your plan early on. Revealing your plan is like showing the reader a road map; it helps him or her to follow the discussion, see your point, and grasp the importance of what you are saying.

One of the best ways to accomplish this is to open your paper with a problem/purpose statement. Such a statement is a concise, informative introduction that does two things. First, it sets up the problem, issue, or thesis on which you will focus. Second, it states the purpose of your particular paper—that is, it tells the reader what you are going to do with your topic and what he can expect to get out of reading further. A good problem/purpose statement not only informs but motivates. It convinces the reader that there is a reason for what you have written—and a reason for him to read it. As you can see, a problem/purpose statement simply combines the introductory problem definition, which was discussed in Chapter 2, with a statement of your rhetorical purpose.

A problem/purpose statement is often simple and direct, as it is in the examples below. It could be a paragraph or a page long; it could be labeled "Introduction" or "Background," or could just come at the beginning. It might be embedded within a dramatic example or an interesting lead-in to your discussion. The particular form your problem/purpose statement takes is not important. Just be sure the information is there, as your reader will be looking for it.

Here are some sample beginnings of papers. The purpose statements are underscored. Notice that in Examples 2 and 3 the beginning sentences define a problem that the reader is also concerned about. And Example 3 includes a preview of how the paper is organized, giving the reader a helpful plan for reading.

EXAMPLE 1   Paper Written for an English Literature Class

For many people the fascination of Shakespeare's <u>Much Ado About Nothing</u> comes from its realism and the witty conversations between the fighting lovers, Beatrice and Benedict. And yet the ending of the play, with the false death and resurrection of Hero, frustrates all our expectations about realism and about "true love." It seems jarring and inappropriate. How can we account for this ending? One way is to look at the play in terms of some of the literary conventions of comedy. In this paper I will try <u>to show how Shakespeare uses these conventions to convey a symbolic meaning behind the realistic lines in the play</u>.

EXAMPLE 2   Report to the College Placement Director

Many students perform poorly in job interviews even
though they are skilled in their subject area and well
qualified for the job. The most frequent problem in such
interviews is that students are unnerved by certain kinds
of questions. Although they can answer any technical
questions concerning their field of study, they have difficulty answering questions about personal motives, weaknesses, and strengths. In addition, they lack experience
in interviewing situations. The purpose of this paper is
<u>to propose a program for giving students an introductory</u>
<u>experience in interviewing and answering the personal</u>
<u>questions interviewers regularly ask.</u>

EXAMPLE 3   Guide to Dealing with Rent Hikes

Recent inflation has created an increased conflict
between realtors and tenants in our area. Landlords need
higher rents to pay for rising costs and to make a profit
from their business. Tenants are also faced with increasing prices and want to keep rents as low as possible.
When landlords raise rents sharply, tenants are faced with
the problem of deciding how to react, since no action is
itself a response.
    The tenants' reaction to a rent hike consists of two
steps: (1) making the right choice among the alternative
actions available, and (2) given that choice, executing it
in the best possible way. This report <u>explores the</u>
<u>tenants' options, the factors to consider in choosing an</u>
<u>option, and the procedures tenants should follow for each</u>
<u>kind of response.</u>

A finished problem/purpose statement looks simple and straightforward but is sometimes hard to write, for this reason: in order to
adapt your statement for the reader, you must switch roles from
researcher to writer. For example, a psychology student who has
been researching the theories of Carl Jung may discover, when for-

mulating her purpose statement, that her implicit purpose has been to "show all the things I know about Jung." Yet she realizes that the intended reader, her professor, will be less interested in the quantity of details she has accumulated than in whether she fully understands Jung's theories. A more realistic purpose for her paper would be "to show I have a clear grasp of Jung's concepts and can contrast them with several other important theories," and her revised statement should reflect this plan.

Problem/purpose statements help not only the reader but the writer. Working on a purpose statement can bring a writer back to the questions of "What is my goal?" and "Who is my reader?"—questions that should always govern the writing process. The importance of designing for a reader and writing reader-based prose will be discussed further in Chapters 9 and 10.

Projects and Exercises

1 Take a paper or another communication on which you might be working. Explore the rhetorical problem, trying to answer these questions:

  a. What exactly do I expect or hope this paper will accomplish for me and for my reader? What do I want my reader to think, feel, or do after he or she has read it? (Can you make your answer operational?)

  b. What is my reader looking for?

  c. What image of myself do I want to project; who am I in this situation?

2 Sketch out a plan for your paper that combines goals and content. Experiment with different ways you could visually represent your thinking on paper: try circles, arrows, flow charts, diagrams—anything that shows how your ideas are connected.

3 Write a problem/purpose statement and ask someone else to role-play the part of your intended reader. Have him (or her) respond by telling you what he would want from such a paper and what your statement has led him to expect. Or evaluate your statement using the checklist below.

  a. Have you defined a problem, critical issue, or thesis on which your paper will focus?

  b. Have you told the reader the purpose of your paper?

  c. Have you given the reader any preview of how your paper is organized, any road map for reading?

If You Would Like to Read More

If you would like to know more about the nature of plans and exploring your rhetorical problem, see:

Flower, Linda, and John R. Hayes. "The Cognition of Discovery: Defining a Rhetorical Problem." *College Composition and Communication* 31 (February, 1980), 21–32. ▪ This study compares the ways in which experienced and novice writers define their own rhetorical problems.

Miller, George, Eugene Galanter, and Karl Pribram. *Plans and the Structure of Behavior*. New York: Holt, 1960. ▪ This stimulating book shows how planning works as a moment-to-moment feature of everyday thinking.

chapter six
Generating Ideas

STEP 3   **Use Creative Thinking**

Use the strategies of creative thinking to explore your own knowledge. Your goal is to discover useful ideas stored in your memory and to create new ideas by forging connections among the old.

STRATEGY 1: Turn off the editor and brainstorm

STRATEGY 2: Talk to your reader

STRATEGY 3: Systematically explore your topic

STRATEGY 4: Rest and incubate

Generating and organizing ideas are like two sides of a coin. They represent two different kinds of thinking every writer needs to do. In this chapter we will take up creative thinking, which is a form of mental *play:* it asks you to plunge into the problem and seek out ideas without trying to edit or tidy them up. This sort of energetic intellectual play lets you be a more creative and productive thinker. Compared to the method of grinding a paper out, creative play can do three things. First, it helps a writer break his or her mental "set" and get out of those well-worn thought patterns which often stifle new ideas. Second, it captures those elusive intuitions which are often censored and lost when a writer only pays attention to fully formed ideas. Finally, it helps a writer to draw inferences and discover new, surprising connections among his or her own ideas.

If creative thinking is a form of *play*, organizing ideas (which we will discuss in the next chapter) is a way to *push* your ideas for all they are worth. Organizing is equally powerful because it lets you work in a systematic, logical way to test out ideas, determine their implications, and fit them into a meaningful whole. And planning, as we have discussed, lets you create the goals that direct both generation and organization of your ideas. Taken together, planning, creative thinking, and organizing form a creative trio. Good writers constantly shift back and forth from one mode of thought to another as they work on a problem. In the heat of writing you can remind yourself to switch strategies by remembering this three-step formula: plan, play, push.

STEP 3 Use Creative Thinking

The four strategies discussed in this chapter cover a wide range of creative techniques. They range from the goal-directed-anything-goes process of brainstorming to the venerable rhetorical method of Aristotle's "topics" and the modern systematic art of tagmemics, to end finally in the only too pleasurable strategy of "rest and incubate." The point of this chapter is simple: there are many ways to get good ideas, and the more alternative strategies you know and can use, the better.

STRATEGY 1: Turn off the editor and brainstorm

Once you have a sense of your goal and the problem before you, brainstorming is a good way to jump in. Brainstorming is a form of creative, goal-directed play. Your brainstorming can take any form you wish, whether it is jotting down notes such as we saw in the planning chapter, or writing out fragments or even whole passages, as long as your goal is to energetically generate ideas.

Brainstorming has three rules: keep writing, don't try to censor or perfect as you go, and keep returning to the problem. You can start in the middle, at the end, or with anything that's on your mind; start anyplace you want, but get started writing or jotting down notes. Don't censor your ideas —write them down. When you come up with an idea or expression that isn't quite right, resist the temptation to throw it out and start again. Instead, write it down so you can later tease out the good idea or intuition that was hidden inside it.

Secondly, don't spend time polishing your prose or making it flow. Because you are not trying to turn out a finished paper in one pass, you don't need to worry about following an outline or writing an introduction and transitions. Express your ideas first, and the connections will be easier to see. Sometimes you won't see how it all fits together, but don't worry, just keep trying to get your ideas into words. Your notes, sentences, and free-floating paragraphs may not look much like a paper, but remember that your goal is to get what you know down in words, not to produce elegant prose.

Finally, try to keep your eye on the problem. Brainstorming is a bit like "free writing" in that it encourages you to follow where your intuition leads. But there is one important difference. Free writing is a form of free association or stream-of-consciousness self-expression: one idea leads to another, which leads to another, like links in a chain. Brainstorming, on the other hand, should be goal-directed thinking. Your ideas radiate out from your central focus like spokes radiating from the hub of a wheel. When your brainstorming flow of thought begins to dry up or strays too far, return to the problem you've defined. Although your thought is encouraged to go off on fresh and productive tangents, it is always returning to focus on the problem at hand.

Brainstorming, then, lets you explore your own knowledge. And, as a bonus, it often lets you write clear, vigorous passages that you will eventually use in your paper.

STRATEGY 2: Talk to your reader

People often come up with their best ideas and most powerful arguments when they are engaged in a face-to-face discussion. You can give yourself this same advantage by acting out such a discussion in your own mind, especially if you play all the parts. Everyone has a natural ability to play various roles, such as the "mature and responsible person" we try to project at a job interview. And with a little thought, we can play the role of our interviewer as well. That is, we can switch parts, take on a hard-nosed, "show me" attitude, and carry on our own simulated discussion.

You can use role-playing to help you get better ideas and *to get them down in words*. Instead of staring at blank paper, imagine yourself walking into your reader's office: you have three minutes to tell this person what you have to say, and you want to make him or her listen. So talk it out and write it down. Or, imagine yourself giving a lecture to fifteen high school students who can't wait to talk back. As you go along, simulate the responses of your various readers and listeners: make them ask you questions (basic and difficult ones), raise objections, or make their own interpretations. For example, what would your reader's first response probably be, and what would you say back to him? To get extra power out of this technique, give yourself different audiences with distinct expectations: a professor or supervisor listening carefully to your logic, a prospective employer looking to see what you can offer her, an enthusiastic audience of beginners sitting in on your lecture, or a friend listening to you over a cup of coffee.

This technique works for two reasons. First, by putting you in a realistic situation with a "live audience" it helps you choose the things you *need* to say out of all the things you *could* say. Secondly, it lets you switch to a "talk" strategy, muttering to yourself as you walk around the room, instead of trying to write finished prose. Whenever you do this, you may have to edit the result a little later. But you are reducing some of the constraints on yourself, and the words and ideas should flow more easily.

STRATEGY 3: Systematically explore your topic

Ever since Aristotle, people have been devising ways to think systematically about complex topics. In classical rhetoric this was called the art of invention. Conducting a systematic exploration of your topic has two important advantages. First, it leads you to see your topic from various points of view, many of which would never have occurred to you. That is, it leads you to see new connections and invent new ideas. Secondly, a powerful systematic procedure not only directs your attention by asking questions, but it asks the right questions. For example, the familiar "Who? What? Where? When? Why? How?" formula of journalism leads you to the heart of an event by asking you to consider its most important features.

We are going to look briefly at three systematic approaches to the art of invention: Aristotelian topics, modern tagmemics, and the use of analogy. Like any serious systematic procedure, these methods work best when you understand and know them well. In-depth coverage of the methods is outside the scope of this book; my purpose is simply to introduce each approach and the kinds of questions it asks, then indicate where you could learn more.

Imagine the following situation. You are working on a paper about reading strategies and have already done a good deal of research and thinking about reading itself. You've decided to focus on the notion of the "active reader" and want to systematically explore everything you know about the subject. Let us see how each of our three methods of exploration could be used in approaching your problem.

First, consider Aristotelian "topics." The *Rhetoric* of Aristotle was designed to instruct public speakers of fifth-century Greece in what Aristotle called the "available means of persuasion." Taken together, these patterns of argument are called the "topics." Each of the "topics" represents a way of organizing ideas, or arguing for a position that most listeners will find logical or persuasive. As you will see from even this short list, Aristotle's "topics" cover some of the basic ways people think about a subject and organize their ideas. Here is how a writer might use the "topics" to explore the subject of the "active reader."

Aristotle's "Topics"	Ideas
Definition	Active reading is a constructive process in which a person seeks information and builds a coherent meaning from a text.
Comparison and contrast	It is unlike passive reading, in which the reader works on the principle of the sponge, trying to absorb each word or sentence in the hope that it will all make sense in the end.
Cause and effect	Active reading leads to greater comprehension because the reader is actively hooking each new idea to things he or she already knows.
Support from evidence	A number of studies show that even brief training in active reading increases both speed and comprehension of complex prose.

A modern method for systematic thinking is called *tagmemics*. It is a powerful tool for analysis because it is both simple and comprehensive. This method is built on the premise that one of the best ways to understand the true nature of a thing is to see it from various perspectives. In particular, it helps to look at your problem or subject as a *particle* (a thing in itself), as a *wave* (something that changes over time), and as part of a *field* (an element within a larger context). Although simple on the surface, tagmemics is a rich and complex approach to generating ideas and well worth learning. With regard to our subject it could lead us to observations such as these:

The Three Perspectives of Tagmemics	Ideas
See your topic as a particle (as a thing in itself)	Active reading is made up of a number of processes, including previewing the text to set up expectations and questions that reading will fulfill; searching for key information as one reads; summarizing the gist of the passage to oneself; and making connections as one reads.
See your topic as a wave (a thing changing over time)	The method of active reading changes with the difficulty of the text and individual passages. Skimming often works for newspapers, but with textbooks, active readers switch from fast previewing and brisk reading of introductions and examples, to slow, careful reading and summarizing of difficult passages.
See your topic as part of a field (as a thing in its context)	Active reading is part of the larger process of comprehension, which includes not only recording new information but integrating it into the elaborate patterns of knowledge the reader already possesses. Active reading makes these intellectual processes more accurate and efficient.

The third technique we will look at depends on the generative power of analogies. It has a simple basic premise that much research on the psychology of creativity supports: namely, one of the best ways to understand a new problem is to see an analogy between it and things you already know. One systematic method that uses analogies, called *synectics*, was developed by a think tank group of inventors, artists, and psychologists who were trying to find creative new solutions to practical problems. Using synectics, a group or individual tries to generate four kinds of analogies to the problem at hand: personal analogies, direct analogies, symbolic analogies, and fantasy analogies. By its very nature, the approach leads you to come up with offbeat, impossible ideas in the hope of finding one startling new insight.

The Four Analogies of Synectics	Ideas
Personal analogy (imagine you are the topic or the solution to a problem)	As an active reader I see myself trying to make each idea my own personal possession. Or it is as if I were trying to explain the text to a child who kept asking questions.
Direct analogy (compare it to something concrete)	It's like using an erector set to build a structure (of meaning). The author gave me the materials and a blueprint, but I built the final structure.
Symbolic analogy (compare it to an abstract principle)	Active reading works on the principle that for every action (the author's), there is a separate and equal reaction (the reader's).
Fantasy analogy (anything goes)	It's like walking right inside the writer's head and getting him or her to answer your questions (even if the author helped draft the questions you want to ask).

Another mode of thinking-by-analogy is simply to change your vocabulary: use the language and concepts from one area you know to understand another. Say your problem is to analyze what your college has to offer, but the college catalog vocabulary of "intellectual community" and "integrated programs" doesn't let you say what you want. If you are familiar with systems engineering, you might assess your college in terms of its work flow and productivity. Or you might switch to the outlook and special language of marketing, asking such questions as "What 'commodities' do colleges typically promise to deliver?" and "How could one test the college's 'advertising claims'?" Often a change in your vocabulary will bring about a change in your "idea set," or way of viewing the problem. By changing terms you tap different pockets of your own knowledge.

STRATEGY 4: Rest and incubate

Sometimes this can be the most productive strategy of all, but only if you do it correctly. That is, before you stop work, make sure you have formulated the next unsolved problem you want to be thinking about. There needs to be something in the "incubator" if it's going to hatch.

People agree that incubation works; nobody understands quite why. The folklore is that your unconscious mind goes to work and solves the problem while you sleep. A more recent explanation of the process says that before people explore a problem in detail, they often create a rather limited or ineffective plan for solving it. Working on the problem, they learn a great deal that doesn't fit into their original plan. What happens in incubation is that people simply *forget* or abandon their old, inadequate plan and are then able to take advantage of all they've learned. For example, after working on the problem and doing a first draft, they come back to their writing with a new, more powerful plan that can work.

Incubation, then, is a strategy you can actively use. Sometimes even half an hour can make a difference. So starting a paper early is a practical decision; otherwise you simply lose the benefit of one of the easiest strategies available, and will probably spend more actual time on the paper. When you use incubation, keep two points in mind: return to your unfinished business from time to time so as to keep it *actively* simmering in the back of your mind. Then, when a new idea or connection comes to you, *write it down*. Most experienced writers carry around note cards of some sort for just this purpose. Don't expect inspiration to knock twice.

Projects and Exercises

1   Hold an in-class workshop to try out the idea-generating strategies described in Step 3. Working in a group or with a friend, try out each of the strategies on some common problem. For example, you might take this as your problem: "Writing is a lot like talking, yet many people who can tell you something have trouble writing it. Why? In particular, why is it that even students who know the material thoroughly have trouble writing papers in college?"

   a. *Brainstorming.* You are the member of a think-tank or professional problem-solving group. Use brainstorming and try to come up with fifteen good ideas on the problem within the next five minutes. Don't just jot down code words, but try to explain briefly what each idea means.

   b. *Talking to the reader.* Break up into two groups to generate ideas for a reader. For example, if your problem was "Why Writing Is Difficult," you could tell the group that they have a late paper and must prepare a statement for a professor explaining why writing is difficult. Let the other group decide what they would say about the same problem to a friend. Then compare your two sets of ideas. Are they different? How?

c. *Systematic exploration.* Break into three groups and analyze a common topic from the three different perspectives of Aristotle's "topics," tagmemics, and analogy. Use each of these systematic methods to create new ideas and develop insight into your subject. Then compare your results. What would you say are the special strengths of each method?

2 Use the creative thinking strategies of Step 3 to write a paper that explores both sides of an issue. Choose an issue about which you yourself have conflicting feelings: for example, the value of grades versus a pass-fail system, the decision to ask a friend out on a date, or the choice of a profession. In one form or another, use all four strategies discussed in this chapter to generate ideas and argue both sides of your question.

3 Use the creative-thinking strategies of Step 3 to analyze some problem that you face. Explore the problem in all its complexity, writing down as much about it as you can. Don't worry if your thoughts are disorganized or even contradictory at this point; simply make a written exploration that gets your ideas down on paper. Ordinarily, much of this sort of idea generation and exploration would be done in your head, leading to a combination of notes and prose. But for this assignment, try to develop a detailed record of your exploration. You might even want to talk it out into a tape recorder and then transcribe your thoughts.

As you explore, try to locate one or two key points that you find confusing or can't express as clearly as you would like. These are points you will want to think about and let incubate.

Now set this written exploration aside for a few days until you have read Chapter 7 on organizing ideas. Then return to your exploration, organize your thoughts, and write a well-structured problem analysis. Turn in this analysis and also the record of your exploration.

4 Exercise 3 asked you to carry out an experiment in which you created a detailed record of your own idea generation and broke your writing process into two separate stages. Write an analysis of your experience, keeping the following questions in mind:

a. How does your written exploration differ from your final paper in organization, content, and style? Why?

b. What happened between drafts? How did time and incubation affect your writing and thinking?

c. What are some of the advantages and disadvantages of this experimental two-part process? How could you integrate the advantages into your normal composing process?

If You Would Like to Read More

If you would like to know more about creativity and other strategies for generating ideas, see:

Aristotle. *The Rhetoric*. Trans. Lane Cooper. New York: Appleton-Century-Crofts, 1932. ■ This is the work that established the study of systematic idea generation called, in classical rhetoric, the art of invention. Aristotle's "topics" are still powerful.

Gordon, William. *Synectics: The Development of Creative Capacity*. New York: Harper & Row, 1961. ■ This book describes how the system of synectics was developed and has proved its worth in industry, both as a way of producing new inventions and as a method for creative problem-solving.

Young, Richard, Alton Becker, and Kenneth Pike. *Rhetoric: Discovery and Change*. New York: Harcourt Brace Jovanovich, 1970. ■ A groundbreaking work in the field of rhetoric, this book presents the tagmemic method for exploring complex problems.

chapter seven

Organizing Ideas

STEP 4

Organize Your Ideas

Use these strategies to develop and focus your ideas. Your goal is to turn good intuitions into precise, well-developed ideas that you can express in clear, logical relationships to one another.

STRATEGY 1: Develop your own code words

STRATEGY 2: Nutshell your ideas and teach them

STRATEGY 3: Build an issue tree

Getting good ideas is half the battle. The other half is making sense out of what you know. The techniques we discussed in Chapter 6 will help you generate a wealth of ideas, but sometimes those ideas will seem more like intuitions than clearly stated arguments. Or they will be in the form of key words or brief notes to yourself that you will have to flesh out in detail for a reader to understand. And sometimes you will end up with a rich but unfocused body of ideas whose only organization is the order in which they occurred to you. This chapter will help you turn such intuitions into clearly stated ideas and then organize and develop those ideas into a logical, well-supported argument.

STEP **Organize Your Ideas**

Each strategy in this chapter suggests ways you can use your own plans, notes, or drafts to develop and organize your ideas. Strategy 1 helps you expand your own loaded expressions into a more meaningful discussion, while Strategy 2 helps you pull key points or concepts out of such a discussion. Strategy 3 gives ideas for organizing all these elements in a clear, logical way. And, as you will notice, these strategies help you start taking your reader into account, even as you explore and organize what you know.

STRATEGY 1: Develop your own code words

Many times writers find that their important, key words in a passage are really "code words." That is, these words carry a great deal of meaning for the writer that they would not carry for the average reader.

For example, what does the expression "problem-solving" mean to you? To some people it means nothing more than the process of doing an algebra problem. But for me, "problem-solving" is not only a basic thinking procedure that gets people through everyday life, but a process that leads to bursts of creative thinking and new insight. And it is also a branch of psychology.

Thus, for me the term evokes a large, complex network of ideas. But just because "problem-solving" is a loaded expression for me — a code word I think with —I cannot simply use it and expect most of my readers to fully understand me, to make the same connections I make. When I use such code words, I must explain and develop the meaning I really have in mind.

A writer's code words can be jargon, special terms such as "problem-solving," or simply complex concepts such as "persona" that some readers wouldn't understand. But often they are merely abstractions, as in the remark, "He has a very interesting job." Here "interesting" is a kind of mental shorthand that stands for a body of related ideas: ideas that may be evident to the writer but are unlikely to be perceived by the reader. In fact, such words may sound like nothing more than vague generalizations or hot air.

Your own code words, then, can sometimes create a problem because they mean much more than they actually express. However, they can also open the door to a very effective strategy for developing and focusing your ideas. Only you, the writer, can tell empty abstractions from solid concepts. For example, ask yourself: "What did I really mean by 'interesting'?" One of the best ways to develop your writing ideas and fill in the gaps for the reader is to show or explain what you mean by your own code words. This strategy is especially useful when you feel you need to develop an argument or reinforce a point, but aren't sure what else to say.

The strategy is simple. First go through your notes or a draft of your paper and locate some of the key words or phrases (ones that you intend to carry much meaning in your paper). Look both for abstractions and for key words and complex concepts that you depend on. Then see if they might also be working as code words, ones that may not convey all your intentions to the reader. Look for words that stand at the center of a whole network of ideas and experience that are *unique to you*. Then ask: "What do I mean by this code word or term?" Try to push that complex meaning into words, using it as a springboard for developing your own ideas. Then transfer this new understanding to your paper.

Example 1 on page 84 shows how many interesting and important ideas can be buried beneath a code word or phrase. In her first draft of a geology paper, the writer had asserted that Alfred Wegener's 1912 theory of continental drift was a "major breakthrough" in the field of geology. She knew this was a strong point she needed to support and develop. After fruitlessly searching for quotes that would support it, she realized that it would be far more effective simply to explain in her own words what she meant. So she used her intuition and her code words as starting points for exploring what she really meant by the theory being a "breakthrough."

Here are some of the ideas she jotted down and eventually worked into her paper. They show how much information she already had on the topic when she began seriously to probe her own network of ideas.

EXAMPLE 1

<u>The theory of continental drift was a major breakthrough</u>
<u>in geology.</u>

It drew on enormous amounts of information from different
fields, including paleontology and physics as well as geology.

It contradicted major assumptions everyone had made about
the rigid nature of continents.

It led to new kinds of studies, such as ones that described and dated the life cycles of continents. It
changed the way people studied geology.

It gave us a whole new image of the earth's surface as
plastic and dynamic.

All in all, it changed both the study of geology and popular notions about the earth. (<u>Note</u>: Use this idea to organize the paragraph.)

Think back for a moment to the writer's original assertion.
Would you as a reader have been able to fill in all of the ideas behind
"breakthrough" that the writer knew but didn't tell you? As a geology
instructor, would you have assumed that the student knew all the
supporting facts she didn't express? Code words are like intuitions.
They offer a starting point for thinking about the reader and for
developing your own ideas.

The next example shows how this strategy can lead you back
through the entire process of planning, generating, and organizing
your ideas. The passage below comes from a draft of the scholarship
application that Joan was writing in Chapter 4. She has underscored
a few of the key terms that are loaded with information for her but
are in danger of just seeming abstract to a reader. Play the role of a
reader on the scholarship committee wondering if this applicant
really understands research well enough to benefit from the scholarship. How would you interpret the terms that are underscored?

EXAMPLE 2

I want a career that will help other people and at the
same time be challenging scientifically. I had the opportunity to do a biochemical assay for a neuropsychopharma-
cologist at ----- Clinic in Chicago. Besides learning the
scientific procedures and techniques that are used, I
learned how to deal with some of the <u>problems encountered</u>
<u>in research.</u> This internship program would let me pursue
further my interest in research, while currently exposing
me to <u>relevant and diverse areas.</u>

chapter seven / Organizing Ideas

The response of a friend to whom Joan showed the draft wasn't very encouraging. According to the friend: "It sounds OK —it's organized and everything—but I felt as if I'd read it before. It's saying things that 'couldn't be wrong,' but I don't have a sense of what you think or what you have actually done. What is a 'relevant area' for you? I don't know, and this draft gives me the feeling you may not know either."

Now look at the notes Joan jotted down (see Example 3) as she thought about one of the phrases underscored in her draft. Then review her revised draft on page 86, with new material underscored. You will notice two interesting things. First, the revision contains the kind of additional, specific details that make Joan's key words meaningful and convincing. In addition, the very process of developing her own code words has led Joan to express a new idea about the benefits of research that was an important but unstated part of her own personal network of ideas. Her code words provided a leaping-off point for generating new ideas.

EXAMPLE 3   Excerpts from the Writer's Notes as She Worked on One of the Underscored Phrases

---

problems encountered in research

practical

Hard to see how research at the Sleep Center tied in with overall program of the Clinic. But you needed to see the big picture to make decisions.

No definite guidelines given to the biochem people on how to run the assay.

Lots of paperwork for even a small study.

rganizational

Difficulty getting equipment
    1. Politics between administrators
        Photometer at the University even though
        the Clinic had bought it.
    2. Ordering time; insufficient inventory; had to
       hunt through boxes for chemicals.
    3. Had to use personal contacts to borrow equip-
       ment. Needed to schedule and plan ahead to do so.

But breakthroughs do occur--pacemaker, artificial limbs, etc.

EXAMPLE 4   Revised Draft with Additions Underscored

Besides learning the scientific procedures and techniques that are used, I learned how to deal with some of
the practical and organizational problems encountered in
research. I saw how the lack of equipment and funds often
calls for real cooperation between departments and careful
planning of one's own project. The experience also helped
me develop more of the patience research requires and recognize the enormous amounts of time, paperwork, and careful steps required for testing a hypothesis that is only
one very small but necessary part of the overall project.

But besides knowing some of the frustrations, I also
know that many medical advancements, such as the cardiac
pacemaker, artificial limbs, and cures for diseases, exist
and benefit many people because of the efforts of researchers. Therefore I would like to pursue my interest
in research by participating in the NIH Internship Program. The exposure to many diverse projects, designed to
better understand and improve the body's functioning,
would help me to decide which areas of biomedical engineering to pursue.

STRATEGY 2: Nutshell your ideas and teach them

Find someone, a fellow student or long-suffering friend, who is willing to listen as you explain the essence of your argument. Then, in
two or three sentences —in a nutshell —try to lay out the whole sub-
stance of your paper. Nutshelling practically forces you to distinguish major ideas from minor ones and to decide how those major
ideas are related to one another. Expressing your argument in a nut-

shell helps you put "noisy," supporting information in its place and focus on the essentials of what you have to say. For example, the box at the beginning of this chapter conveys in a nutshell what the main ideas in the chapter will be.

Besides helping people to separate main points from interesting but merely supporting ones, nutshelling has another benefit. In trying to condense their thoughts, people often synthesize or combine ideas and create a new concept that expresses or encompasses all they have in mind. For instance, Joan did this in Example 3, when she looked at her notes and decided that a number of points could be grouped and labeled an "organizational" problem. This process of conceptualizing is probably the writer's most difficult yet also most creative action. And nutshelling helps you do it.

The second part of this strategy, teaching, takes the process one step further. Once you can express your idea in a nutshell to yourself, think about how you would *teach* those ideas to someone else. How would you have to introduce or organize your brief discussion so someone else would understand and remember it? Like nutshelling, trying to teach your ideas helps you form concepts so that your listener gets *the point*, not just a list of facts. Furthermore, as a teacher you have to think about which concepts will be most meaningful to your reader. In explaining the dangers of germs to a five-year-old, for example, you would probably find "dangerous things" a more effective organizing concept than "public health problems." Nothing helps you stand back, evaluate, and reorganize your ideas more quickly than trying to teach them to someone else who doesn't understand.

Even if you don't have a live audience to talk to, there is an easy and practical way to use this strategy of nutshelling and teaching when you write. Simply imagine your intended reader sitting before you, think about what you want that person to learn or do when you're through, and then try to teach your ideas in writing so that you get results.

STRATEGY 3: Build an issue tree

Most of the idea-generating strategies described so far ask you to think and write without the straightjacket of an extensive outline. However, one of your goals is to produce a paper with a tight, logical structure. Experienced writers resolve this dilemma in the following way: they try to *pull* an outline *out* of the ideas they generate, rather than write to *fill* an outline *in*. Building an issue tree is a technique for organizing the ideas you generate.

What is an issue tree and why use one?

As noted in Chapter 1, an issue tree is a sketch like an upside-down tree that puts your ideas in a hierarchical order. As you know, in a hierarchy, the top-level idea is the most inclusive. All the other ideas are a response to it or a part of it like subsystems in a larger system. This does not mean that they are less important (a subsystem of the body, such as the brain, can be crucial), but they are less inclusive.

Issue trees have two main things to offer writers. First, they let you sketch or test out ideas and relationships as you write. At the same time they let you visualize the whole argument and see how all the parts might fit together. Issue trees can also help you generate new ideas. A traditional outline, written before you start the paper, only arranges the facts and ideas you already know. An issue tree highlights missing links in your argument and helps you draw inferences and create new concepts.

In the sections that follow we will look at ways of using an issue tree to organize your brainstorming, to develop a paper, and to test the organization of your first draft.

USING AN ISSUE TREE TO ORGANIZE YOUR BRAINSTORMING

To show how useful an issue tree can be in organizing ideas, we will watch a writer in action, using a tree to organize his ideas and write an essay. Here is the assigned topic:

> In England there is a saying that every Englishman is branded on his tongue. Is this true in the United States? Do a person's speech traits — from pronunciation, to pitch, to choice of words—mean anything in the American social system?

Figure 7-1 shows the first three steps a writer might take in answering this question.

1. Generate some ideas on the problem. At this point the writer's goal is simply to answer the question, "Do speech traits communicate anything to me?" and generate some ideas. These are jotted down like a list.
2. Find a key word or phrase for each idea.
3. Put the key words in a hierarchically organized tree.

In Figure 7-1, the line connecting "speech traits are social markers" and "education" simply tells us that there is a general relationship between the two. It will be up to the writer to eventually make that relationship more explicit (for example, is education a cause or an effect of speech traits?). As we will see, an issue tree can help you create concepts that give order and meaning to your own ideas.

FIGURE **7-1** *Organizing brainstorming into a tree*

Brainstorming   *Key Words*

As with the British, Americans' traits differ according to upper,   class
middle, and lower class

They are like social markers or tags that identify people   social markers

Affected by education   education

Biggest source must be the region one grows up in   region

Tree

SPEECH TRAITS ARE SOCIAL MARKERS

class   education   region

Sometimes the best organization of one's ideas is self-evident, as it was for the ideas in Figure 7-1. But when it isn't, when things seem confusing, an issue tree can help you spot the missing links in your thinking and generate new concepts that will organize your ideas. For example, Figure 7-2 shows a set of ideas our writer generated after reading a number of studies on people's responses to voice. These ideas didn't neatly fit onto the tree. "Breathiness," "throatiness," and "pitch" are clearly related to the top-level idea of speech traits as social markers, but they certainly do not belong on the same level with "class," "education," and "region." Nor are they subordinate to (a part of) those larger categories. Taken as a group, however, they add up to another kind of social marker that would be comparable to a regional or class trait. The question is, what should the writer call it?

The writer's task is to generate a new concept that sums up these facts. In other words, he must examine the material and propose a new unifying idea. In this case the unifying idea he arrived at was that speech traits also suggest or reflect a person's sex role (see Figure 7-3).

FIGURE **7-2**   *Using an issue tree to spot missing concepts*

Brainstorming   *Key Word*

Breathiness is considered a "sexy" trait in women.   breathiness

Throatiness (i.e., a husky, quite deep voice) is considered   throatiness
"unfeminine" in women but mature in men.

A wide pitch range is heard as "effeminate" in men and as   pitch
"flighty" or "frivolous" in women.

Trees

SPEECH TRAITS ARE SOCIAL MARKERS

class   education   region   ~~breathiness~~   **wrong**

SPEECH TRAITS ARE SOCIAL MARKERS

class   education   region

                                        ~~breathiness~~   **wrong**

SPEECH TRAITS ARE SOCIAL MARKERS

class   education   region   ?   **needs a
                                                        new concept**

                        breathiness   throatiness   pitch

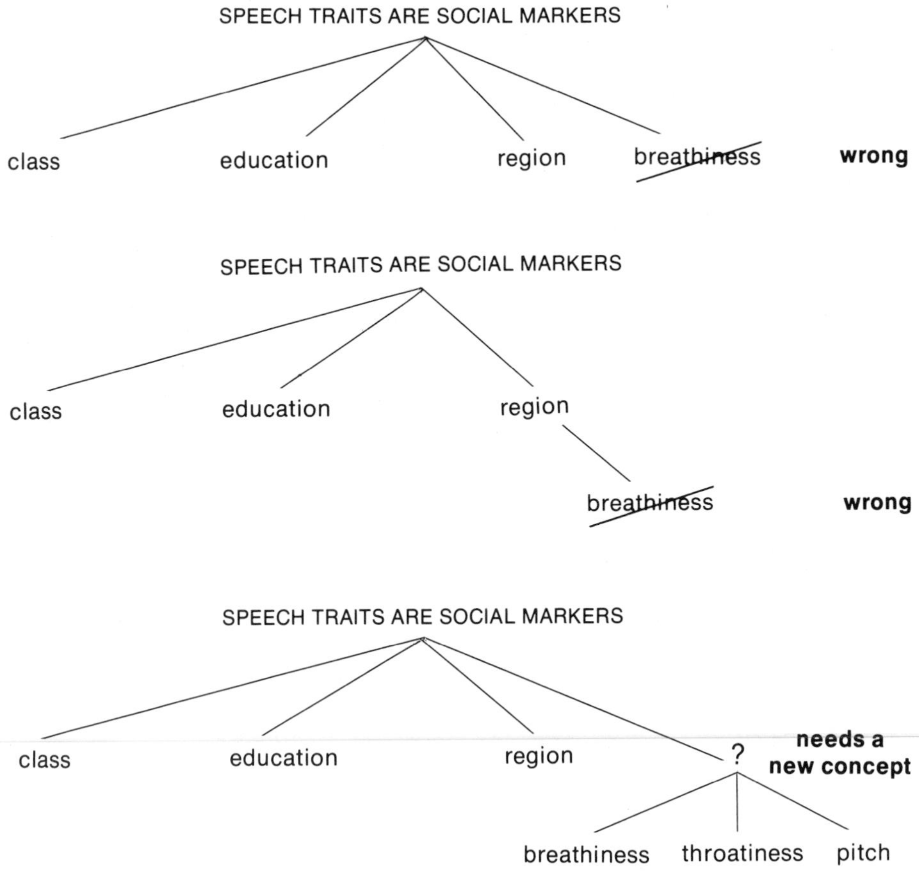

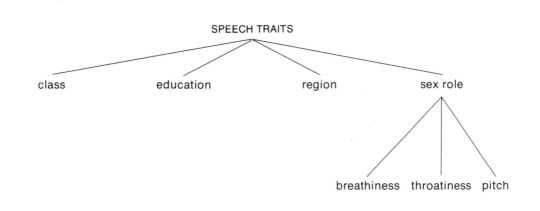

FIGURE **7-3**   *Grouping ideas under a unifying concept*

SPEECH TRAITS

class   education   region   sex role

breathiness   throatiness   pitch

Creating a unifying idea or concept from facts is something we do all the time. The problem is that in the heat of writing, when ideas just don't seem to jell, people often continue to flounder rather than stop, think, and *create* new organizing ideas. At such times the writer needs to turn from searching his or her memory for the "right" word (because it isn't there) and start looking for relationships and developing new ideas. An issue tree helps do this.

USING AN ISSUE TREE TO DEVELOP A PAPER

You can also use an issue tree to help develop or flesh out a paper. As you think and write, your issue tree will keep changing, reflecting your developing set of ideas. For example, our essay writer eventually decided not to treat the issue of education and decided that he had two major ideas to discuss on the subject of speech traits. Here are his notes for the beginning of the essay:

Speech traits are an important means of communication in
the United States. First of all, <u>listeners</u> use them to
determine someone's social identity, especially in the
areas of class, regional background, and sex role. In addition, <u>speakers</u> use them, either deliberately or unconsciously, to communicate certain things as well.

    (what things? to project a self-image maybe?
    or fit in with a group?)

As Figure 7-4 shows, the writer's working tree reflects this two-part reorganization of his ideas. And it shows exactly where he needs to support those ideas with more evidence and examples. So again he turns to brainstorming, now with the goal of refining and supporting his major points. Notice how his thinking is working in two directions, from the bottom up and from the top down. Sometimes he starts with an inclusive idea such as "listeners interpret regional speech traits" and tries to work from the top down to support that idea with more facts and examples. Sometimes he starts with facts and examples, such as the facts about New Yorkers, and works from the bottom of the tree up, finding relationships and creating a new idea.

The revised tree shows how much of the writer's final argument was created in the process of organizing and developing his ideas, that is, in the process of building a tree. An issue tree, then, offers a writer three important things:

1. It is a flexible tool for thinking that develops as your ideas develop.
2. It helps you visualize, organize, and support the ideas you have.
3. It signals when you must stop to look for relationships and create new unifying ideas.

FIGURE **7-4**   *Developing a paper*

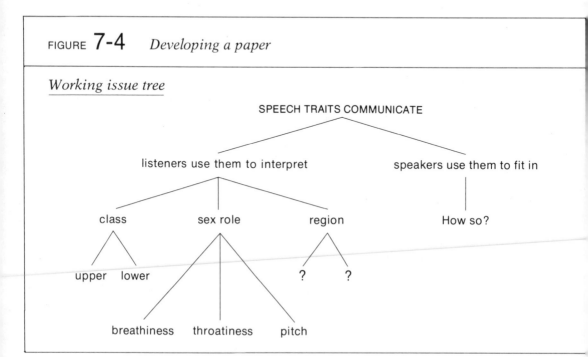

Working issue tree

(continued)

FIGURE 7-4 (*continued*)

Brainstorming

How do listeners interpret regional speech traits?

SUPPORTING
FACTS

→

Northerners sometimes stereotype people with a Southern drawl as "slow and easy-going."

An Eastern twang makes people think of a wealthy, boarding-school upbringing.

How do speakers use them?

In informal situations many New Yorkers drop "r's" so "guard" and "god" sound the same. In formal situations they keep the "r."

Likewise the "ing" that is fully pronounced in the schoolroom (as in "hitting") becomes shortened to "in" on the schoolyard (hittin').

NEW CONCEPT

→

People alter their pronunciation depending on where they are.

People often use slang in informal situations and standard English in formal ones.

NEW CONCEPT

→

People adjust their word choice depending on the situation.

Revised issue tree

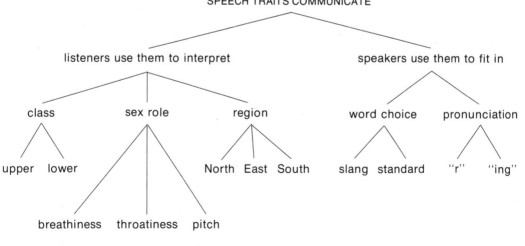

SPEECH TRAITS COMMUNICATE

listeners use them to interpret — speakers use them to fit in

class — sex role — region — word choice — pronunciation

upper   lower — North   East   South — slang   standard — "r"   "ing"

breathiness   throatiness   pitch

By this point in the writing process, the issue tree has done its job and the writer is well into writing paragraphs, but knowing as he writes how each part fits logically into the whole.

USING AN ISSUE TREE TO TEST YOUR FIRST DRAFT

One of the best ways to compare your *thought* with what you actually *wrote* is to do a tree of your own first draft or, if you can, ask a reader to do this for you. The procedure is simple: from your draft, pull out all the main ideas (use a brief phrase such as "statistics show decline"). You might jot these down in the margin of your paper. Make sure you don't include any ideas that are in your head but not on the paper. Although you can expect readers to see connections and fill in *some* organizing ideas as they read, you can't expect them always to arrive at the same interpretation you did. By building an issue tree, you can find out what your paper is actually saying. The tree will reveal the focus and underlying structure of your prose.

In the next example, a tree diagram is used to look at the underlying structure of individual paragraphs. When you apply this technique to a whole paper, you might want to work in larger units and let each point on your tree summarize the point of an entire paragraph. The two paragraphs below, taken from the beginning of a student's paper, demonstrate two of the most common problems a tree will uncover: a top-heavy or unfocused organization (seen in the first paragraph) and a runaway branch (seen in the second). Read the first paragraph and then look at Figure 7-5 on page 96, which shows the structure of the discussion as a reader saw it.

EXAMPLE 4

───

The Writing Problem

America has a writing problem. Like the Constitution, American education is based on democratic principles, which means it is committed to teaching reading, writing, and arithmetic to everyone as a basic right, like the right to vote. The history of American education is the history of an attempt to turn these principles into practice for everyone. In 1975, Newsweek magazine, in a famous exposé article entitled "Why Johnny Can't Write," started a crusade against poor writing. The vivid, even shocking examples in this article came from colleges all over the country. Other disturbing findings on writing skills have come from various sources, including the Na-

tional Assessment of Educational Progress, the College
English Education Board, and the Department of Health, Education, and Welfare. However, many people have been most
appalled by the statistics on basic literacy itself.
These statistics are especially revealing. The majority
of Americans use only the simplest sentence structures and
the most elementary vocabulary.
     Many things have led to this decline——the schools
themselves, television, and our changing social values.
In an attempt to create relevant, attractive courses, many
schools have understressed the old-fashioned basics of
reading and writing. The long-term impact of television
has lulled people into a more simplistic speaking style.
Writing, on the other hand, is essentially book talk,
which goes as far back as the invention of movable type.
But today students spend time watching television that
they might have spent reading 20 years ago. Studies have
shown that many students watch more than 8 hours of TV per
day. TV has in fact replaced books, newspapers, and even
movies as our primary source of entertainment and information. Instead of actively participating in learning, people prefer the more passive experience of watching "the
tube." According to Marshall McLuhan, "literary culture
is through." It belonged to the world of the printing
press. And who wants to watch a printing press?

Consider the first paragraph of this draft. It is hard to see the
paragraph's focus: is the main idea the democratic ideal and the
failure of education, is it the decline of writing skills, or is it the
drama of the *Newsweek* crusade? According to the writer, he really
had intended to focus on how American education was failing to
teach writing. Figure 7-5 compares the tree the reader saw with the
tree the writer really wanted to produce. Notice that all the reader
saw was a list of facts, whereas the writer really had intended to use
those facts to support the idea that skills had declined.
     In sketching his intended tree, the writer uncovered another
problem. Although he felt his comments about democratic ideals
were relevant, he really didn't want to discuss that issue in this paragraph. He realized it would make more sense to discuss it in a later
section about how the writing problem is also a failure to meet the
historical goals of American education. Sketching out a tree of the
paragraph helped the writer take a bird's eye view of his organization

The reader's tree

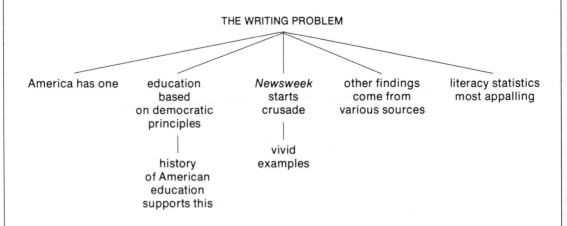

THE WRITING PROBLEM

America has one   education based on democratic principles   *Newsweek* starts crusade   other findings come from various sources   literacy statistics most appalling

history of American education supports this

vivid examples

The writer's intended tree

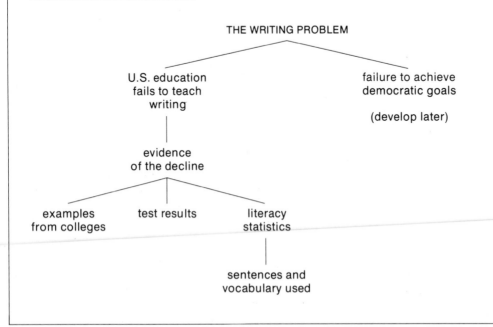

THE WRITING PROBLEM

U.S. education fails to teach writing   failure to achieve democratic goals

(develop later)

evidence of the decline

examples from colleges   test results   literacy statistics

sentences and vocabulary used

and compare his private mental tree (or the one he would like to have) with the idea structure his prose actually presented to the reader. Below is a revision of the first paragraph in which the writer tries to maintain a clear focus and show the reader how each sentence and point are connected to his main point.

EXAMPLE 5

───

                    The Writing Problem:
              A Failure of American Education

        According to the startling Newsweek article of 1975
    ("Why Johnny Can't Write"), the U.S. educational system is
    failing to equip its students with sound writing skills.
    The article displayed a number of examples of poor writing
    from colleges all over the country. But more definitive
    support came from test results reported by the National
    Assessment of Educational Progress, the Department of
    Health, Education, and Welfare, and the College English
    Education Board. These were supported by the even more
    appalling statistics on basic literacy itself; for exam-
    ple, the majority of Americans use only the simplest sen-
    tence structures and the most elementary vocabulary.

───

    A second problem that a tree will reveal is the presence of a long, trailing branch. In the second paragraph of Example 4, the author began discussing causes of this decline, and one idea led to another, to another, and yet another. Each idea was a response to the one before, but they got further and further from the writer's top-level idea. The branch simply ran away with the writer and produced an unbalanced paragraph in which very little time was spent on his major, top-level topics. In the process of composing, the writer remembered a number of interesting ideas about television and other media, so his ideas did seem to "flow" as he wrote. But in sketching the tree, he realized that he had given too much space to one supporting idea (watching television) and little or no space to his points that schools neglect basics and that changes in social values are causing the decline.

    Figure 7-6 gives a vivid picture of the structure of this paragraph and places it in the context of the other major points the writer wanted to cover, in both the paragraph and the entire paper. As you

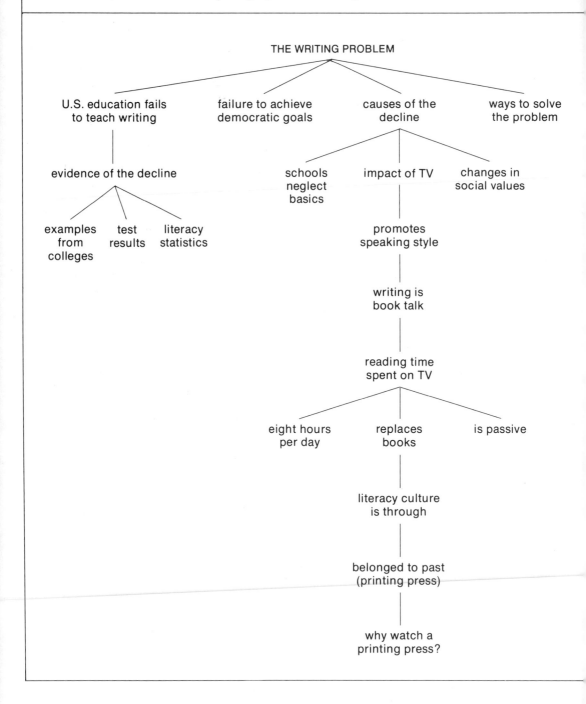

FIGURE **7-6** *The second paragraph: a runaway branch*

THE WRITING PROBLEM

U.S. education fails to teach writing

failure to achieve democratic goals

causes of the decline

ways to solve the problem

evidence of the decline

schools neglect basics

impact of TV

changes in social values

examples from colleges

test results

literacy statistics

promotes speaking style

writing is book talk

reading time spent on TV

eight hours per day

replaces books

is passive

literacy culture is through

belonged to past (printing press)

why watch a printing press?

can see, he intended to focus on American schools and education, but the interesting topic of television simply ran away with his paragraph.

Whether you actually sketch a tree or read your prose looking for its underlying hierarchical structure, you can use this technique to test for the focus and connections your reader is likely to see.

Using questions to develop an issue tree

Sometimes a writer will develop a skeleton of an issue tree but not know where to go from there. One way to break this block is to start asking questions about each item in the tree. This method simply makes a natural process more systematic. When you write you are often carrying on a question-and-response dialogue with your reader or yourself. Children, as we all know, can build endless chains of reasoning with the single question "Why?" or "How?" Other questions that frequently arise in a reader's mind are "What do you mean?" (which asks for a more expanded definition) and "Such as?" (which is a reaction to a vague, overly abstract idea that lacks supporting examples). As a writer, you can anticipate the reader's questions, as well as generate more material, by asking such questions of yourself. Some useful ones are:

> What do you mean?
> How so?
> How do you know?
> Such as?
> Why?
> Why not?
> So what?

The questions that are most applicable will depend on the type of paper. A journal article exploring a question of scientific fact will rely heavily on the question "What evidence?" ("How do you know?"), while one concerned with pragmatic or technological issues would probably concentrate more on asking "How?", "Why?", and "So what?" Figure 7-7 shows how a writer has used the questioning method to develop ideas for a paper on running. Notice how each new point is a response to the point above it. Unlike an outline, an issue tree allows you to keep adding more points one under the other, in any direction you wish.

This technique, also called *issue analysis*, is often used in a formal, systematic way to examine large policy questions such as: "Should we build more nuclear power plants?" Issue trees help

FIGURE **7-7**   *A tree generated through the questioning method*

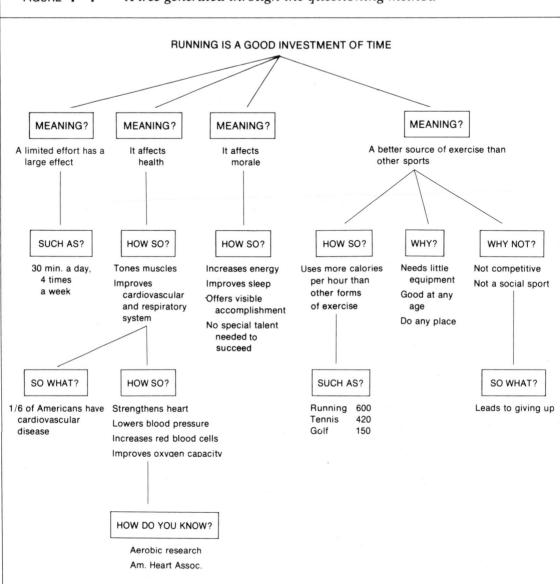

RUNNING IS A GOOD INVESTMENT OF TIME

| MEANING? | MEANING? | MEANING? | | MEANING? |

A limited effort has a large effect

It affects health

It affects morale

A better source of exercise than other sports

| SUCH AS? | HOW SO? | HOW SO? | HOW SO? | WHY? | WHY NOT? |

30 min. a day, 4 times a week

Tones muscles
Improves cardiovascular and respiratory system

Increases energy
Improves sleep
Offers visible accomplishment
No special talent needed to succeed

Uses more calories per hour than other forms of exercise

Needs little equipment
Good at any age
Do any place

Not competitive
Not a social sport

| SO WHAT? | HOW SO? | SUCH AS? | SO WHAT? |

1/6 of Americans have cardiovascular disease

Strengthens heart
Lowers blood pressure
Increases red blood cells
Improves oxygen capacity

Running	600
Tennis	420
Golf	150

Leads to giving up

| HOW DO YOU KNOW? |

Aerobic research
Am. Heart Assoc.

people deal with such enormous problems because they offer a way of systematically stating and organizing all the major points such a decision should cover. In addition, a systematic use of questions such as "Why?" and "So what?" helps people to reason carefully about an issue by considering it from a variety of viewpoints.

Projects and Exercises

1 Use the strategies in Step 4, "Organize Your Ideas," to help test and improve the first draft of a paper on which you are currently working.

   a. *Develop code words.* Go through your first draft and circle three or four words that are functioning as code words for you. Then, on a separate sheet, brainstorm all the things that come to your mind when you use those expressions. Use your brainstorming to go back and develop and clarify those ideas for your reader.

   b. *Nutshell and teach your ideas.* Try to state the main points of your paper in a nutshell, then try to teach those ideas to another person. You might also test how well you communicated by having your listener tell you back, in his own words, what he thought you meant. If he didn't see your point, try again. Then use this experience and your own new ideas to go back and focus your paper better for a reader.

   c. *Develop an issue tree.* On a separate sheet of paper, do an issue tree of the draft you have just written. Then find someone who is familiar with the issue-tree concept and ask him to read your paper and from it develop his own tree. Tell him to write items down in his own words as much as possible and to tree your argument as he sees it on the first reading. If he is at all confused in trying to follow the paper, you want his tree to reflect that. Ask him not to put down any of his own ideas on what he thinks you should have said. Then compare the two trees and try to account for the differences. What happened and why?

2 Take a controversial question such as, "Should smoking be allowed in public places?" Or, "Is a liberal arts education still one of the best preparations for any career?" Do a systematic analysis of the issue, using the questioning method ("How so?", "Why?", etc.) outlined earlier. Make sure your analysis looks at both the pros and the cons. Then write a short paper that takes a stand and argues for one side while acknowledging the strengths of the other. Use an issue tree to focus and organize your ideas, and be sure to give your reader an introductory problem/purpose statement that previews your paper (see Chapter 5).

3 When you have completed a draft of a paper, you can use this short checklist to test its overall structure:

   a. Have I given the reader an introductory problem/purpose statement that sets up a problem or thesis on which my paper will focus? (This idea will be at the top of your issue tree.)

   b. Is each paragraph organized around an idea, not just a list of facts? (If not, you can use an issue tree to help create the missing, higher-level concept under which all your points will fit.)

c. Can you and your reader see the overall hierarchical structure of your paper? Does each section, paragraph, and idea fit into the structure in a logical way? (If it doesn't, you probably need to rethink some of your top-level unifying ideas. Try using an issue tree to play with other possible organizations and concepts.)

If You Would Like to Read More

If you would like to know more about strategies for organizing ideas, see:

Simon, Herbert. "The Architecture of Complexity." *Proceedings of the American Philosophical Society*, 106 (December, 1962), 467–482. Reprinted in Herbert Simon. *The Sciences of the Artificial*. Cambridge, Mass.: M.I.T. Press, 1969. ▪ This essay, by one of the creators of information processing theory, discusses the role of hierarchical structures in human thought.

Wojick, David. "Planning for Discourse." *Water Spectrum*, Winter, 1975–76 and Summer, 1978. ▪ This offers an introduction to issue trees in their original setting, the analysis of complex policy issues.

chapter eight

Two Case Studies:
A Research Paper and
a Consulting Report

I n the case study of Joan (Chapter 4) we watched a writer trying to generate ideas and make meaning out of her own experience. The two writers we will look at here face a different part of the writing problem. They have done a lot of research and have a great deal to say, but must transform what they know to meet the needs of their readers. For Kate this will mean meeting the expectations of a professor and responding to an assignment; for Matt this means designing a consulting report so it will be read and used —so it will actually make something happen. In watching Kate and Matt's papers develop we will see how both writers have to actually rethink and reorganize their ideas in order to design their papers for a reader.

Case study: Kate

Kate, a sophomore, is writing her first college research paper and facing that great unknown: "What does the teacher want?" or, more accurately, "What is it academic readers in general expect?" Kate is still making the transition from high school writing to college writing and is trying to figure out how to write a serious academic paper that does more than just display what she knows. This case study describes some of the processes she went through in trying to get an answer.

Kate's assignment, from a course in cognitive psychology, was a relatively open-ended one: "Write a paper on creativity based either on your own experimental project or on a biographical study of some 'creative person.' In doing so, treat some of the theories and principles covered in this course." Papers by other students ranged from studies of Einstein and Shakespeare to one on "Walt Disney: An American Original." Kate had enjoyed her own research on Charles Darwin, and the writing problem really began when she sat down to do a draft of the paper. At this point, Kate had done her homework well, although she felt the research would have been easier if she'd had an idea of exactly what to look for in the first place. Nevertheless, she had accumulated a great deal of information and it even fell into a rather tidy outline.

Kate's plan was to start with a catchy beginning, something like, "Creativity is a thing envied by those who feel they are noncreative. Quite often a noncreative person will marvel at other people's abilities and talents and exclaim on their impossibility and unbelievability. . . ." Then she planned to work through her outline, which is shown below, filling in the material she had found in the library.

I. Definition of creativity
II. Darwin's theory of evolution
   A. Social effects —controversy at the time
   B. Main points of the theory
III. Darwin's biographical background
IV. Four theories of creativity
   A. Romantic
   B. Freudian
   C. Wallas' stages
   D. Problem-solving

Everything seemed ready to go, but the minute she began to write she knew this was going to be a second-rate paper: boring to write and dull to read. Although it looked well organized, there was nothing holding it together, no reason to write. Kate felt she would simply be plodding through each topic on the outline and writing it up. This method —outline the topic and fill in the blanks —had worked well enough in high school, but she feared it wouldn't produce an effective academic paper. It was hard to imagine a good reason for anyone to read it —or write it.

Here was the dilemma: Kate had worked hard on the course and on Darwin, and had learned a lot, but her paper wouldn't show that she could *do* something with her information. Perhaps a "flash of inspiration" could have saved the paper, but the more frustrated and helpless she felt, the less likely she was to become inspired. Kate felt stuck.

It's hard to say whether frustration, common sense, or the lateness of the hour was responsible, but the next step in Kate's writing process was a return to the basics. She and four friends sat down one night to figure out what the reader's expectations really were, or, as they put it, "If I were the professor, what would I want?"

JAY: Well, I can tell you what I *wouldn't* want. I wouldn't want someone to recite the textbook back at me and feed me another summary of creativity theory. There are 25 papers to read from this class. I'd climb the walls if everyone just repeated the ideas back to me.

ANN: I don't think I'd be so keen on reading large chunks of straight biography either. I'd keep asking myself, "What's the point?"

KATE: O.K., I agree, but you've just demolished two-thirds of my paper. What did I do all that research for if I can't use it? And the assignment says to treat some of the principles of the course. You have to work that stuff in to show you've learned something.

CHEN: Well, if *I* were assigning this paper, here's what I'd want. Naturally I'd want you to show me you know the course material, but what I'd really want to see is if you can *use* those theories —not just repeat them. I'd expect you to *apply* the theory to some new problem like explaining what made Darwin or Shakespeare creative. The exam will show if you've read the text; I think a paper like this should show you can *think*.

ANN: I agree with that. I'm working as a grader for a freshman history class, and we were told to look for two things: if the person can discuss the readings well, that's a "B" paper; but in order to get an "A," they have to come up with their own ideas and be able to support them. That's what a real historian has to do, of course. So we're supposed to treat these papers as if they were going to be submitted to a magazine or journal. I think what Professor Howard wants is for everyone to learn the material and then be able to think like a historian and really *use* it.

KATE: All right, but how do I use creativity theory? What is there to analyze about Darwin? He made a huge splash —though, of course, come to think of it, he wasn't the first person to talk about evolution; Lamarck was. Would you still call him creative? ... You know, what I could do is use the theory to test Darwin —was he truly a "creative" thinker —and at the same time test the various creativity theories. Do they really account for a person as important as Darwin?

JAY: Now I think you're getting somewhere. Chen was right about applying the theories, not just repeating them. It sounds as if you've come up with a real problem or issue to analyze here. The paper is even starting to sound interesting. I think it would meet the professor's expectations because you'd be using the material in the course to support your own thinking.

Actually, talking this over may help me with my own paper I'm doing for the course, on Thoreau. I was working up sort of a straightforward informal outline, but maybe I should pursue a thought that kept occurring to me when I was doing my research. One of the most perplexing things about Thoreau is that today everyone thinks he's a genius, but in the 1860s no one thought he was creative at all. The botanists thought he was incompetent, and the poets thought he was just imitating Emerson. I think I could tie this contradiction into some of the creativity theories we've been studying.

According to Kate the discussion went on for another hour, but the main ideas that emerged were relatively simple ones:

1. Professors who read academic papers have two very clear expectations. Naturally they want to see that you are learning, but they also expect you to show your ability to think: to use your knowledge to *create* and *support* your own ideas.
2. One important way of coming up with new ideas is to identify a problem, conflict, issue, or contradiction associated with your topic. Papers that merely "cover" a topic are often only schoolroom exercises. But once you define a real problem or issue within that topic, you have created a real-world writing problem: you have a reason to write and your reader has a reason to listen to you.

Example 1 shows the new plan and introduction that Kate developed. Compare it to her old outline and notice these two differences: First, Kate's paper is no longer a survey of information. Instead, it is organized around a problem or question that the reader (and Kate) will find compelling. Darwin's biography and theory no longer sit in a section of their own. Instead Kate *uses* the information she found in the library to support her own ideas about Darwin's creativity.

Secondly, the paper now has a hierarchical structure. Kate's old plan was a list of topics. Now she states her two top-level ideas in the first paragraph and organizes the paper around them. Notice too that Kate isn't using a traditional topic outline. Her new outline is more a plan for what she wants to accomplish in each section and a reminder of what information she should use to do that. What follow are the first draft of her problem/purpose statement, which sets up the issue she intends to address, and a plan for what she wants to do in the rest of the paper.

EXAMPLE 1

THE CREATIVITY OF CHARLES DARWIN

Introduction

    In 1859 Charles Darwin, a British naturalist, published <u>The Origin of Species</u>, and its impact on the world was tremendous. Indeed, <u>Origin</u> is probably the most influential biology book ever written, and some historians even go so far as to claim that this book ranks second only to the Holy Bible. And yet, Darwin's ideas were not strictly new; he did not actually "create" the notion of evolution. Was he just a controversial thinker rather than a creative one?

    In this paper I will look at the creativity of Charles Darwin by asking two questions. Does Darwin's work support or contradict current psychological definitions of creativity? And secondly, what is the best way to account for Darwin's own kind of creativity? Which of the major theories best fits the facts of Darwin's life and work?

Discuss point 1: Is Darwin "creative"?

    Define creativity. (Use Hayes, p. 215: "a novel, surprising, and potentially useful act.")

    Does Darwin fit? Yes, because

1. He contradicted the theory of the special creation of man held by the church and the general public.

2. His notion of natural selection raised a controversy in the scientific community as well.

3. While Lamarck proposed the idea of evolution before Darwin, Darwin was the first to make the theory scientifically plausible. (Use quote from Farish, p. 333: "No one had ever presented evolutionary theory so forcefully and so well documented.") Back this up with description of Darwin's biological knowledge and research methods.

Sum up answer to point 1

(continued on next page)

EXAMPLE 1 (*continued*)

<u>Discuss point 2</u>: Which theory fits Darwin?

    1. Romantic inspiration. No.
          Discuss the 20-year development of Darwin's
          theory and cover his four key principles
          here.

    2. Freudian sexual energy theory. Possible.
          Mention limited biographical evidence from
          Darwin's 5-year voyage on the <u>Beagle</u>.

    3. Four-stage theory--Wallas. Partially true.
          Discuss the biographical information that
          fits this pattern, but note the misfit with
          the third stage.

    4. Problem-solving theory. Best fit.
          Show how Darwin spent years of study and
          slowly pieced his ideas together, trying to
          fill in gaps in order to form an integrated
          theory.

<u>Sum up answer to point 2</u>

Case study: Matt

Matt was given the following assignment in a writing course: "You are a free-lance consultant. (1) Find and analyze a real-world problem involving communication that you have encountered at school, in an organization, or on a summer job. Your goal is to help your 'client,' so (2) write a proposal or consulting report that will help your reader understand and actively deal with this problem. Design your report around your reader's needs: write in order to make something happen."

    The problem Matt chose was a dramatic one, at least to him: inadequate communication equipment was putting him in danger. Working as a flagman on a summer road crew, Matt had been ignored, shouted at, and even threatened by irate and unconcerned drivers who either didn't see the flagman or resented being stopped. From *his* point of view, the problem was vivid and clear-cut: the paving company's desire to cut unnecessary costs had led them to ignore his need for greater protection. And from his point of view the solution was clear-cut too: the company should buy more safety equipment. In this case we will see Matt coming to see the problem from his reader's point of view and adapting his report to meet both his own goals *and* his reader's needs.

Matt's first step was to write the following proposal. Put yourself in the shoes of Michael Shipton, the president of the New Haven Road Company, as you read this. How would you respond to the way Matt defines the problem and to his proposal?

PROJECT PROPOSAL

The New Haven Road Company has failed to provide adequate safety measures for flagmen. The flagman is the most ex-posed person on a road crew and the one in the greatest danger from oncoming traffic, since he is the first person on the edge of the construction area. In addition, he is the first person to hear complaints from drivers about the inconvenience the construction is causing them. As a flagman I have had drivers shout at me and even threaten to run me down. Others pay no attention and cause work stoppage by driving right into the work area. Despite these dangers, many of the available precautions are not being used.

New Haven Road Company could correct this failure by the purchase of new equipment and by the measures de-scribed below:

1. Walkie-talkies $100

2. Signs $350

3. Night and weather gear $100

4. Lobbying for more detours, enforcement of speed
   limits, police protection

Three people read Matt's draft, and they all saw two problems. The first was that Matt's primary audience, Michael Shipton, might never get beyond the first line. Matt's vision of the flagman's problem was so vivid that he had never considered the reader's perspective. Therefore he started out by essentially attacking his reader, charging him with failure to solve a problem he perhaps didn't even know about. Matt then focused the rest of the proposal on himself and the problem he faced. It seemed unlikely that this description of the problem —although quite reasonable from Matt's point of view— would motivate his reader, at least in any positive way.

The second difficulty with Matt's analysis was that it jumped abruptly from a brief description of a problem to a set of solutions. That is, it didn't really analyze the problem; it was simply trying to sell someone a ready-made and packaged solution. Again, from Matt's point of view, this was a good recommendation. He had a good package to sell.

As a writer, then, Matt needed to do two things differently. First, he needed to show Shipton that a problem really existed, by analyzing that problem. Only then would his package of recommendations seem necessary. As it was, he had put the cart considerably before the horse. Secondly, he had to show Michael Shipton that this was a mutual problem, and one that he, Michael Shipton, had a reason to solve. There is always danger in construction work; Matt had to show that on some level, he and New Haven Road had a mutual goal in improving flagman safety.

Matt responded to his readers' comments with some important changes. As you will see in the final draft of his report, he didn't pussyfoot around the issue of inadequate safety measures. What he did was put that "failure" in a positive context. He developed a mutual goal that he and his reader could share and in doing so he put the whole problem in perspective. Protecting the flagman not only would make Matt's job easier but was a way to increase safety and traffic control for the whole crew and, in turn, to reduce the rate of work stoppage that had been plaguing the company. In addition, Matt found a way to demonstrate in dollars and cents that his recommendations would actually solve an overtime problem for the company.

We could say that Matt designed his report for an audience by rethinking his information from his reader's point of view. He also established the format of the report with the reader in mind. The executive summary gives a busy reader what he needs to know: the problem and the writer's recommendations. The rest of the report uses headings to let the reader know what is coming and to help him locate information he might want to use later.

1000 Morewood Avenue
Pittsburgh, Pennsylvania 15213

March 14, 1980

The covering
letter reminds
the reader why
he should read
the report, by
reviewing its
background
and previewing
its contents.

Mr. Michael Shipton
President
New Haven Road Company
400 Brown Road
New Haven, Connecticut   06512

Dear Mr. Shipton:

　　Enclosed is the report on flagman safety that you
and I discussed last week. As you know, I have worked
with NHRC for two summers and have had the chance to
talk to members of a number of road crews, many of
whom feel the need for greater precautions. The increasing number of work stoppages in the last few
years suggests that this is a growing problem. In my
report you will find a recommendation for six measures
that I believe not only will increase safety and cut
down costly work stoppage but will pay for themselves
within a year.

　　Thank you for your help and cooperation in carrying out this study. If I can be of any further assistance, please call me.

                    Sincerely,

                    Matthews Earl Ward

                    Matthews Earl Ward

The title tells the reader what the paper has to offer.

Flagman Safety:
A Plan for More Efficient Road Crews

presented to

Michael Shipton

President

New Haven Road Company
New Haven, Connecticut

By Matthews Earl Ward

March 14, 1980

The table of contents lets the reader find specific sections and previews the hierarchical organization of the report.

Table of Contents

1

Summary

In the past three years, New Haven Road Company (NHRC) road crews have had an increasing number of work stoppages due to traffic problems. The ability of flagmen to stop traffic and prevent it from entering the work area depends on advance warning for approaching traffic and adequate safety precautions for the flagmen. On the basis of my practical experience and interviews with other road crew members, I believe we could significantly increase traffic control by increasing the safety precautions for flagmen, often at minimal cost. Six alternatives are presented here:

1. Walkie-talkies

2. Effective marking of work areas

3. Rain and night gear

4. Greater use of detours

5. Greater enforcement of 35-mph speed limit

6. Better police protection

I recommend that NHRC adopt the first three alternatives immediately and consider ways to implement the final three.

Note how this summarizes the problem and solution. Packed with information, it gives a busy reader the gist of the report. Since it may be all some readers will read, it should make your case.

I. Why Flagman Safety?

Flagmen are the key to coordinating the flow of
traffic around a work area. Their job requires almost
continuous concentration on the traffic patterns in
front of them and behind them. A flagman also needs
to know the position of the road crew within the work
area. Unfortunately, the dangers presented by oncoming cars often interfere with the flagman's concentration and his control of the traffic flow. Because
these disruptions cause work stoppages, they often result in the work crew having to work overtime and can
turn a profitable project into a loss. Thus, it makes
sense to attempt to make the flagman's job safer and
the traffic control more effective.

Why Hasn't This Problem Received Major Attention?

There are two major reasons why flagman safety
has not been a major concern of NHRC. First, road
crew managers apparently have not seen the link between overtime costs and flagman safety. More often
the complaint from the main office is that excess
overtime occurs because the workers are lazy.

Secondly, even when crew managers do see the connection, they don't know what to do about it. They
seem to be waiting for the union to come up with demands on behalf of the flagmen. This is not to say
that management is insensitive to the safety of flagmen, but rather that they expect the union to bring up
the matter if anything is wrong. Unfortunately, the
company can't wait for the union to act, since the
union is rarely swayed by the flagmen. Flagmen in the
union are vastly outnumbered by the laborers, who are
all too happy to accept the overtime caused by the
work stoppages, which are, in turn, caused by the lack
of flagman safety.

I hope that a review of several alternative
safety measures and a delineation of the costs and
benefits of each will show just how necessary and beneficial these measures could be.

Sources of Information

I gathered a great deal of first-hand information
when I worked as a flagman for NHRC during the summers

of 1978 and 1979. More recent data have come from
members of the 1980 NHRC road crews in several informal interviews. All men interviewed had two or more
years of experience with the company and were members
of the Laborer's International Union (LIU) Local 1066.

II. Alternatives

The alternatives open to NHRC fall into two basic
categories. The first set involves the use of gear
and equipment that can be purchased and used immediately. The second set of alternatives is concerned
with legislation and law enforcement that will involve
lobbying efforts with state and local officials. The
potential benefits from these latter options are far
more uncertain than the benefits of the new gear.
Therefore, the lobbying alternatives will be treated
briefly, and no attempt will be made to delineate
their costs and benefits.

Additional equipment and gear

Walkie-talkies: One highly effective measure would be
to provide flagmen at either end of a work area with
walkie-talkies. These not only would let flagmen know
about the situation behind them but would help them
know when to let traffic go through the work area.
With a walkie-talkie, the flagman no longer has to
worry about cars hitting him from behind. While this
may seem to be a remote possibility, it has happened
to me and other flagmen. And it goes without saying
that my flagging was much less effective than usual in
the days following this incident.

A good set of walkie-talkies will cost roughly
$100. They need only avert one hour of overtime (this
is approximately equal to the amount of overtime caused
by one work stoppage) for ten men in order to pay for
themselves (calculations of overtime are based on $10/hr.).

Walkie-talkies are not a safety cure-all, however, since they only permit the flagman to know the
situation behind him. The situation in front of him
remains uncertain. If drivers of oncoming cars do not
know that a work area exists ahead, they may enter the
area at high speeds. In this dangerous situation the

The headings
in this section
let readers
locate or skip
different
subsections and
emphasize the
hierarchical
organization.

flagman must decide whether he can stop the car in time
or if he should get out of the way and let the car
go into the work area, endangering the work crew. Thus,
the danger affects not only the flagman, but the crew.

<u>Effective marking of work areas</u>. Another important
way to reduce the danger of fast-moving traffic is to better post the work areas. While NHRC has made some efforts at marking its work areas, these have generally
not been effective because the marking signs are too
inconspicuous, are frequently set up in low-visibility
spots, and look too much like speed limit signs to catch
the attention of oncoming drivers. The large, diamond-
shaped, orange construction signs currently being used
by other companies seem to be the best solution.
   The cost would be as follows:

Two sets (3 signs each)	$300
Extra time setting up for visibility	50
	$350

To pay for this alternative, 35 man-hours of overtime
would need to be saved. Most likely the measure would
pay for itself in the first month of use.
   Even effective marking, however, will not completely end the problem. Drivers will not notice the
unlit signs during rainy weather or at night, when
flagmen are harder to see.

<u>Rain and night gear</u>. To avoid the problems brought on
by bad weather and night work, two things are needed.
First, the signs marking the work area should be
lighted. Second, the flagmen should be equipped with
flashlights and provided with bright-colored (yellow
or orange) water-resistant jackets. These items will
make it easier for drivers to see the flagmen and the
work areas. The cost of this alternative--roughly
$100, or 10 man-hours of overtime--should be recovered
over the course of a year.

<u>Lobbying</u>

<u>Greater use of detours</u>. Detours are probably the best
way to avoid work stoppages. However, many state and
local ordinances heavily restrict the use of detours.

The transition between sections ties both of them back to the main problem, reminding us again of the overall organization of the report.

If some of these restrictions could be lifted through
lobbying efforts, much time would be avoided in setting up traffic flow around the work area.

Greater enforcement of 35-mph speed limit. In areas
where detours cannot be set up, NHRC could lobby for
increased enforcement of the 35-mile per hour speed
limit in construction areas, which is now generally
ignored.

Better police protection. A problem that sometimes
confronts the flagman is irate drivers. An impatient
driver will quite often run a flag or threaten the
flagman unless allowed to go through the work area.
Although failure to follow a flagman's signals is a
felony and punishable by heavy fines and imprisonment,
policemen are currently present only on large construction jobs, so there is seldom any deterrent to
offenders. NHRC could lobby for increased policing of
all construction jobs.

III. Summary of Recommendations

The use of any or all of the six alternatives:

		Costs
1.	Walkie-talkies	$100
2.	Effective marking of work areas	350
3.	Rain and night gear	100
4.	Greater use of detours	
5.	Greater enforcement of 35-mph speed limit	
6.	Better police protection	

should greatly increase the ability of the flagmen to
do a good job with increased safety. This, in turn,
will permit the work crew to operate more profitably
because of improved traffic control, reductions in
work stoppages, and reductions in overtime. The cost
of these recommendations is small and the benefits po-
tentially great. NHRC can't afford not to try them.

[In the original report, Matt's appendix of equipment sources
followed this page.]

Projects and Exercises

The following assignments will take you some time to complete. As you can see, they draw on the skills of planning, generating, and organizing ideas, which we have already covered, and on the additional skills of designing for a reader and editing, which will be discussed in the chapters to come. Exercises 1 and 2 ask you to incorporate all of these skills into a single research or problem-solving paper; Exercise 3 gives a checklist for evaluating your first draft.

1 *A research project.* Every academic or professional field raises its own set of interesting and complex questions. For example, what are the pros and cons of selecting different advertising media, does the modern detective novel have roots in earlier literature, or how does air pollution actually affect people and the environment? Select a topic you would like to know more about, then find a critical issue or problem within that topic and write a research paper focused on that issue. Direct your paper to a reader who might be interested in the issue you pose but who is not an expert in the field.

2 *A problem-solving project:* Assume you are a free-lance consultant with special expertise in solving communications problems. You have recently noticed a problem involving communication—it might be on your job, at school, or in some organization to which you belong. For example, you might want to solve a problem for other students by writing a short handbook on getting through self-paced courses at your school, or write a manual for new summer employees at the place you work. Just be sure to address a real problem someone faces.

Do some additional study of the problem until you feel you have at least a rough grasp of where the difficulties lie. At this point you might want to prepare a proposal that outlines the problem and your intentions to the reader, your client. Then, write a consulting report that carefully and imaginatively analyzes the problem and offers some solutions. Remember that your primary goal is to help a real reader solve a real problem, so keep that reader's needs and viewpoint in mind.

3 Once you have written a draft of your paper in Exercise 1 or 2, use the following checklist to see how well you have handled various aspects of the total paper. As you will see, the checklist also offers a preview of ideas that will be covered in the coming chapters.

The problem analysis:

- Is there an effective problem/purpose statement?
- Does the paper define a real problem (instead of just describing a situation or recommending a new program)? And is this problem centered around a shared goal? *(or)* Does the writer state a clear issue or thesis that the research paper will explore?

The overall structure of ideas:

- Is the paper organized around an issue tree that is focused on the problem or thesis?
- Does the paper provide cues, such as headings, that help the reader see this top-level organization?
- Is the overall structure reader-based rather than writer-based?

The structure of sentences and paragraphs:

- Has the writer chunked his or her ideas and provided organizing ideas for the reader? Is the function of each paragraph clear?
- Has the writer provided *cues* for the reader, such as overviews and transitions, that make the relationship between paragraphs or sentences clear?
- Do the paragraphs have a reader-based organization?

Editing:

- Does the paper use vigorous prose?
- Does the writing make the underlying relationships of ideas clear?
- Is the writing proofread and free of errors?

Overall academic or professional quality:

- Does this paper show the overall attention to research, analysis, and presentation that you would expect from a professional consultant or problem analyst?
- Will this report have a real intellectual or functional value for its intended reader?

chapter nine

Designing for a Reader

STEP 5   **Know the Needs of Your Reader**

The first step in designing your writing to be read is to understand the needs, attitudes, and knowledge of your particular reader, and to help that reader turn your written message into the meaning you intended.

STRATEGY 1: Analyze your audience

STRATEGY 2: Anticipate your reader's response

First drafts are often satisfying; they seem to say just what one meant. But when writers come back a day, a week, or a year later, they often discover a gap between what they were thinking and what their writing actually conveyed. If you are writing to be read, it is what you communicate to your reader that finally counts —not what is in your head. If you want to be understood, it is usually not enough simply to *express* your ideas. One of the secrets of communicating your ideas is to understand the needs of your reader and to transform writer-based thought into reader-based prose. The next two chapters will help you design your writing so someone else not only will read it, but will understand and remember it.

In trying to design for the reader, one question people often ask is: "How soon should I start thinking about my reader? Where does this step fit in the total writing process?"

The answer is that it can fit nearly anywhere. It may occur during planning, when you try to identify the audience; during idea generation, in which you may develop your code words to help the reader understand; and during organizing, when you nutshell and teach your ideas with the reader in mind. Thus, designing for the reader occurs during many stages of the writing process. It could be said that this step is nested, or embedded, within other phases, much as a set of Chinese boxes is nested within one another.

Nesting also occurs on a broader level. The general steps of planning, generating, organizing, and editing are often performed "out of order" or one within the other. As you know from your experience, writers use the steps we have been discussing in this book but do not always use them in a 1, 2, 3 order like stair steps to a finished paper. They may generate ideas first, then go back to plan, then organize and edit while revising some of their plan, and so forth.

The process of designing for a reader, which will be discussed in this and the following chapter, is one that occurs throughout the act of writing. You may use the process as part of one particular step, such as planning, or you may stop between steps—say, between generating and organizing—and decide to focus in on your audience before proceeding further. Therefore, designing for a reader is nested not only within each writing step but within the total writing process: you turn to it whenever you feel a need to pause and concentrate in depth on your reader. That moment could come in the middle of planning, while you are organizing ideas, or before you begin the second draft of the paper. Whenever such a time comes, Steps 5 and 6 will help you think and write for your reader.

STEP 5   Know the Needs of Your Reader

The goal of the writer is to create a momentary common ground between the reader and the writer. You want the reader to share your knowledge and your attitude toward that knowledge. Even if the reader eventually disagrees, you want him or her to be able for the moment to *see things as you see them*. A good piece of writing closes the gap between you and the reader.

STRATEGY 1: Analyze your audience

The first step in closing that gap is to gauge the distance between the two of you. Imagine, for example, that you are a student writing your parents, who have always lived in New York City, about a wilderness survival expedition you want to go on over spring break. Sometimes obvious differences such as age or background will be important, but the critical differences for writers usually fall into three areas: the reader's *knowledge* about the topic; his or her *attitude* toward it, and his or her personal or professional *needs*. Because these differences often exist, good writers do more than simply express their meaning; they pinpoint the critical differences between themselves and their reader and design their writing to reduce those differences. Let us look at these three areas in more detail.

Knowledge / This is usually the easiest difference to handle. What does your reader need to know? What are the main ideas you hope to teach? Does your reader have enough background knowledge to really understand you? If not, what would he or she have to learn?

Attitudes / When we say a person has knowledge, we usually refer to his conscious awareness of explicit facts and clearly defined concepts. This kind of knowledge can be easily written down or told to someone else. However, much of what we "know" is not held in this formal, explicit way. Instead it is held as an attitude or image — as a loose cluster of associations. For instance, my image of lakes includes associations many people would have, including fishing, water skiing, stalled outboards, and lots of kids catching night crawlers with flashlights. However, the most salient or powerful parts of my image, which strongly color my whole attitude toward lakes, are thoughts of cloudy skies, long rainy days, and feeling generally cold and damp. By contrast, one of my best friends has a very different cluster of associations: to him a lake means sun, swimming, sailing, and happily sitting on the end of a dock. Needless to say, our differing images cause us to react quite differently to a proposal that we visit a lake. Likewise, one reason people often find it difficult to discuss religion and politics is that terms such as "capitalism" conjure up radically different images.

As you can see, a reader's image of a subject is often the source of attitudes and feelings that are unexpected and, at times, impervious to mere facts. A simple statement that seems quite persuasive to you, such as "Lake Wampago would be a great place to locate the new music camp," could have little impact on your reader if he or she simply doesn't visualize a lake as a "great place." In fact, many people accept uncritically any statement that fits in with their own attitudes —and reject, just as uncritically, anything that does not.

Whether your purpose is to persuade or simply to present your perspective, it helps to know the image and attitudes that your reader already holds. The more these differ from your own, the more you will have to do to make him or her *see* what you mean.

Needs / When writers discover a large gap between their own knowledge and attitudes and those of the reader, they usually try to change the reader in some way. Needs, however, are different. When you analyze a reader's needs, it is so that you, the writer, can adapt to him. If you ask a friend majoring in biology how to keep your fish tank from clouding, you don't want to hear a textbook recitation on the life processes of algae. You expect the friend to adapt his or her knowledge and tell you exactly how to solve your problem.

The ability to adapt your knowledge to the needs of the reader is often crucial to your success as a writer. This is especially true in writing done on a job. For example, as producer of a public affairs program for a television station, eighty percent of your time may be taken up planning the details of new shows, contacting guests, and scheduling the taping sessions. But when you write a program proposal to the station director, your job is to show how the program will fit into the cost guidelines, the FCC requirements for relevance, and the overall programming plan for the station. When you write that report your role in the organization changes from producer to proposal writer. Why? Because your reader needs that information in order to make a decision. He may be *interested* in your scheduling problems and the specific content of the shows, but he *reads* your report because of his own needs as station director of that organization. He has to act.

In college, where the reader is also a teacher, the reader's needs are a little less concrete but just as important. Most papers are assigned as a way to teach something. So the real purpose of a paper may be for you to make connections between two historical periods, to discover for yourself the principle behind a laboratory experiment, or to develop and support your own interpretation of a novel. A good college paper doesn't just rehash the facts; it demonstrates what your reader, as a teacher, needs to know —that you are learning the thinking skills his or her course is trying to teach.

Effective writers are not simply expressing what they know, like a student madly filling up an examination bluebook. Instead they are *using* their knowledge: reorganizing, maybe even rethinking their

FIGURE 9-1   *Audience chart for primary audience: the new store manager*

CRITICAL FEATURES OF THE READER		
KNOWLEDGE	ATTITUDE	NEEDS
Has general knowledge of bookstore operations but not a detailed under-standing of how things work here. Doesn't know what tasks I've added to my job description.	Sees it as a student job—no responsibility. Assumes I'm a temporary.	General list of tasks. Time they take. Background or experience required. Needs info to give new trainees.

ideas to meet the demands of an assignment or the needs of their reader.

Sometimes it is also necessary to decide who is your primary audience as opposed to your secondary audience. Both may read your paper, but the primary audience is the reader you most want to teach, influence, or convince. When this is the case, you will want to design the paper so the primary reader can easily find what he or she needs.

A sample audience analysis

Margo Miller is a college student who works in the bookstore at her university. She has been asked by the new store manager to write a job description of her position as an administrative assistant in the paperback department. The manager, Dot Schwartz, said she wanted to know what tasks the position involved and needed information that would help in evaluating Margo's performance and in hiring and training an eventual replacement should Margo leave the position. Dot mentioned that new trainees might be shown the description for guidance in performing the job.

Margo's audience chart in Figure 9-1 pinpoints the critical features of her primary reader, the store manager, Dot Schwartz. Although there is much more Margo could find out about Dot, such as age and education, and so forth—observe how her notes and thinking focus on the critical facts—the facts most relevant to her purpose in writing.

Knowledge	Dot Schwartz, the new manager, knows a lot about bookstore operations in general, but she probably doesn't know what, exactly, I do as an administrative assistant and what tasks I've added to my job since I've been here. In terms of the tasks I've added, the amount of *new knowledge* I'll need to convey will be rather small, so that aspect of the report should be easy to handle.
Attitudes	When I took this job it was mostly a matter of typing and filing. However, through my own efforts I've now often become responsible for dealing with salespeople, ordering certain paperbacks, and designing window displays. I suspect Dot's image of my job is an inadequate one that doesn't recognize the importance of what I'm doing. She may see it as simply a part-time student job, but I see it as a training position that's allowing me to gain increased experience and responsibility. This difference in our images of the job could be critical when I ask for a raise in the fall. So in this report I need to revise Dot's inadequate image of my job and close the gap between our differing attitudes.
Needs	If asked, I could give a very detailed account of my job: exact facts, figures, people, and procedures. But I don't think that's what my reader needs. Dot asked for the report in order to carry out her overall job as a bookstore manager, not to get involved in minutiae. She's interested in the basic tasks involved, how long they generally take, and, since trainees may be coming in, what kinds of background or experience to look for.

Clearly the reader's needs here dictate a quite special organization of Margo's knowledge.

Margo also has a secondary audience for this report: the new trainee who will eventually read it. This reader is quite different in some ways from the manager, as Margo's audience chart in Figure 9-2 shows. Again, here are Margo's notes and thinking:

Knowledge	This reader probably won't know the difference between a back order and on O. P. title, so I'll need to explain procedures and terms in more detail.
Attitude	Given the official description of this as a part-time job, a new trainee may not realize the opportunities it offers or the amount of planning and organization required to do it well.
Needs	The new assistant may be using this report to learn the job, so, unlike the manager, he or she will need a report organized around when and how to do things. However, since the manager is still my primary audience, I probably should put this detailed information in a chart or separate section at the end.

chapter nine / Designing for a Reader

FIGURE **9-2** *Audience chart for secondary audience: the new trainee*

CRITICAL FEATURES OF THE READER		
KNOWLEDGE	ATTITUDES	NEEDS
Probably won't know basic terms or procedures.	May think of it as a "simple" part-time job. Might not recognize the opportunities or demands really involved.	Needs to know what to do and how to do it: an operational description of the job.

By analyzing her audiences and their particular needs, Margo now knows enough to design a report that not only will achieve her ends but will be effective for her two quite different readers.

What about other situations, when you must write for a general reader? In the following example, Margo has decided to adapt her thoughts about her job to a very different use. She wants to submit an article to the *University Times* for a series the paper is running on jobs at the university. Even though this audience represents a cross-section of the university's students, faculty, and staff, Margo's audience analysis turns up some concrete ideas that will help her plan the paper. Here are her thoughts about the article:

These readers may have a limited knowledge of what it means to run a bookstore beyond selling books (knowledge). *Furthermore, as with the store manager, their image of my job will be colored by their conception of part-time jobs* (attitudes). *Since I want to show how part-time jobs can be good career training, I'll have to deal directly with those attitudes. Finally, these readers will also need or expect something from the article* (needs). *Some people might want to learn things relevant to themselves, or might simply want some entertainment. Many people are reading the series in order to find out about various types of jobs they might like to apply for. It may be possible to meet all these needs if I structure the article well.*

Margo also needs to keep in mind her secondary audience, the *University Times* editor. Although the editor is himself seeking to meet the needs of his audience, he also has special requirements the writer must meet. For example, he needs articles under 1,000 words that are focused on the series topic and are written in an engaging, partly journalistic style. To be successful with both her audiences, Margo needs to meet them halfway.

We can sum up this discussion of audience analysis by noting three things you can do:

1. Find out who your reader will be. If you have more than one, decide which audience is primary. Which reader or kind of reader will your paper be designed primarily for?

2. Then begin to explore what you know about your reader's knowledge, attitudes, and needs. Locate those characteristics of your reader that will be critical in light of your purpose in writing.

3. Then plan how you are going to close the gap between you and your reader to make your paper effective.

STRATEGY 2: Anticipate your reader's response

Let us now shift focus from a particular audience or type of audience to the reader's actual process of understanding. When you think about it, we ask a great deal when we expect people to translate a few words presented on a page into a complex meaning or an image that resembles what we originally intended. As we all know, merely reading a message is not the same thing as understanding, much less remembering, it.

The question then is, what happens when a reader tries to turn a *message* into a *meaning*? And what can a writer do to increase the chances that the reader will comprehend and retain the *writer's* meaning?

How does the communication process work?

We often talk about communication as if it were a physical process rather like sending goods in a delivery truck to the reader. We say that a writer *conveys* his message, *expresses* his ideas, or *gets* his point *across*. In this view, the writer's duty is simply to pack all his meaning into the message before it is delivered. Then the reader

FIGURE **9-3**   *Delivering an idea: a simplified model of communication*

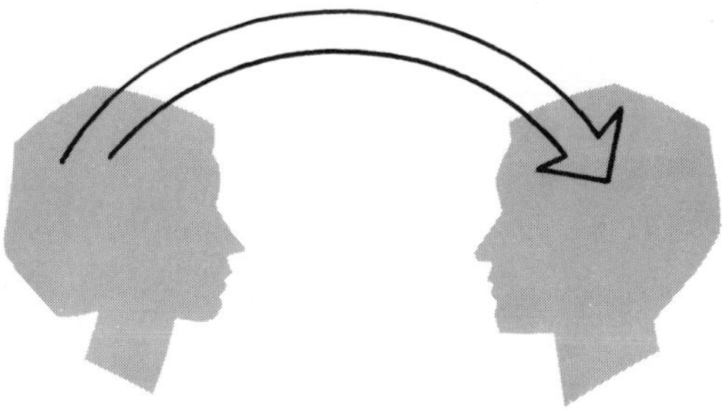

idea transmitted to reader

writer puts idea into words

reader gets the picture;
no loss of meaning

supposedly gets the message and sees the writer's point of view. Figure 9-3 depicts this concept of communication.

One problem with this model is that it turns the writer into a delivery boy. Communication, it seems to say, is the same as simply expressing what's on your mind. If your meaning has been placed (somewhere) in the message, then the reader can dig it out. But unfortunately readers can, and quite often do, read information yet fail to get your meaning or your point. This model of the communication process misleads us by suggesting that a writer's meaning or ideas can simply be transferred intact to someone else.

During World War II a more sophisticated version of the communication process was developed by electrical engineers who were trying to increase the amount of information transmitted through electronic equipment such as radios and telephones. This model of how communication works (see Figure 9-4) depicts the writer as a combination of a radio announcer and a transmitter that sends the messages out on air waves.

In this model the writer, or sender, has a meaning in mind. He "encodes" that meaning into a message, and it is this message that is sent to the reader. The message could take the form of a signal sent out on air waves, a hastily scrawled note tacked on the back door, or a twenty-page paper with pictures and graphs. The point is that the sender has to *encode* his meaning in some form in order to send it. And some senders are better at turning meaning into code than others. A powerful radio transmitter sends off a good-quality

FIGURE 9-4   *A model based on communication theory*

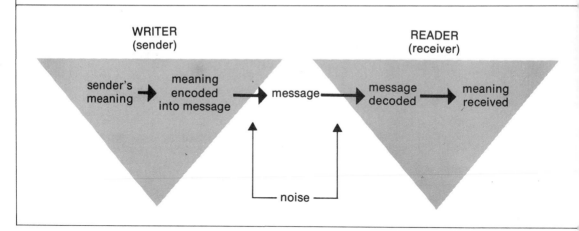

signal; a good writer is able to send messages that accurately express his or her meaning. The first hurdle in the communication process, then, is turning meaning into a message.

This model also reminds us that there are many opportunities for *noise* or interference in this process. While the radio operator may worry about thunderstorms, the writer must worry about everything from misspellings and bad grammar to poor organization and fuzzy thinking—all the things that make his coded message a little less clear.

When the message finally reaches the reader, he, like a radio receiver, must repeat the process of decoding the message back into a meaning. The reader, like a secret agent with a cryptogram, must interpret a meaning. And again the chance for noise enters: if the reader is tired, is confused by the subject, or misses a key word, the communication process breaks down a little more.

As you can see, it is a long way from the meaning the sender had in mind to the meaning that the receiver eventually decodes at the end of the line. The value of this model is that it graphically demonstrates that no matter what you *mean*, and even no matter what message you *send*, all that finally counts is the decoded meaning that the reader finally *receives*.

This model, however, has a limitation: it can't help us understand how readers actually decode messages. To know that, we would need a cognitive or mental model that describes some of the thinking strategies readers use to transform messages into meanings as they read. The discussion that follows will show that readers are not passive recipients who simply *see* the writer's point. In order to comprehend a message, they actually create a meaning in their own mind.

The creative reader

What happens when readers go about decoding messages and creating meanings? The first thing to notice is that they just don't *remember* all the things we tell them. (Imagine trying to repeat every major and minor idea that was presented in the preceding chapter of this book.) Instead of remembering all the details, readers do something much more creative—they draw inferences as they read and use the writer's ideas to form their own concepts. In other words, readers remember not what *we* tell them, but what they tell *themselves*. You can demonstrate this process for yourself with the following exercise.

Here is an excerpt from the "Personal Experience" section of Henry Morris' application for a summer job in accounting. As personnel director, you have been asked to evaluate six such applications. Your job is to read each one and come up with a set of distinctive qualities that characterize each candidate. How would you characterize Henry Morris from his statement below?

> During high school I managed the concession stand for our home basketball games. Later I worked at the nearby A & W Root Beer stand during summers, and for three years I kept the books at my father's local soda bottling plant. I have taken a number of math courses and have had two courses in acounting. I am currently taking courses in small business managment.

Before reading further, write down several sentences that you would use to characterize this applicant.

You now might want to compare your reactions to those of a group of students who were shown the statement. First they listed in the left column the main facts about Henry they all agreed were important (see Figure 9-5). Then everyone proceeded to describe the Henry they had just read about. Here are some of the conclusions they reached about Henry:

LISA: He seems like a good bet for the job—first, because he's had a lot of practical accounting experience. And then he's had a couple of courses on the subject, plus the math. On top of that, he seems pretty enterprising to have taken all those courses and gotten himself those summer jobs.

FIGURE **9-5** *Drawing inferences from facts*

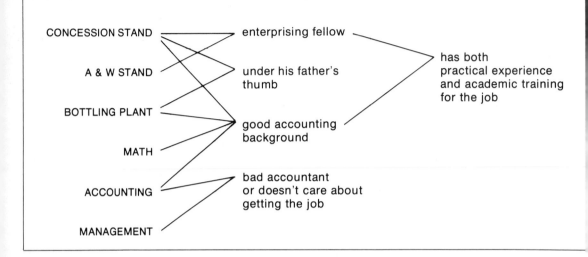

JOSÉ: It sounds as if he's had accounting experience all right, but all he's done is work at his father's plant. And maybe he only had the job at the concession stand because of his father's plant. He doesn't seem very enterprising if he hasn't gone out and found another accounting job to get more varied experience.

TIM: His accounting experience does look impressive: three years is a lot of experience for a young guy coming into a summer job. But his application is so sloppy. He misspelled both "accounting" and "management" in just that one paragraph. Accountants are supposed to be good with details. Maybe he didn't proofread the statement before he sent it, but in that case he seems very careless or not really interested in the job.

Note that from even small details in the text, such as misspellings, the students had arrived at some sweeping conclusions. Furthermore, the chances are good that a real personnel director might have the same response. As you can see from this example, when people are trying to understand a passage, they constantly are drawing inferences and making their own meanings.

This experiment demonstrates two things. The first is that readers do not passively absorb a writer's information; they make meaning as they read. And secondly, the meanings they make are often surprising leaps of imagination. The obvious question, then, is why are readers so creative with our prose? Why must they draw inferences and form concepts?

THE PROBLEM OF SHORT-TERM MEMORY

One reason for this phenomenon is the limitations of the human short-term memory, which forces us to "chunk," or group, information in order to understand it. When it comes to reading, or in fact processing any kind of new information, people are remarkably inefficient. This is because our short-term, working memory, or conscious attention, can only handle a limited number of inputs at one time. This is in contrast to the apparently unlimited storage capacity of long-term memory.

Imagine yourself sitting in a lecture. All incoming information — the voice of the speaker, the words on the blackboard, that idea you were trying to remember, and the person smiling at you across the room — all this information clamors for a portion of your limited conscious attention. We are often caught like jugglers with too many balls in the air.

To test the limits of your own short-term, working memory, multiply 12 × 14 in your head. Now try multiplying 789 × 678 in your head. Do it now.

Notice how hard it is to keep track of your partial answers, carryovers, and the current multiplication task at the same time. You can see why one of our major limitations as thinkers and problem-solvers is the nature of our short-term memory. Although we must deal with highly complex problems, we are unable to actively hold in mind and consider more than a few separate items at a time. Cognitive psychologists set the critical limit at 7 ± 2 bits of information.

Furthermore, in comparison with other processing systems, such as a computer, we are neither particularly fast nor accurate. As a communication channel the human voice can process 25 "bits" of information per second, whereas most electronic channels are designed to process between 10^4 and 10^5 bits in that same second. According to cognitive psychologist George Miller, it is a charity to call us a channel at all. We are more like a bottleneck.

THE POWER OF CHUNKING

Fortunately, we human beings have another trick up our sleeve that makes us remarkably good at thinking. This is the ability to "chunk" information: to look at a whole milling array of facts and perceptions, all shouting for immediate individual attention, and to reduce that throng down to a single chunk. ("Oh, that's one of those whatchamacallits again.") A chunk may be a concept, a category, a term — anything that enables a person to organize miscellaneous data. Telegraph operators use this process when they learn to perceive a string of rapid dashes and dits as meaningful chunks such as words and phrases. You and I do it when, instead of thinking "There are 48 individual cars (in Aztec Red, Seafoam Green, Harvest Gold, etc.) jammed up around the 5th and Penn Avenue intersection honking their horns at 5:34 P.M. Tuesday afternoon . . . ," we simply think to ourselves, "rush hour traffic jam," and go on with our conversation. In order, then, to compensate for the limitations of short-term memory, people sort information into chunks they can manage. In the act of processing new information—such as your job application—they actively organize it into chunks or categories such as "good accountant."

But what determines *how* the reader will chunk new information and *which* inferences they will draw? We naturally like to think that readers carefully mine our prose for *the* meaning we intended. But much recent research in psychology shows that it is more accurate to think of readers as hard at work using our information like a set of tinker toys, to build an idea structure of their own. And if our writing doesn't help them build it, that final structure may or may not resemble our own. In attempting to read and understand a message—to make meaning—a creative reader:

1. Tries to fit new information into an old framework he or she already knows.

   Therefore: The writer should supply that framework by creating a context for his or her ideas.

2. Develops expectations and uses them to actively process and understand the text.

   Therefore: The writer needs to create (and then fulfill) accurate expectations that will help the reader anticipate the writer's meaning.

3. Sorts and organizes information into an unconscious hierarchical structure built around a few key concepts or chunks.

   Therefore: The writer needs to make the hierarchical structure he or she has in mind clear to the reader.

Let us look at these three processes of the reader in more detail.

Readers need a framework, or context, for new ideas / In 1938 Orson Welles threw thousands of people into panic with a radio broadcast reporting a Martian invasion of England. Why? Because his audience had the wrong framework. Those who tuned in during the middle thought they were hearing a news broadcast, not a mere radio drama called "The War of the Worlds."

Readers make sense out of new information by putting it into context. When they aren't given a clear context for such information, they are likely to do two things. The first is to supply their own: a worried reader, anticipating disagreement and afraid that no one likes him, will interpret your helpful suggestion as yet another criticism. A second possibility is that the reader will not understand you at all. Even the simplest information may be hard to understand and impossible to remember if the reader has no context for making sense out of it.

To demonstrate this for yourself, try this experiment. Read the following passage through once (and only once).

> The procedure is actually quite simple. First you arrange things into different groups. Of course one pile may be sufficient depending on how much there is to do. If you have to go somewhere else due to lack of facilities that is the next step, otherwise you are pretty well set. It is important not to overdo things. That is, it is better to do too few things at once than too many. In the short run this may not seem important, but complications can easily arise. A mistake can be expensive as well. At first the whole procedure will seem complicated.
>
> Soon, however, it will become just another fact of life. It is difficult to foresee any end to the necessity for this task in the immediate future, but then one never can tell. After the procedure is completed, one arranges the materials into different groups again. Then they can be put into their appropriate places. Eventually they will be used once more and the whole cycle will then have to be repeated. However, that is a part of life.*

Now shift your attention for a minute or so by saying the alphabet backwards or reading a page at random from this book. Then, without looking at the passage again, try to write down all you can remember about the passage.

How much did you remember? When psychologists John Bransford and Nancy McCarrell ran this experiment they found that their subjects did very poorly, even though the passage describes a very common activity for which everyone has a framework: washing clothes. When another group of subjects was given the passage and told at the beginning that it was a description of washing clothes, the subjects had an immediate framework. Not only did they appear much less frustrated with the task, but they remembered much more of the passage. By creating a context for their readers, Bransford and McCarrell were able to more than *double* their readers' comprehension and recall.

Professional writers and magazine editors often go to great lengths to establish a context for their articles. Consider the article

---

* John D. Bransford and Nancy S. McCarrell, "A Sketch of a Cognitive Approach to Comprehension," in *Cognition and Symbolic Processes*, ed. Walter Weiner (Hillsdale, N.J.: Erlbaum, 1974).

shown below, from the March 1979 issue of *Ms.* magazine. It creates a context in five different ways, each one more specific than the last.

(1) The heading tells us we are reading the magazine's monthly column on *money*.
(2) This month it will be on money and *housing*, the picture says.
(3) In particular it's on *buying* your own house, we learn from the title.
(4) Buying, that is, with a *low down payment*, the subtitle adds.
(5) And it is especially pertinent if you are a *woman*, we learn in the first sentence.

(1)

MONEY

(2)

(3)

How To Buy A House on Your Own...with a Little Help from Uncle Sam

(4)

Under one government program, you can buy a house for $1 down.

(5)

BY EMILY VAN NESS

I never dreamed that as a single woman I would ever be able to own a house. Like many women, I assumed that on my salary (about $14,000 a year) and with today's staggering new-home prices, I would continue to be a "renter" all my adult life—unless I struck it rich or decided to get married and pool my resources.

Then, while apartment-hunting last year in New Jersey, I came across an ad in a local paper for a three-story, brick house in Trenton for only $30,000, 10 percent down, and an unbelievably low 7½ percent mortgage. (Today most conventional lenders are requiring a cash down payment of at least 20

Consider the difference if the article had had an ambiguous title or heading and had started out with "While apartment hunting last year in New Jersey, I came across an ad in a local paper for a three-story brick house in Trenton...." Unless you knew it was a short story (and had faith that it would get better soon), your reaction would probably have been: "So what? Why should I read this?" As you can see a context not only helps a reader make sense of things, it also creates expectations that lure him or her on. And this brings us to the second point about readers.

Readers develop expectations and want those expectations met / General context, as we have seen, gives readers a rough idea of what is coming by setting up a framework with empty slots waiting to be filled. Sometimes the very type of article or paper arouses firm expectations. For example, whenever I read a movie review I expect to find some discussion of the theme or plot, some background on the actors, and an evaluation by the critic—but not a description of the ending. If you depart too greatly from your genre—whether it is a stockholders' report, a highly structured essay assignment, or a résumé—you are likely to confuse or disorient your reader.

Although you can sometimes use expectations readers already have, as a writer you also have the power to create expectations in the reader's mind. Exam graders, for example, are strongly influenced by a dazzling first answer or a weak beginning. If an article or paper begins in a vague fashion, the reader's expectation may be: "This paper sounds as if it's going to be full of hot air, so I can just skim." Perhaps the writer is building slowly up to a point or plans to save his best ideas for last, but it is hard to overcome the powerful effect of a reader's initial expectations.

Cues in the text—whether they are key words you introduce, "teaser" sentences that suggest interesting material to come, or simply a preview of the contents—help generate expectations. But cues can backfire too. In Henry Morris' accounting application (see page 131), some readers saw Henry's misspellings as evidence that he would be a poor accountant. Readers often generate expectations from relatively small, and sometimes inadvertent, cues in the text. These expectations may be so strong that the reader simply won't see what you have to say.

Once a reader's expectations are aroused, they actively clamor to be fulfilled. So it is important to follow through on what your initial paragraphs promise. A reader quickly becomes impatient with wandering prose that seems not to be moving toward the points initially previewed.

Setting up and fulfilling expectations also serve another very important function—they make people remember things. The best way to make your point vivid and memorable is to set up a strong expectation and then fulfill it. Expectations are a valuable way of circumventing short-term memory. If you know what you are looking for, it is much easier and faster to process all that information. Plus, by giving the reader a context and building up expectations, you are equipping him with a set of hooks for retaining what you want him to know.

Readers organize ideas into natural hierarchies / A final way readers understand and remember what you tell them is by organizing your discussion in a general hierarchical way. If you don't do it for them, they will do it themselves—and the result may be far from what you had intended.

The important things about hierarchies, as you know, are that they create a focus by distinguishing major points from minor ones and they show how ideas are related to one another. In general, a reader will want to get a feel for the structure of any discussion very quickly; it is hard to hold many unrelated ideas in mind for long. A writer, on the other hand, might want to present all the facts first and then reveal his point, hoping the reader will keep everything in mind until he does so. Unfortunately, when readers don't see the focus and structure of your ideas, they will probably just build an organization of their own to comprehend the discussion. And the structure they build may not be the one you had in mind at all.

To demonstrate for yourself just how creative readers can be, try the following "headless paragraph" experiment. The six sentences listed below come from a paragraph written by a student on the topic of "The Writing Problem of College Students." Without a topic sentence and without the transitions and connections between the sentences, it is hard to see just how the ideas in this paragraph were organized. Read the six sentences and then jot down in a sentence or two what you think the main point of the paragraph was.

The Headless Paragraph

- Students aren't practicing.
- College atmosphere produces tension.
- Students are afraid of getting a "D."
- Writing is time-consuming.
- Writing is usually done under time pressure.
- Writing courses are not required, so students must take a heavy course load to learn how.

When this experiment was conducted with a group of 18 college sophomores the results were surprising to the student who had written the paragraph containing these ideas. Out of eighteen readers, no one came up with the same organizing idea she had had in mind. Three had concepts that accounted for much of the paragraph, such as: "Students have difficulty in writing due to the pressures imposed upon them by grades, time, and the tension of college life." Three other readers focused on an inclusive or high-level idea, pressure, but neglected other points such as practice.

Altogether, only six of the eighteen came up with an organizing idea that could incorporate most of the information in the paragraph. Of the other twelve readers, four came away with concepts that accounted for only a limited part of the paragraph, such as "Students don't have enough time." And seven ended up with ideas that were not contained in the sentences at all! For example, these readers thought the topic sentence should be "Students aim to please teachers," or "There is too much competition in college," or "Writing should not be required," or "Writing should be required in college." These readers simply took the writer's information and hooked it onto a framework of their own. They used it to support something they already believed. The final reader in this group of eighteen even dropped the subject of writing altogether and said that the major idea of the paragraph was that "Students are more interested in grades than in learning. Their selfishness produces artificial pressures." This statement came as quite a shock to the original author.

As you can see, some readers created a focus or structure that was at least close to what the writer had intended. Their topic sentence created a tree that was at least able to account for most of the information. But some of the readers, in their need to create some sort of organization, interpreted the paragraph in unexpected, even drastic ways.

Here, for comparison, is the paragraph that the writer finally developed after receiving input from her classmates. Note how she employed a topic sentence to create expectations and used cues along the way to show how the ideas were related.

> Students often have trouble writing in college because of a combination of bad habits and high pressure. To start with, students don't practice. This is partly because of time limitations: learning to write is time-consuming, and since writing courses are not required, students have to take a heavy load in order to learn how. Some students do have the time to practice but fail to do so because writing in the high-pressure atmosphere of college produces anxiety and tension. Many students are so afraid of getting a "D" that they avoid writing altogether —until the day before the paper is due. Furthermore, college papers are usually done under time pressure, which simply increases the tension of writing.

Anticipating the creative reader

We can sum up this discussion of the creative reader in this way. Because of the characteristics of the human mind, readers must actively construct meanings from the messages they receive. In order to make meaning, readers rely very heavily on expectations and on structure. In fact, these two things are so important that if the writer doesn't provide expectations and a clear structure, the reader will make up his own. And the framework the reader builds may not be the one the writer intended. In order to help the reader read efficiently and comprehend your meaning, you need to do three things:

1. Try to organize or chunk your information around clear, explicitly stated ideas or concepts. If you want your reader to "see your point," make that point explicit. Don't expect him or her to automatically draw the same conclusion or come up with the same topic sentence you would.
2. Organize your explicit concepts and their supporting information into a clear hierarchical structure for the reader. De-

cide which ideas are major and which are minor, and show how *you* want them to be related.

3. Preview both your concepts and your structure. Set up expectations all through your paper so your reader will know what is coming. Put your ideas in a framework that will help build expectations and make your points forceful and memorable when they come.

Projects and Exercises

1 You are writing an article on eating out for people who are following a low-carbohydrate diet, and you plan to include a paragraph on fast-food restaurants. Use the data in the table below for source material, and write a paragraph tailored to your audience. How will you chunk the data? What concepts should you use?

NUTRITIONAL CONTENT OF POPULAR FAST FOODS

Item	Calories	Protein (grams)	Carbohy-drates (grams)	Fat (grams)	Sodium (milli-grams)
HAMBURGERS					
McDonald's Big Mac	541	26	39	31	962
Burger Chef Hamburger	258	11	24	13	393
FISH					
Arthur Treacher's Fish Sandwich	440	16	39	24	836
Long John Silver's Fish (2 pieces)	318	19	19	19	not available
OTHER ENTREES					
McDonald's Egg McMuffin	352	18	26	20	914
Taco Bell Taco	186	15	14	8	79
Dairy Queen Brazier Dog	273	11	23	15	868
SIDE DISHES					
Burger King French Fries	214	3	28	10	5
Arthur Treacher's Cole Slaw	123	1	11	8	266
McDonald's Chocolate Shake	364	11	60	9	329
McDonald's Apple Pie	300	2	31	19	414

Source: The New York Times, September 19, 1979. © 1979 by The New York Times Company. Reprinted by permission.

Now use the table for a different purpose. You are giving a talk to a group of heart patients who must follow a low-fat, low-salt diet, and you plan to mention fast food. Write a paragraph advising them of good and poor fast-food choices.

2 Here is part of the entry for Margaret Fuller from the *Dictionary of American Biography*. Use it to write a brief statement about Margaret Fuller to include in a paper you are writing for a history class, on nineteenth-century American attitudes toward women.

FULLER, SARAH MARGARET (May 23, 1810–July 19, 1850), Marchioness Ossoli, journalist, critic, social reformer, was born in Cambridgeport, near Boston, Mass. of typical Puritan ancestry. Her father, Timothy Fuller, was a lawyer and a graduate of Harvard . . . Mr. Fuller took full charge of the education of his daughter, who was a precocious child and a model pupil. . . . At the age of six she was introduced to Latin and two years later she was reading Ovid. Shakespeare, Cervantes, and Moliere were also read before she had reached her teens. . . .

. . . Margaret's friendships with the intellectual leaders of her time began at an early age. She . . . read with Frederic Henry Hedge the German authors whom Carlyle had made the fashion and confided in William Henry Channing "her secret hope of what Woman might be and do, as an author, in our Republic" (*Memoirs*, II, 7-8). Often satirized as a blue-stocking, she became along with Emerson the butt of many gibes aimed at Transcendentalism. She was accepted in this circle on a par with men like Alcott and Thoreau and developed in its atmosphere her talents as a talker.

From 1839 to 1844 her famous "conversations" were held in Boston. . . . The purpose of the course, as her prospectus said, was to supply "a point of union to well-educated and thinking women, in a city which, with great pretensions to mental refinement, boasts, at present, nothing of the kind." ". . . Her pupils, whom Harriet Martineau once peevishly described as "gorgeous pedants," were drawn from the most intellectual and cultivated circles of Boston society. From her discussions with this group, she derived material and inspiration for her volume, *Woman in the Nineteeth Century* (1845). Though comparable with Mary Wollstonecraft's *Vindication of the Rights of Woman* (1792), the book did not attract the same degree of popular attention. It touched on all the issues of the future woman's movement, however . . . although its view of woman's rights was too comprehensive and its tone too philosophical to gratify the militants of those early days. When the outcome of the Civil War made suffrage a burning issue, the ideas of Margaret Fuller were allowed to fall into the background. . . .

Margaret began her career as a journalist with the editorship of the *Dial*, the organ of the Transcendentalists. Ralph Waldo Emerson and George Ripley were joint editors with her. As editor-in-chief she was to have received two hundred dollars a year, but Emerson doubts whether even this modest salary was ever paid. . . . The common criticism was that the *Dial* was too feminine. . . . While "far from being an original genius," as she once said of herself, she was one of the best of American critics.*

---

* From *Dictionary of American Biography*, Volume VII, edited by Allen Johnson and Dumas Malone. Copyright 1931 by American Council of Learned Societies. Reprinted by permission of Charles Scribner's Sons.

Now consider this information from another viewpoint. Many people see Margaret Fuller as a representative nineteenth-century American writer and literary figure. Given the limited information you have here, write an introductory paragraph for an imaginary textbook discussing two or three important characteristics of such New England writers. Try to create concepts out of the facts before you.

If You Would Like to Read More

If you want to know more about readers and how to design your writing with them in mind, see:

Bransford, John D. *Human Cognition: Learning, Understanding and Remembering*. Belmont, Calif.: Wadsworth Publishing, 1979. ■ This is an excellent introduction to the most recent research and theories about human thinking processes.

Farnham-Diggory, Sylvia. *Cognitive Processes in Education*. New York: Harper and Row, 1972. ■ This book offers a good introduction to the many psychological issues that affect education and learning.

Mathews, J. C. and Dwight Stevenson. *Designing Technical Reports: Writing for Audiences in Organizations*. Indianapolis: Bobbs-Merrill, 1976. ■ This book gives excellent guidance on professional writing in all kinds of organizations, with special emphasis on the writing of technical reports. It also offers a very detailed and effective way of analyzing one's readers in a technical organization.

Miller, George. "The Magical Number Seven, Plus or Minus Two: Some Limits on Our Capacity for Processing Information." *Psychological Review*, 63 (March 1956), 81–96. In *The Psychology of Communication*, New York: Basic Books, 1967. ■ This is a witty and well-written introduction to the research that has been done in information processing, authored by one of the pioneers in the field.

chapter ten

Writing Reader-Based Prose

As we saw in the preceding chapter, simply expressing yourself isn't always enough; it's no guarantee that you are actually communicating with someone else. This chapter will focus on specific rhetorical strategies you can use to design your writing for a reader.

Some people are rightly suspicious of the notion of rhetorical strategy when they equate it with such things as "mere rhetoric," empty eloquence, or the sophist's art of persuading by any means available. The rhetorical strategy we will discuss is, instead, an attempt to fulfill your goals by meeting the needs of your reader. It is, in essence, a plan for communicating.

Why is such a strategy necessary? We have already looked at one reason: the creative reader needs the help of a context, a clear structure, and guiding expectations to effectively read your prose. Writing a message down is one thing; communicating your meaning is an art that requires planning. Shortly we will look at a second reason for conscious strategy, which grows out of the private nature of the writer's own composing process.

STEP 6 Transform Writer-Based Prose into Reader-Based Prose

Good writers know how to transform writer-based prose (which works well for them) into reader-based prose (which works for their readers as well). Writing is inevitably a somewhat egocentric enterprise. We naturally tend to talk to ourselves when composing. As a result, we often need self-conscious strategies for trying to talk to our reader.

STRATEGY 1: Set up a shared goal

The first strategy for adapting a paper to a reader is to create a shared goal. Try to find a reason for writing your paper and a reason for reading it that both you and your reader share. (Remember that your desire to convey information will not necessarily be met by your reader's desire to receive it.) Then organize your ideas and your arguments around this common goal. You will need to consider the knowledge, attitudes, and needs of your reader, as discussed previously.

A shared goal can be a powerful tool for persuasion. To illustrate, try this exercise:

> You have just been commissioned to write a short booklet on how to preserve older homes and buildings, which the City Historical Society wants to distribute throughout a historical section of the city in an effort to encourage preservation. Most of your readers will simply be residents and local business people. How are you going to get them, first, to read this booklet and, second, to use some of its suggestions?

Take several minutes to think about this problem, then write an opening paragraph for the booklet that includes a shared goal.

To test the effectiveness of your paragraph, consider the following two points about shared goals:

1. A shared goal can *motivate your audience* to read and remember what you have to say. Does your paragraph suggest that the booklet will solve some problem your reader faces or achieve some end he or she really cares about? An appeal to vague goals or a wishy-washy generalization such as "our heritage" is unlikely to keep the reader interested. Use your knowledge to fill some need your reader really has.

In a professional situation think of it this way: Your reader has ten letters and five reports on her desk this morning. Your opening statement with its shared goal should tell her why she would want to read your report first and read it carefully.

2. A shared goal can *increase comprehension*. People understand and retain information best when they can fit it into a framework they already know. For example, the context of "home repair" and "do-it-yourself" would be familiar and maybe attractive to your readers. In contrast, if you defined the goal as "architectural renovation" or "techniques of historical landmark preservation" you would make sense to members of the historical society but would have missed your primary audience, the local readers. They would probably find that context not only unfamiliar but somewhat intimidating.

Offer your readers a shared goal—one for which they already have a framework—that helps them turn your message into something meaningful to them.

Here are examples of three different introductory paragraphs written for this booklet. After reading each one, consider how you would evaluate its power to motivate and aid comprehension. Then read the reaction of another reader, which follows each paragraph.

1. This booklet will help you create civic pride and preserve our city's heritage. In addition you will be helping the Historical Society to grow and extend its influence over the city.

   A reader's response:

   I suppose civic pride is a good thing, but I'm not sure I'd want to help create it. This paragraph makes me feel a little suspicious. What does the Historical Society want from me? I'll bet this is going to be a booklet about raising money so they can put up city monuments.

2. This booklet is concerned with civic restoration and maintenance projects in designated historical areas. It discusses the methods and materials approved by the City Historical Society and City Board of Engineers.

A reader's response:

I guess this is some booklet for city planners or the people who want to set up museums. "Methods and materials" must refer to all those rules and regulations that city contractors have to follow. I wouldn't want to get mixed up with all that if I were doing improvements on my own home.

3. If you own an older home or historical building, there are a number of ways you can preserve its beauty and historical value. At the same time you can increase its market value and decrease its maintenance costs. This booklet will show you five major ways to improve your building and give you step-by-step procedures for how to do this. Please read the booklet over and see which of the suggestions might be useful to you.

A reader's response:

This might be a good idea. I don't know if I'd want to buy the whole package, but I think I'll read it over. What is it—five things I could do? I might find something useful I could try out. I'm particularly concerned about the maintenance costs. Maybe I can find something here on insulation.

Note that in the final example the writer not only has identified shared goals but has given the reader a sort of mental map for reading and understanding the rest of the booklet.

Sometimes a shared goal is something as intangible as intellectual curiosity. But it is the writer's job, in whatever field, to recognize goals or needs that his reader might have and to try to fulfill them. Philosopher Bertrand Russell set forth his shared goal in this way in his introduction to *A History of Western Philosophy:*

Why, then, you may ask, waste time on such insoluble problems? To this one may answer as a historian, or as an individual facing the terror of cosmic loneliness. . . . To teach how to live without certainty, and yet without being paralyzed by hesitation, is perhaps the chief thing that philosophy, in our age, can still do for those who study it.*

To sum up, the first step in designing your paper for a reader is to set up a shared goal. Use it in your problem/purpose statement, and you might also use it as the top level of your issue tree when you generate ideas. A good shared goal will motivate your reader by providing a context for understanding your ideas and a reason for acting on them.

---

* Bertrand Russell. *A History of Western Philosophy* (New York: Simon and Schuster, 1945), p. xiv.

STRATEGY 2: Develop a reader-based structure

Most of us intend to write reader-based prose, to communicate with our reader. But for various reasons, people often end up writing writer-based prose, or talking to themselves. For example, the following excerpts are from letters written by students applying for summer jobs. They had been asked to include some personal background and experience.

Do some detective work on these paragraphs and try to describe the hidden logic that you think is organizing each one. Compare the paragraph to some other way you could write it. Why did the writers choose to include the particular facts they did, and why did they organize them in these particular ways?

Terry F.:

I was born in Wichita, Kansas, on December 4, 1962. After four years there my family moved to Topeka, Kansas, where I attended kindergarten. The next year my family moved to Rose Hill, Iowa. I went to first grade there and my family moved again. I started second grade in Butler, Pennsylvania, and finished it in Pittsburgh, Pennsylvania, where I still live today. . . . I took the college curriculum in high school, which included English, history, science, French, and mathematics, and am currently a college sophomore.

I would like this job for two reasons. First, I could use the money for school next year. Second, the experience would be very helpful. It would help me get a job in that specific area when I graduate.

Katherine P.:

As a freshman I worked as a clerk in a student-managed store, Argus. . . . I became acquainted with the university personnel manager and was offered the position of Argus personnel manager for the semester beginning August, 1979. I accepted and held the job until December of 1979, when a managerial position was eliminated. With managerial staff reduced to two people, responsibilities were adjusted and I was offered the position of purchasing agent. Again I accepted.

Notice that in these examples there is a logic organizing each paragraph, but it is the logic of a story, based on the writer's own memories and, in Terry's case, personal needs. The needs of the reader have not been considered. This is writer-based prose: writing that may seem quite clear and organized to the writer but is not yet adequately designed for the reader. In each case, the potential employer probably wanted to know how the applicant's background and experience could fit his or her needs. But neither paragraph was organized around that goal.

Why do people write to themselves when they are ostensibly writing to a reader? One reason is a natural mental habit that psychologists call "egocentrism": thinking centered around the ego or "I." Egocentrism is not selfishness but simply the failure to actively imagine the point of view of someone else as we talk or write. We see this all the time in young children who happily talk about what they are doing in a long, spirited monologue that has many gaps and mysterious expressions. They may speak in code words or private language which, like jargon in adults, is saturated with meaning for the user but not for the listener. Although a bystander may be totally in the dark, the child seems to assume everyone understands perfectly.

Part of a child's cognitive development is growing out of this self-centeredness and learning to imagine and adapt to another person's state of mind. But we never grow out of our egocentrism entirely. When adults write to themselves, it is usually because they have simply forgotten to consider the reader.

There is another very good reason adults write writer-based prose. If you are working on a difficult paper, it is often easier to discover what you know first and worry about designing it for a reader later. An interesting study called the New York Apartment Tour experiment* demonstrated people's tendency to explain in a self-oriented way. The experimenters, Charlotte Linde and William Labov, posed as social workers and asked a number of people to describe their apartments. They found that nearly everyone gave them a room-by-room verbal tour and used similar procedures for conducting it. Although neither the experimenters nor the speakers were actually in the apartments, the descriptions were phrased as though they had been. For example, the description typically starts at the door; if the nearest room is a big one, you go on in ("from the left of the hall you go into the living room"); if the nearest room is small, the speaker merely refers to it and makes a comment ("and there's a closet off the living room"). Then the speaker suddenly brings you back to the entrance hall ("and on the right of the hall is the dining room"), without having to retrace steps or repeat previous rooms. The intuitive, narrative procedures used in conducting this verbal tour were very efficient for remembering all the details of the apartment.

Linde and Labov found that 97 percent of the people questioned used this sort of *narrative* tour strategy. Only 3 percent gave an *overview* such as, "Well, the apartment is basically a square." The reason? The narrative tour strategy is a very efficient way to retrieve

---

* Charlotte Linde and William Labov, "Spatial Networks as a Site for the Study of Language and Thought," *Language*, 51 (1975), pp. 924–39.

information from memory—that is, to survey what you know. In this case it allows you to cover all the rooms one by one as you walk through your apartment. Yet it is almost impossible for another person to reproduce the apartment from this narrative tour, whereas the overview approach, which only 3 percent used, works quite well. As in writing, an organization that functions well for thinking about a topic often fails to communicate that thinking to the listener. A strategy that is effective for the speaker may be terribly confusing to a listener.

Note, however, that in draft form, writer-based prose can have a real use. Since this type of writing comes naturally to us, it can be an efficient strategy for exploring a topic and outwitting our nemesis, short-term memory. If a writer's material is complicated or confusing, he may initially have to concentrate all his attention on generating and organizing his own knowledge. He might simply be too preoccupied to simultaneously imagine another person's point of view and adapt to it. The reader has to wait. But you don't want to make the reader wait forever.

You can usually recognize writer-based prose by one or more of these features:

1. An *egocentric focus* on the writer.
2. A *narrative organization* focused on the writer's own discovery process.
3. A *survey structure* organized, like a textbook, around the writer's information.

There are times, of course, when a narrative structure is exactly right—if, for example, your goal is to tell a story or describe an event. And a survey of what you know can be a reasonable way to organize a background report or survey. But in most expository and persuasive writing, the writer needs to *re*organize his or her knowledge around a problem, a thesis, or the reader's needs. Writer-based prose just hasn't been reorganized yet.

A reader's test

Below are two versions of a report that will be used as a test case. The writers were students in an organizational psychology course who were also working as consultants to a local organization, the Oskaloosa Brewing Company. The purposes of the report were to show progress to their professor and to present a problem analysis, complete with causes and conclusions, to their client. Both readers — academic and professional—were less concerned with what the students had done or seen than with *how* they had approached the problem and *what* they had made of their observations.

To gauge the reader-based effectiveness of this report, read quickly through Draft 1 and imagine the response of Professor Charns, who needed to answer these questions: "As analysts, what assumptions and decisions did my students make? Why did they make them? And at what stage in the project are they now?" Then reread the draft and play the role of the client, who wants to know: "How did they define the problem, and what did they conclude?" As either reader, can you quickly extract the information the report should be giving you? Next try the same test on Draft 2.

DRAFT 1

Group Report

(1)   Work began on our project with the initial group decision to evaluate the Oskaloosa Brewing Company. Oskaloosa Brewing Company is a regionally located brewery manufacturing several different types of beer, notably River City and Brough Cream Ale. This beer is marketed under various names in Pennsylvania and other neighboring states. As a group, we decided to analyze this organization because two of our group members had had frequent customer contact with the sales department. Also, we were aware that Oskaloosa Brewing had been losing money for the past five years, and we felt we might be able to find some obvious problems in its organizational structure.

(2)   Our first meeting, held February 17th, was with the head of the sales department, Jim Tucker. Generally, he gave us an outline of the organization, from president to worker, and discussed the various departments that we might ultimately decide to analyze. The two that seemed the most promising and more applicable to the project were the sales and production departments. After a few group meetings and discussions with the personnel manager, Susan Harris, and our advisor, Professor Charns, we felt it best suited our needs and Oskaloosa Brewing's needs to evaluate their bottling department.

(3)   During the next week we had a discussion with the superintendent of production, Henry Holt, and made plans for interviewing the supervisors and line workers. Also, we had a tour of the bottling department that gave us a first-hand look at the production process. Before begin-

ning our interviewing, our group met several times to for-
mulate appropriate questions to use in interviewing, for
both the supervisors and the workers. We also had a meeting with Professor Charns to discuss this matter.

(4)   The next step was the actual interviewing process.
During the weeks of March 14–18 and March 21–25, our group
met several times at Oskaloosa Brewing and interviewed ten
supervisors and twelve workers. Finally, during this past
week, we have had several group meetings to discuss our
findings and the potential problem areas within the bottling department. Also, we have spent time organizing the
writing of our progress report.

(5)   The bottling and packaging division is located in a
separate building, adjacent to the brewery, where the beer
is actually manufactured. From the brewery the beer is
piped into one of five lines (four bottling lines and one
canning line) in the bottling house, where the bottles are
filled, crowned, pasteurized, labeled, packaged in cases,
and either shipped out or stored in the warehouse. The
head of this operation, and others, is production manager
Phil Smith. Next in line under him in direct control of
the bottling house is the superintendent of bottling and
packaging, Henry Holt. In addition, there are a total of
ten supervisors who report directly to Henry Holt and who
oversee the daily operations and coordinate and direct the
twenty to thirty union workers who operate the lines.

(6)   During production, each supervisor fills out a data
sheet to explain what was actually produced during each
hour. This form also includes the exact time when a
breakdown occurred, what it was caused by, and when production was resumed. Some supervisors' positions are
production-staff-oriented. One takes care of supplying
the raw material (bottles, caps, labels, and boxes) for
production. Another is responsible for the union workers'
assignments each day.

     These workers are not all permanently assigned to a
production-line position. Men called "floaters" are used,
filling in for a sick worker or helping out after a break-
down.

(7)   The union employees are generally older than thirty-
five, some in their late fifties. Most have been with the
company many years and are accustomed to having more
workers per a slower moving line....

DRAFT 2

MEMORANDUM

TO: Professor Martin Charns

FROM: Nancy Lowenberg, Todd Scott, Rosemary Nisson,
      Larry Vollen

DATE: March 31, 1977

RE: Progress Report: The Oskaloosa Brewing Company

Why Oskaloosa Brewing?

Oskaloosa Brewing Company is a regionally located brewery manufacturing several different types of beer, notably River City and Brough Cream Ale. As a group, we decided to analyze this organization because two of our group members have frequent contact with the sales department. Also, we were aware that Oskaloosa Brewing had been losing money for the past five years and we felt we might be able to find some obvious problems in its organizational structure.

Initial Steps: Where to Concentrate?

After several interviews with top management and a group discussion, we felt it best suited our needs, and Oskaloosa Brewing's needs, to evaluate the production department. Our first meeting, held February 17, was with the head of the sales department, Jim Tucker. He gave us an outline of the organization and described the two major departments, sales and production. He indicated that there were more obvious problems in the production department, a belief also suggested by Susan Harris, the personnel manager.

Next Step

The next step involved a familiarization with the plant and its employees. First, we toured the plant to gain an understanding of the brewing and bottling processes. Next, during the weeks of March 14–18 and March 21–25, we interviewed

---

ten supervisors and twelve workers. Finally, during the past
week we had group meetings to exchange information and discuss
potential problems.

The Production Process
     Knowledge of the actual production process is imperative
in understanding the effects of various problems on efficient
production. Therefore, we have included a brief summary of
this process.
     The bottling and packaging division is located in a sepa-
rate building, adjacent to the brewery, where the beer is actually manufactured. From the brewery the beer is piped into
one of five lines (four bottling lines and one canning line) in
the bottling house, where the bottles are filled, crowned, pasteurized, labeled, packaged in cases, and either shipped out or
stored in the warehouse.

Problems
     Through extensive interviews with supervisors and union
employees, we have recognized four apparent problems within the
bottling house operations. The first is that the employees'
goals do not match those of the company.... This is especially
apparent in the union employees, whose loyalty lies with the
union instead of the company. This attitude is well-founded,
as the union ensures them of job security and benefits....

As a reader, how would you describe the difference between these
two versions? Each was written by the same group of writers, but
the revision came after a discussion about what the readers really
needed to know and expected to get from the report. Let us look at
the three things that make Draft 1 a piece of writer-based prose.

NARRATIVE ORGANIZATION

The first four paragraphs of the draft are organized as a narrative, starting with the phrase, "Work began...." We are given a
story of the writers' discovery process. Notice how all of the facts are
presented in terms of *when* they were discovered, not in terms of

their implications or logical connections. The writers want to tell us what happened when; the reader, on the other hand, wants to ask "why?" and "so what?"

A narrative organization is tempting to write because it is a pre-fabricated order and easy to generate. Instead of having to create a hierarchical organization among ideas or worry about a reader, the writer can simply remember his or her own discovery process and write a story. Papers that start out, "In studying the economic causes of World War I, the first thing we have to consider is. . . ." are often a dead giveaway. They tell us we are going to watch the writer's mind at work and follow him through the process of thinking out his conclusions.

This pattern has, of course, the virtue of any form of drama —it keeps you in suspense by withholding closure. But only if the audience is willing to wait that long for the point. Unfortunately, most academic and professional readers are impatient and tend to interpret such narrative, step-by-step structures either as wandering and confused (does he have a point?) or as a form of hedging.

EGOCENTRIC FOCUS

The second feature of Draft 1 is that it is a discovery story starring the writers. Its drama, such as it is, is squarely focused on the writer: "I did/I thought/I felt." Of the fourteen sentences in the first three paragraphs, ten are grammatically focused on the writers' thoughts and actions rather than on the issues. For example: "Work began . . . ," "We decided . . . ," "Also we were aware . . . and we felt. . . ." Generally speaking, the reader is more interested in issues and ideas than in the fact that the writer thought them.

SURVEY FORM OR TEXTBOOK ORGANIZATION

In the fifth paragraph of Draft 1, the writers begin to organize their material in a new way. Instead of a narrative, we are given a survey of what the writers observed. Here, the raw facts of the bottling process dictated the organization of the paragraph. Yet the client-reader already knows this, and the professor probably doesn't care. In the language of computer science we could say the writers are performing a "memory dump": simply printing out information in the exact form in which they stored it in memory. Notice how in the revised version the writers try to *use* their observations to understand production problems.

The problem with a survey or "textbook" form is that it ignores the reader's need for a different organization of the information. Suppose, for example, you are writing to model airplane builders about wind resistance. The information you need comes out of a physics text, but that text is organized around the field of physics; it starts with subatomic particles and works up from there. To meet the needs of your reader, you have to adapt that knowledge, not lift it intact from the text. Sometimes writers can simply survey their knowledge, but generally the writer's main task is to *use* knowledge rather than reprint it.

To sum up, in Draft 2 of the Oskaloosa report, the writers made a real attempt to write for their readers. Among other things the report is now organized around major questions readers might have, it uses headings to display the overall organization of the report, and it makes better use of topic sentences that tell the reader what each paragraph contains and why to read it. Most important, it focuses more on the crucial information the reader wants to obtain.

Obviously this version could still be improved. But it shows the writers attempting to transform writer-based prose and change their narrative and survey pattern into a more issue-centered hierarchical organization.

Consider another example of how a writer transformed a writer-based paragraph into a reader-based one. The first draft below is full of good ideas but has a narrative organization and egocentric focus. We can almost see the writer reading the book. Her conclusions (which her professor will want to know) are buried within a description of the story (which her professor, of course, knows already).

Writer-based draft:

In *Great Expectations,* Pip is introduced as a very likable young boy. Although he steals, he does it because he is both innocent and good-hearted. Later, when he goes to London, one no longer feels this same sort of identification with Pip. He becomes too proud to associate with his old friends, cutting ties with Joe and Biddy because of his false pride. And yet one is made to feel that Pip is still an innocent in some important ways. When he dreams about Estella, one can see how all his unrealistic, romantic illusions blind him to the way the world really works.

We know from this paragraph how the writer reacted to a number of things in the novel. But what conclusions did she finally come to? What larger pattern does she want us to see?

Reader-based revision:

In *Great Expectations* Pip changes from a goodhearted boy into a selfish young man, yet he always remains an innocent who never really understands how the world works. Although as a child Pip actually steals something, he does it because he has a gullible, kindhearted sort of innocence. As a young man in London his crime seems worse when he cuts his old friends, Joe and Biddy, because of false pride. And yet, as his dreams about Estella show, Pip is still an innocent, a person caught up in unrealistic romantic illusions that he can't see through.

The revised version starts out with a topic sentence that explicitly states the writer's main idea and shows us how she has chunked or organized the facts of the novel. The rest of the paragraph is clearly focused on that idea, and words such as "although" are used to show how her observations are logically related to one another. From a professor or other reader's point of view, this organization is also more effective because it clearly shows what the writer learned from reading the novel.

Below is a good example of a writer who has focused all of his attention on the object before him. He has given us a survey of what he knows about running shoes, although the ostensible purpose of the paragraph was to help a new runner decide what shoe to buy.

Writer-based draft:

Shoes are the most important part of your equipment, so choose them well. First, there are various kinds. Track shoes are lightweight with spikes. Road running flats, however, are sturdy, with ½" to 1" of cushioning. In many shoes the soles are built up with different layers of material. The uppers are made in various ways, some out of leather, some out of nylon reinforced with leather, and the cheapest are made of vinyl. The best combination is nylon with a leather heel cup. The most distinctive thing about running shoes is the raised heel and, of course, the stripes. Although some tennis shoes now have such stripes, it is important not to confuse them with a real running shoe. All in all, a good running shoe should combine firm foot support with sufficient flexibility.

In this draft the writer has focused on the shoe, not the reader who needs to choose a shoe. How would we decide between leather, nylon, and vinyl? Or judge what is "sufficiently" flexible? Why does it matter that the soles are layered; was the writer trying to make a point?

Reader-based revision:

Your running shoe will be your most important piece of running equipment, so look for a shoe that both cushions and supports your foot. Track shoes, which are lightweight and flimsy, with spikes for traction in dirt, won't do. Neither will tennis shoes, which are made for balance and quick stops, not steady pounding down the road. A good pair of shoes starts with a thick layered sole, at least ½" to 1" thick. The outer layer absorbs road shock; the inner layer cushions your foot. Another form of cushioning is the slightly elevated heel which prevents strain on the vulnerable Achilles tendon.

The uppers that will support your foot come in vinyl, which is cheaper but can cause blisters and hot feet; in leather, which can crack with age; and in a lightweight but more expensive nylon and leather combination.

The best nylon and leather shoes will have a thick, fitted leather heel cup that keeps your foot from rolling and prevents twisted ankles. Make sure, however, that your sturdy shoes are still flexible enough that you can bend 90° at the ball of your foot. Although most running shoes have stripes, not all shoes with stripes can give you the cushioning and flexible support you need when you run.

Notice how the revision uses the same facts about shoes but organizes them around the reader's probable questions. The writer tells us what his facts *mean* in the context of choosing shoes. For example, vinyl uppers mean low cost and possible blisters. And the topic sentence sets up the key features of a good shoe—cushioning and support—which the rest of the paragraph will develop. The reader-based revision tells us what we need to know in a direct, explicit way.

Creating reader-based prose

In the best of all possible worlds we would all write reader-based prose from the beginning. It is theoretically much more efficient to generate and organize your ideas in light of the reader in the first place. But sometimes that is hard to do. Take the assignment: "Write about the physics of wind resistance for a model airplane builder." For a physics teacher this would be a trivial problem. But for someone ten years out of Physics 101, the first task would be remembering whatever they knew about wind resistance or friction at all. Adapting that knowledge to the reader would just have to wait.

In general, write for your reader whenever you can, but recognize that many times a first draft is going to be more writer-based than you may want it to be. Even though the draft may not work well for your reader, it can represent a great deal of work for you and be the groundwork for an effective paper. The more complex your problem and the more difficult your material, the more you will need to transform your writer-based prose to reader-based prose. This is not an overly difficult step in the writing process, but many writers simply neglect to take it.

In order to transform your paper to more reader-based prose, there are four major things you can do, all of which should be familiar by now:

1. Organize your paper around a problem, a thesis, or a purpose you share with the reader—not around your own discovery process or the topic itself.
2. With a goal or thesis as the top level of your issue tree, organize your ideas in a hierarchy. Distinguish between your

157

major and minor ideas and make the relationship between them explicit to the reader. You can use this technique to organize not only an entire paper but sections and paragraphs.

3. If you are hoping that your reader will draw certain conclusions from your paper, or even from a portion of it, make those conclusions explicit. If you expect him or her to go away with a few main ideas, don't leave the work of drawing inferences and forming concepts up to your reader. He or she might just draw a different set of conclusions.

4. Finally, once you have created concepts and organized your ideas in a hierarchy focused on your reader and your goals, use cues—which we will discuss shortly—to make that organization vivid and clear to the reader.

STRATEGY 3: Give your reader cues

Part of your contract with a reader, if you seriously want to communicate, is to guide him or her through your prose. You need to set up cues that help the reader see what is coming and how it will be organized. This means, first of all, creating expectations and fulfilling them so that when your point arrives, your reader will have a well-anchored hook to hang it on. This was discussed in the preceding chapter (pp. 136–37). In addition, you want the reader to know which points are major, which are minor, and how they are related to one another. By using various kinds of cues and signposts, you can guide the reader to build an accurate mental tree of your discussion.

Readers, of course, come to your prose with built-in expectations about where these cues will be. For example, they expect:

- To find the most important points of a discussion stated at the beginning and summarized in some way at the end.
- To find a topic sentence that tells them what they will learn from a paragraph.
- To find the writer's key words in grammatically important places such as the subject, verb, and object positions.

It is to your advantage to fulfill these expectations whenever you can.

Writers have a number of tools and techniques they can use to *preview* their meaning, *summarize* it, and *guide* the reader. Figure 10-1 lists some of the most common. Check this list against the last paper you wrote. How many of these tools did you take advantage of?

FIGURE **10-1** *Cues for the reader*

Title Table of contents Abstracts Introduction Headings Problem/purpose statement Topic sentences for paragraphs	*Cues that preview your points*

Sentence summaries at ends
  of paragraphs
Conclusion or summary
  sections
	Cues that summarize or illustrate your points

Pictures, graphs, and tables
Punctuation
Typographical cues:
  different typefaces,
  underlining, numbering
Visual arrangement:
  indentation, extra white space,
  rows and columns
	Cues that guide the reader visually

Transitional words Conjunctions Repetitions Pronouns Summary nouns	*Cues that guide the reader verbally*

The conventions of format on a page also work as familiar cues to the reader. Figure 10-2 shows a typical format for papers and reports.

Draft 2 of the Oskaloosa Brewing report (pp. 152–53) offered a good example of how headings, topic sentences, and previews of conclusions can provide reader cues. Here is another piece of writing that was designed with the reader in mind. It comes from Thomas

FIGURE **10-2** *Common format for typewritten paper*

```
          THIS IS A TITLE: THE SUBTITLE QUALIFIES IT


     The first sentence in this paragraph is a topic sentence,
which announces the topic and previews the argument or point of
the paragraph.  The remainder of the paragraph often previews
the rest of the paper, introducing the main points to be
covered.

THIS IS A MAJOR HEADING

     Major headings are placed flush left, often set in caps,
and, in typewritten manuscript, usually underlined.  In print
they are often set in boldface type.  Ideally a reader should
be able to see the shape of your discussion simply by reading
the title and major headings.  Make the wording of major head-
ings grammatically parallel, if you can, as the major and minor
headings are in this example.

     This Is a Minor Heading

     Unlike a major heading it is indented and typed in capital
and lower-case letters.  It should be clearly and logically re-
lated to the major heading that precedes it.

          The fact that this passage is indented says it
          is either a long quotation or an example.  The
          additional space around it and the single spac-
          ing signal that it is a different kind of text,
          and let readers adjust their reading speed and
          expectations.
```

Miller's book *This Is Photography,** in a chapter called "Action." One of the first previews the reader sees on the page is a photo of a pole vaulter effortlessly sailing over a bar and a place kicker completely off the ground with his right foot at the top of his kick. The caption reads, "These look like top speed but . . . ."

---

* Thomas Miller and Wyatt Brummitt, *This Is Photography* (Rochester, N.Y.: Case Hoyt Corp., 1945).

In the passage below, I have italicized and footnoted certain portions for discussion later. As you read the italicized parts, try to figure out what effect the writer was hoping to have on you by using the cues he did.

Poised Action[1]

In many sports,[2] particularly in races, movement is constant enough to permit picture making in terms of calculated speeds. *But there are other sports*[2] in which the action is spasmodic, defying calculation. *In those sports,*[2] the instants when action is poised are, pictorially, just as vivid and interesting as the moments when action is wildest. *Take pole vaulting, for instance.*[2] At the very top of the vault, with the vaulter's body flung out horizontally over the bar, action is relatively quiet —yet it's the best pictorial moment in this field event. This peak instant can be "stopped" with much less shutter speed than either the rise or fall.

Baseball[3] has a number of moments which are full of *poised action.*[3] The pitcher winds up and *then*[4] unwinds to throw his speed-ball. *In that instant,*[4] between winding and unwinding, action is suspended, yet a picture of it tells a story of speed and power. *An instant later,*[4] having released the ball, the pitcher is *again*[4] poised —all his energy having gone into the delivery. *There's another pictorial moment.*[5] *To picture either of these moments you need to work swiftly, but a high shutter speed is less important to your success than an understanding of the sport and of the personal style of the athlete before your lens.*[6]

Even in boxing,[7] a good photographer gets his pictures as the blows land, not as they travel. *There was that famous instance*[8] at the Louis-Nova fight in '41. Two photographers, on directly opposite sides of the ring, saw a heavy punch coming and shot just as it landed. Both used Photo-flashes, of course, but —one of the lamps failed to work. The photographer whose light had failed discovered, on developing the film, that he had a picture —a most unusual and vivid silhouette —*made by the light of his competitor's flash.*[9] The fighters hid the other man's flash bulb, so the silhouette effect was perfect —and dramatic. *The only moral to this yarn*[10] is that experience teaches pressmen and other pro's that there are right instances for any shots. The photographers on opposite sides of the ring were right —and right together, within the same hundredth of a second.

Here are comments on the writer's cues:

1. In the original, this heading is set in boldface type.
2. These cues make the relationship between each of the sentences explicit. They lead us along; many sports are contrasted to other sports. We are told something additional about "other sports" and then given an example.

3. A topic sentence ties a new subject, "baseball," to the old topic, "poised action."

4. These words and phrases reinforce our sense of the timing and sequence of the action.

5. The writer recaps his discussion by redefining it not just as an action, but in the larger context now of photographs representing "pictorial moments."

6. This sentence is a recap on an even larger scale. In it the writer draws a conclusion based on both this paragraph and the preceding one, and ties the paragraphs to the larger goal of the book and the chapter: how to take good action photographs.

7. This topic sentence and its introductory phrase are performing two functions: they introduce a new subject, boxing, and tie it neatly to the old framework with the words "even in."

8. We are told to see this as an example of the writer's point. He doesn't let us simply be entertained by the story; he uses it.

9. This line was also in italics in the original, to emphasize how unusual the occurrence was. Note that in the phrase just before this one—"a most unusual and vivid silhouette"—the writer used dashes to highlight the significance of the facts. Both italics and dashes are attention-getting cues, though they can be overdone.

10. The writer draws a particular conclusion from all of this that is tied to the point of his book, and he signposts his conclusion quite clearly so we won't miss it: "The only moral to this yarn is . . ."

STRATEGY 4: Develop a persuasive argument

People often write because they want to make something happen: they want the reader to do something or at least to see things their way. But sometimes expressing a point of view isn't enough, because it conflicts with the way the reader *already* sees things. We are faced with the same old problem of communication: your image of something and your reader's are not the same. What kinds of argument can you use that will make him or her see things *your* way? In this section we will look at the nature of arguments and at one type, the Rogerian argument, that can help you persuade another person to see things differently.

Winning an argument versus persuading a listener

When people think of arguments they usually think of winning them. And the time-honored method of winning an argument is by force ("You agree or I'll shoot.") or, in its more familiar form, by authority ("This is right because I [your mother, father, teacher, sergeant, boss] say it is."). The problem with force or authority is that, short of brainwashing, it often changes people's behavior but not their minds.

A second familiar form of argument is debate. Yet many people who learn to debate in high school discover that in the real world their debate strategies can indeed prove their point—but lose the argument. Debate is an argumentative contest: person A is pitted against person B, and the winner is decided by an impartial judge. But in the real world, person A is trying not to impress a judge but to *convince* person B. The goal of such an argument is not to win points but to affect your listener, to change his or her image of your subject in some significant way. And, as you remember, that image may be a large, complex network of ideas, associations, and attitudes. The goal of communication is to find a common ground and create a shared image, but debate typically polarizes a discussion by pitting one image against the other.

Let us look for a moment at the possible outcomes of an argument or discussion in which the two parties have firmly held but differing images. Ann has decided to take a year off to work and travel before she finishes college and settles on a career. Her parents immediately oppose the idea. To them, this plan conveys an image of "dropping out" and wasting a year, with the possibility that Ann might not return to school. Furthermore, they have saved money to help put her through school and see this prospect as an indication that she doesn't value their plans, hopes, and efforts for her.

For Ann, on the other hand, taking a year off means getting time and experience that would enable her to take better advantage of college. She hopes it will help her decide what sort of work she wants to do, but more importantly she sees it as a chance to develop on her own for a while. In her mind, the goal of going to college isn't getting a degree but figuring out what things you want to learn more about.

Clearly Ann and her parents have very different images of taking a year off. Assume you are Ann in this situation. What are the possible outcomes of an argument you might have with your parents?

One outcome, and usually the least likely one, is that you will totally reconstruct your listeners' image so they see the issue just as you do. You simply replace their perspective with yours. Reconstruction can no doubt happen if your audience has an undeveloped image of the subject or sees you as a great authority, but argument strategies that set out to reconstruct someone else's ideas completely —to *win* the point —are usually ill-founded and unrealistic. They are more likely to polarize people than to persuade them.

A second alternative is to modify someone else's image, to add to or clarify it. You do this when you clarify an issue (for example, taking a year off is not the same as "dropping out") or when you add new information (Ann's college even has a special program for this and might give her some course credit for work experience). As a writer this is clearly the most reasonable effect you can aim for. In doing so you respect the other person's point of view while striving to modify those features you can reasonably affect.

The third possible outcome of an argument may be the most common: no change. Think for a minute of how many speeches, lectures, classes, sermons, and discussions you have sat through in your life and how many of those had no discernible effect on your thinking. If we think of an argument as debate in which a "good" argument inevitably wins, we forget that it is possible for even a "correct" argument to have absolutely no effect on our listener.

To sum up, the goal of an argument is to modify the image of your listener —and that this is not the same as simply presenting your own image. A successful argument is a reader-based act. It considers attitudes and images the reader already holds.

However, a great roadblock stands in the way of modifying a listener's image. Many people perceive any change in their image of things as a threat to their own security and stability. People's images are part of themselves, and a part of how they have made sense of the world. To ask them to change their image in any significant way can make people anxious and resistant to change. When this happens, communication simply stops.

Arguments that polarize issues often create just this situation. The more the speaker argues, the more firmly the listener clings to his own position. And instead of listening, the listener spends his time thinking up counter-arguments to protect his own position and image. So the critical question for the writer is this: how can I persuade my reader to listen to my position and maybe even modify his or her image without creating this sense of threat that stops communication?

Rogerian argument

Rogerian argument, developed in part from the work of Carl Rogers, is an argument strategy designed not to win but to increase communication in both directions. It is based on the fact that if people feel they are understood —that their position is honestly recognized and respected —they may cease to feel a sense of threat. Once the threat is removed, listening is no longer an act of self-defense, and people feel they can afford to truly listen to and consider other ways of seeing things.

The goal of an argument, then, is to induce your reader at least to consider your position and the possibility of modifying his or her own. One way to make this happen is to demonstrate an understanding of your listener's position *first*. That means trying to see the issue from his or her point of view. For face-to-face discussions, Carl Rogers suggested this rule of thumb: before you present your position and argue for your way of seeing things, you must be able to describe your listener's position back to your listener in such a way that he or she *agrees* with your version of it. In other words, you are demonstrating that you not only care about your listener's perspective but care enough to actively try (and keep trying) to understand it. So Ann in our example would have begun the discussion with her parents by exploring with them their response to her leaving college and the reasons behind their feelings.

What does this mean for writers who don't have the luxury of a face-to-face discussion? First, you can use the introduction to your paper, including your shared goal, to demonstrate to your reader a thorough understanding of his or her problems and goals. This is your chance to look at the question from your reader's point of view and show how your message is relevant to them.

Secondly, try to avoid categorizing people and issues. This puts people into camps, polarizes the argument, and stops communication. For example, Ann may well have felt that her parents were being old-fashioned and conventional to resist her idea, but establishing that point would have done little to change their minds. A Rogerian argument, by contrast, would begin by acknowledging the parents' plans and hopes for her and recognizing the element of truth in their fear of her "dropping out." They know that, despite good intentions, many people don't come back to college. In taking a Rogerian approach, Ann might also begin to understand the issues more clearly herself. One of the hidden strengths of a Rogerian argument is that, besides increasing one's power to persuade, it also opens up communication and may even end up persuading the persuader. It increases the possibility of genuine communication and change for both the speaker and listener.

The first draft of Ann's letter started like this:

Dear Mom and Dad,

I wish you would try to see my point of view and not be so conventional. Things are different from when you went to school. And you must realize I am old enough to make my own decisions, even if you disagree. There are a number of good reasons why this is the best decision I could make. First, . . .

Although this letter created a "strong" argument, it was also likely to stop communication and unlikely to persuade. Here is the letter Ann eventually wrote to her parents, which tries to take an open Rogerian approach to the problem.

Dear Mom and Dad,

As I told you the other night on the phone, I want to consider taking a year off from college to work and be on my own for a while. I've been thinking over what you said because this is an important decision and, like you, I want to do what will be best in the long run, not just what seems attractive now. I think some of your objections make a lot of sense. After all the effort you've put into helping me get through college, it would be terrible to just "drop out" or never find a real career that I could be committed to.

I know you're also wondering if I recognize what an opportunity I have and are probably worrying if I'm just going to let it slip through my fingers. Well, in a way I'm worried about that too. Here I am working hard, but I don't really know where I want to go or why. It's time for me to specialize and I can't decide what to do. And it's that opportunity I'm afraid of losing. I feel I need some time off and some experience so I can make a better decision and really take advantage of my last year here.

But there's still the question of whether I would be dropping out. The college actually has a program for people who want to take a year off, and they even encourage you to enter it if you have some idea of what you'd be doing. So, as far as the school is concerned, I'd be in a well-established leave of absence program. But the fact is, people do drop out. They don't always come back. What would a whole year away from school do to me? You're right, I can't really be sure. But I think my reasons are good ones, and I'm working on a plan that would let me earn credit while I work and come back to school with a clearer sense of where I want to go. Can you offer me any more suggestions on ways I could plan ahead?

Love,
ANN

Projects and Exercises

1 Here are some mini-cases, dealing with a college environment, in which you need to create a goal that both you and your reader share. Write an introduction that sets up a shared goal and then discuss why you think it would work.

a. You would like the chairperson of your department to contribute some money to a fund that would allow coffee hours and socials for majors in the department. You know she has a rather tight budget this year. What can you say to her?

b. You would like the faculty members in your department to coordinate their exams and papers better so that students' work will be spread out more evenly over the term. For them, this would be just one more thing to try to plan their syllabus around. They have given you five minutes to talk at the faculty meeting.

c. You have been given the responsibility of getting voluntary compliance to the "no smoking" rule in the redecorated conference classrooms, which are rather small and cozy and are used for group meetings. Find a shared goal.

2 The following paragraph comes from a student paper analyzing a form that was currently being used for student evaluation of the department's courses. See how many characteristics you can find that make this a writer-based discussion. Then reread the paragraph, decide what the main ideas are, and try to transform it into a piece of reader-based prose. Remember you will need a topic sentence that previews the main points for the reader and transitions that show how sentences are related.

> In order to improve the course evaluation form, it was first necessary to know how the current form is viewed by students and faculty, so the following survey of opinion was taken. From the faculty viewpoint, the form seems subjective. Many feel that the goals of their course are not as simple as the form sets them out to be. And the form has the aura of a popularity contest. When students were asked about the purpose of the form, a majority felt it was designed to mollify disgruntled students. Only a few marked the box "improves faculty performance" on the questionnaire. It also appeared that many students fill out the evaluation form just to let off steam. Attitudes about the form's effectiveness were further indicated by the questions students often asked while the survey was being conducted. The most common of these were "Why aren't the results published?" and "How does the administration use these evaluations?"

3 Write a brief narrative that describes your first experience with something new, such as moving into an apartment, going to a new class, joining Weight Watchers, or learning to play squash. Then think of some group of readers who might benefit from your experience. Contemplate what they are like and write a short, reader-based article or essay that adapts your knowledge and experience to their needs.

If You Would Like to Read More

If you want to know more about readers and their responses, see:

Clark, Herbert and Eve Clark. *Psychology and Language: An Introduction to Psycholinguistics*. New York: Harcourt Brace Jovanovich, 1977. ■ This is a readable and wide-ranging survey of the ways language works.

Holtzman, Paul. *The Psychology of the Speakers' Audience*. Glenview, Ill.: Scott, Foresman, 1970. ■ This writer describes communication in terms of the listener's experience.

Linde, Charlotte and William Labov. "Spatial Networks as a Site for the Study of Language and Thought." *Language*, 51 (1975), pp. 924–39. ■ This article contains the original discussion of the apartment tour experiment.

chapter eleven
Editing for Purpose and Style

STEP 7

Review Your Paper and Your Purpose

Check over your paper in a goal-directed way, testing it against your plans and your reader's probable response.

STRATEGY 1: Match your paper against your goals and plans

STRATEGY 2: Simulate a reader's response

STEP 8

Test and Edit Your Writing

Edit your paper to achieve a clear, direct prose style.

STRATEGY 1: Edit for economy

STRATEGY 2: Edit for a forceful style

Writers who depend on inspiration are often reluctant to reread their papers. Their image of the writing process assumes that when ideas finally come, they should not be altered or need improvement. Perfect-draft writers have spent so much time laboring over their sentences that they simply don't want to see them again. But a problem-solving writer treats editing and revising as useful steps in composing because they break the process up and make it much easier to handle. Many of the problems that could block a writer are easily solved when the writer returns to the work as an editor. Even more important, editing is an inexpensive method (in terms of time and effort) for making dramatic improvements in your writing. Like strategies for designing for a reader, editing lets you concentrate on *communicating*.

STEP 7   **Review Your Paper and Your Purpose**

A recent study* comparing a group of experienced and inexperienced writers revealed that the novice writers all viewed revision as nothing more than a time to proofread and "clean up" their prose, whereas the experienced writers regularly used revision as a more literal *re-vision* —a chance to re-see and improve their text. Proofreading and minor wording changes are important, but don't be lured into merely skimming the surface of your writing when you could be conducting a more active, goal-directed review. In fact, many writers review first and proofread later in order to get a fresh response to their text.

STRATEGY 1: Match your paper against your goals and plans

To get an overall view of your paper, try to let it sit for at least part of a day—the longer the better. Otherwise you get bogged down in details. First, review your goals (What did you expect this paper to accomplish?) and review your plans (How were you going to structure it? What tone of voice did you want to project? etc.). Then study the paper with these high-level goals in mind. Test it not only to see if it fits your goals and plans but to see if your plans changed in midstream. Since this often happens, make sure your entire paper

_____

* Nancy Sommers, "Revision Strategies of Student Writers and Experienced Writers," *College Composition and Communication,* 31 (December, 1980).

fits your best and final plan. Try to see your paper as a whole, as a coherent rhetorical entity.

If you don't like the match or the result, it may be time to return to Step 1 and do some more planning.

STRATEGY 2: Simulate a reader's response

Naturally, once you have matched the paper against *your* goals, the next step is to test it against the reader's needs. There are two ways to do this: one is with a live reader, the other is by yourself.

Ask a friend to read your paper and jot down two things: first, a nutshell or capsule statement of what he thinks you are trying to do or say (in his own words, not yours) and second, an outline or diagram of your major points and how they are related. If you are even more daring, have him try this some time after he has read the paper to see what really stands out in his memory.

Then, of course, you compare this reader's version against your own. To keep everything honest, you should jot down your own nutshell and outline *before* you read his. Bear in mind that there is always the chance your reader will misread or forget, but consider this as a signal that you need to increase your cues or redesign some part of your presentation. It also helps to know where your reader felt bored, because that is usually a signal that you have confused him or that your point is unclear.

If you don't have a live reader, you can simulate a reader's response in a number of ways. The simplest is to role-play, as was discussed in Chapter 6. Think yourself into the role of your reader responding to individual sentences in your text: what is she looking for, what does she need to do after reading this, and how would she react to what I just said? If you would like a more elaborate response, simulate a scenario in which you have a dialogue with the reader. Have her ask you questions such as "What do you mean?", "How do you know?", "Such as?", and "Why?" whenever your intuition tells you a real reader might do the same.

Many people find it very helpful to read their own writing out loud. Try it if you have some privacy. Listening to yourself out loud sometimes cuts out that private voice in your mind that fills in all the gaps between ideas and makes everything sound smooth and coherent. Reading out loud also helps you hear how your style sounds and see if your prose "flows" or doesn't.

Finally, if you are fresh out of friends, imagination, or privacy, there is a fourth technique called a highlighter test. You can simulate the comprehension process of a typical busy reader by going over your paper with a highlighter pen in hand and marking off all the titles, headings, and sentences to which convention of position in the paper give special significance. Assume that these are the major elements your reader will see and perhaps remember. Now check to see if these highlighted parts contain the major information you wanted the reader to focus on and retain. Ideally the highlighted items will identify the goals of your paper and the top-level elements of your issue tree. If they don't, what have you given the reader instead?

STEP 8   Test and Edit Your Writing

No matter how well they speak on their feet, few people can write their most vigorous, direct, or logical prose on a first draft. In fact, if you are working in an organization or attending an institution such as college, it may even seem natural to write in the padded style of organizational prose. If you are working with technical material, it may come naturally to write with a great deal of jargon or technical language. Or, if you are trying to juggle a number of facts and ideas, it may be easiest to write out a paragraph that looks more like a list than a well-balanced tree. When writing this way comes most naturally to you but you know it won't work for your reader, the most efficient procedure is to *write* it—however it comes—and then *edit*.

Some writers will ask, "Why not make each sentence and paragraph perfect the first time so you won't have to look at them again?" The answer is that if you separate the two operations of generating and editing, it is easier for you and you can get better results. The ultimate goal is always polished, reader-based prose. What changes are the immediate subgoals on which you choose to concentrate. Certain things, including organization and style, are sometimes better handled by an editor than an idea generator. *Editing can come at any point in the composing process*—after you have written a phrase, a sentence, a paragraph, or an entire draft. Sometimes editing is simply a final stage for fixing up details. But it is always a powerful strategy for writing.

The method is essentially the same one used in generating ideas and designing them for a reader. A writer-based prose style or unedited draft may be a reasonable and natural way to say what you have to say at that particular moment. Once your thoughts are out of short-term memory and down on paper, you can come back as an editor with a much clearer sense of where you are going and what you want those words to do.

The editing techniques you will learn in this chapter are not concerned with frills, or with adding commas and dotting "i's." For an experienced writer, editing is a major tool for making meaning. A writer may in fact spend more time editing and restructuring a first draft than he or she did generating it. Once you know a few basic editing techniques, you will be able to transform sentences, paragraphs, and even entire discussions into far more effective statements of your meaning.

Knowing how to edit a first draft doesn't guarantee that you will produce elegant writing. But it does mean that you will be able to cope with three major problems professional writers have, and that you will be better able to write:

- Economical prose that says exactly what you mean,
- Forceful prose that holds your reader's attention,
- Logical prose that expresses the hierarchical structure of your ideas.

STRATEGY 1: Edit for economy

The goal of this editing strategy is to help you write clear, direct statements that come quickly to the point and say exactly what you mean. Probably the most frequent complaint made about college and professional writing is that it is stuffy and inflated or overly technical and full of jargon. And yet, it is often written by dynamic people who can think clearly and speak forcefully when they are face to face. These people often use inflated or "institutional" language because they hope it will sound more impressive.

The problem with institutional language is that it handicaps the writer who really has something to say, burying his or her point beneath a load of excess language. Think of all the college catalogues, final reports, or political statements you never finished reading. As readers of such institutional prose, we all know how readers respond to an inflated style. It makes us mentally rewrite sentences to find the point and we soon begin to skip, skim, and read with diminishing attention. If you really have something to say and want to keep a reader alert and reading, you need to write economical prose that comes to the point.

Institutional prose and the abstraction ladder

A direct prose style is much like the style people use when they speak. One of the chief differences between an institutional style and a personal speaking style is the level of abstraction. In fact, one decision you make every time you speak or write is how abstract or concrete you want to be.

Say someone asks you, "What do you expect to be doing tomorrow afternoon?" There are a number of ways you could convey your situation, ranging from abstract at the top to concrete at the bottom:

Abstraction Ladder

Expect to still be living and breathing, if all goes well.

Will be busy.

Will be busy part of the afternoon.

Have a previous appointment at 4:30.

Have my Friday afternoon tennis match at 4:30 with Joyce at the Stanton Avenue courts.

The level of abstraction you choose in replying will depend on who asked you and why. For example, on the phone you might choose to tell Ms. Howard, the chairperson of a committee to which you belong, that you "will be unable to make the meeting because of a previous appointment at 4:30." However, ten minutes later when talking to a friend, you might translate that highly abstract "previous appointment" into: "Oh, I have my usual tennis match with Joyce at the Stanton courts." One difference between the two statements is their level of abstraction.

When you write you likewise have a range of options, going from general, abstract terminology at the top to specific, concrete information at the bottom. In choosing your abstraction level, each choice carries an advantage and a price. By going to the top of the ladder and using nice, fuzzy abstractions you gain the advantage of breadth — and if you are high enough it's hard to be wrong. Weather forecasters do this when they say, "Unfavorable weather patterns may materialize in the near future." However, the problem with abstractions is that they are likely to be misinterpreted or just plain ignored. If you say "It's going to rain like hell between now and 3 A.M.," you've put yourself on the line, but you can be sure your listeners will pay attention. In writing, you'll usually get much better results with concrete language.

Likewise, a vivid, direct prose style works because it cuts out unnecessary padding and puts powerful words in powerful places.

This lets the main words and major ideas stand out prominently and, because the prose is direct and to the point, encourages the reader to listen.

Key-word editing

One method that can help you achieve such a style is key-word editing. The method has five steps:

1. Divide the sentence into meaningful units.
2. Identify the key words or phrases in each unit.
3. Cut out unnecessary words, and build your statement around the key terms.
4. Pack in more concrete words when possible.
5. Let the actors act.

Consider this verbose sentence from a student paper:

> The condition of excessive redundancy that exists in such a great degree in the academic paper assignments produced by members of the student body should be eliminated by grading policy and the example-setting capabilities that lie at the disposal of those who instruct such students.

The editor's first step is to divide the sentence into its natural, meaningful units. The next step is to pick out the key words and phrases in each unit —in other words, look for words that seem to be carrying the weight of the sentence's meaning. Thus:

> The condition of excessive *redundancy* / that exists in such a great degree in the academic *paper* assignments / produced by members of the *student* body / should be eliminated by *grading* policy and the *example*-setting capabilities / that lie at the disposal of those who *instruct* such students.

The third step is to cut out as much of the nonfunctional padding as possible and try to write a sentence around the key words.

> Redundancy in student papers should be eliminated by grades and the example set by the instructor.

The fourth step is to try to pack the sentence with concrete information where possible, replacing abstractions with more specific words. For example, since "redundancy" could mean wordiness or repetition or both, the writer needed to ask himself: "What exactly am I trying to say?" He decided he meant:

> *Wordiness and repetition* in student papers should be eliminated by grades and the example set by the instructor.

The final step is to let the actor act. Usually the person or thing that carries out the action of the sentence should also be the grammatical subject.

> *Instructors* should use grades and their own example to eliminate wordiness and repetition in student papers.

Here is another example. Try the key-word editing technique on this sentence, then compare your result to the revision that follows.

> In the event of your participation in a charter flight, the thing which should be noticed is the fact that there is a possibility of a change in fare necessitated by a last-minute change in fuel prices.

Writer's Stages of Revision

Steps 1 and 2: Divide into meaningful units; identify key words

In the event of your *participation* in a *charter flight* / the thing that should be *noticed* is the fact that / there is a *possibility* of a *change in fare* / necessitated by a *last-minute change in fuel prices*.

Step 3: Cut out unnecessary words; build around key terms

In participation in a charter flight, the possibility of a change in fare necessitated by a last-minute change in fuel prices should be noted.

Steps 4 and 5: Pack in more concrete words; let the actor act

When you sign up for a charter flight, remember that a last-minute change in fuel prices can increase your fare.

Note that in the final revision the writer realized that the real actor was "you," the passenger, and translated the vague "change in fare" into the concrete "increase your fare."

The primary goal of key-word editing is to *put powerful words in powerful places*. As you could see in the first-draft sentences, the words that carried the writers' meaning were buried in verbiage. The subject and verb are the two most powerful parts of a sentence, and as readers we rely on those parts to contain the writer's essential information. The object position is also a strong one. In the first draft of the airline paragraph, the words in the powerful subject, verb, and object positions only told us: "the *thing is* the *fact*."

Key-word editing, therefore, helps you say what you want to say by putting powerful words in these grammatically powerful places.

Naturally you won't always want to use such a spare, economical style, but it is important to know how to write direct, concise sentences when you need them. When you try to write economical prose think of yourself as giving a brief, well-prepared oral presentation. Imagine yourself in your reader's office: you have 3 minutes to tell him or her the gist of what you have to say. Concentrate on the essential points you want that person to remember. Think about the structure and emphasis of what you have to say, rather than making your phrases flow. You may well find that your key words are emerging, your excess words are dropping away, and you have become more direct and concrete.

STRATEGY 2: Edit for a forceful style

If you still feel your writing sounds heavy-handed, indirect, or verbose, other trouble-shooting techniques may help. Try some of these editing approaches:

1. Lower the noun/verb ratio

Test the following sentence for vigor by counting the ratio of nouns to verbs: Nouns/Verbs = ____ / ____ . Then rewrite the sentence using more verbs and fewer nouns.

> The effect of the overuse of nouns in writing is the placing of excessive strain upon the inadequate number of verbs and the resultant prevention of the flow of thought.

Note that the original sentence contained one verb and eleven nouns, few of which were serving any useful purpose. Here is a revised version with a ratio of two verbs to seven nouns:

> Using too many nouns in writing places strain on verbs and prevents the flow of thought.

Note that in some sentences you simply have to use many nouns —for example, you have a compound subject involving four or more essential nouns. But if you improve the ratio of verbs to nouns as much as possible, your prose will be more forceful.

2. Transform heavy nouns back into verbs

Many of the heavy, polysyllabic nouns that make prose hard to read were made in the first place by adding a Latin ending to a verb.

Often, your sentences will improve if you transform these nouns back into their original form. The five Latin endings below are the most common ones to watch for.

Remove this Latinate *ending*	from a *noun*	to produce a *verb*
-tion	resumption	resume
-ment	announcement	announce
-ing	dealing	deal
-ion	decision	decide
-ance	performance	perform

3. Avoid weak linking verbs

The verb "to be" can be used as a linking verb ("The water is hot") or as an auxiliary or helping verb ("The water is boiling furiously"). The verb can take these forms:

be	is	was	been
am	are	were	being

When used as linking (or state-of-being) verbs, these words are simply saying that "something = something else." They can't act. If you want to state a definition, linking verbs are often very powerful ("To be or not to be, that is the question"). If, however, you are discussing an action, whether it is physical, mental, or metaphoric, linking verbs can weaken your sentence.

For example, you might write: "Galileo's telescope was helpful in the explosion of the myth of an earth-centered universe." But by using a form of "to be" you waste some of the potential of the powerful verb slot in your sentence. To make the sentence more forceful, transform the words "helpful" and "explosion" into verbs: "Galileo's telescope helped explode the myth of an earth-centered universe." Look for ways to change linking verbs into action verbs.

4. Transform negative expressions

Sentences containing several negative expressions ("No, I didn't know that the book was not on the shelf") are more difficult to comprehend than positive expressions ("I thought the book was on the shelf"). Negatives require increased mental processing time, and they decrease the chance that a person will correctly remember what he or she has read. Studies have even shown that implicit negatives such as "forgot" (didn't remember), "absent" (not present), and "hardly," "scarcely," and "few" have a similar effect.

Obviously, negative expressions are necessary at times. But remember that they can dilute the forcefulness of your statements and make your writing difficult to read. Test the following paragraph. Is the meaning clear on a first reading? How many negatives does the passage contain? Revise the paragraph and see how many negatives it is really necessary to use.

> To avoid assuming the rapid decrease in temperature implied by the weather charts described above, other factors, used to make a prediction from past data, were not ignored. We feel the method can scarcely fail to predict the direction of temperature change for the not-so-distant future.

According to the writer, who hoped that all these extra qualifications would make her prose sound more scientific, what she really meant was:

> In order to make a prediction from our past data and not simply assume a rapid decrease in temperature that the weather charts imply, we used a variety of factors in the calculation. We feel this method will effectively predict the direction of temperature change for the near future.

5. Transform passive constructions into active ones

Passive expressions, like negative ones, are harder to understand and harder to remember. The difference between an active and a passive construction is a simple one. In an active construction, the subject *acts:*

S   V
Moe made a decision.

In a passive construction, the subject is *acted upon:*

S   ⌐—V—⌐
A decision was made by Moe.

While this example was a simple one, complex passive constructions create problems. Often readers must mentally transform such constructions into active ones as they are reading in order to comprehend them. If you use a number of passives, your reader may not be willing to put in that extra effort; furthermore, you are forcing him to waste energy on processing your prose when he should be concentrating on what you have to say. Passive constructions may also twist your meaning, because they push the actor, which should be the subject of the sentence, into a less significant grammatical position.

To transform a passive construction into an active one, try these techniques:

1. Find the hidden actor in the sentence and let him (or it) act.
2. Convert an important noun in the sentence into a verb.

Usually, going from passive to active means switching from an impersonal to a personal style.

Passive:
Negotiation of a contract with the Downtown Jazz Club was conducted by our agent after an initial booking was used to establish contact. Performances are planned to start in two weeks.

Active:
Our agent negotiated a contract with the Downtown Jazz Club after establishing contact through an initial booking. We plan to begin performing in two weeks.

There are, of course, many times when a Latinate noun, a passive verb, or a negative expression is exactly what you want to say. For example, passives let you put emphasis on the result of an action when the actor is not important, as in: "My telephone has finally been repaired." The important thing is to know how to make your prose direct and vigorous when you need to, and to recognize the effect your choice will have on a reader. A thank-you note that says, "The assistance received from the members of your department was appreciated," doesn't convey the warmth and sincerity of a more direct statement such as, "I sincerely appreciated the help everyone in your department gave me."

If you believe in an idea and want to stand up for it —but still be serious and formal —you can do it in active, direct language. Which of these conclusions to a planning report would you be more likely to act on?

The conclusions drawn from the Co-op Board's study indicate that it seems advisable under present circumstances to initiate the adoption of the new work-sharing plan. If a presentation of all the facts of the plan is duly made to the co-op members, our opinion is that their approval will be forthcoming.

or

As a result of our study, we believe the Co-op Board should adopt the work-sharing plan. Once the members fully understand the plan, we think they will favor it.

Projects and Exercises

1 Revise these sentences using the key-word editing technique.

   a. The thing that tended to bring about the manager's decision to stop hiring was the crisis caused by the sudden departure with company funds of the accountant.

   b. The key factor in the inflation of the cost of health care in the United States at this time would appear to be the unnecessary duplication of medical services.

   c. There has been an increase in the number of publications of pornography that sell at newsstands from zero in 1953 to a number well over thirty in the last five years.

   d. Although a great many of our citizens do not have any wish to see pornography that is of a soft-core nature in our public drugstores, the dictates of the "high percentage" rule allow the storeowner to be paid extra sums of money by the distributor to enable the display of magazines of this nature.

2 For each passage below, figure the noun/verb ratio, note the heavy nouns and negative expressions, and locate any linking or passive verbs. Then rewrite each paragraph to make it as forceful as you can. Score your results and compare them to the original paragraph.

   a. Wanda Stevens, secretary, called public attention Friday to the organization of a demonstration to be held by the Walton Community Council. The demonstration is planned as a protest against the slowness of the city's clearance effort in a vacant lot in the Walton area. Usage of the lot as a playground by local children is not unusual, although it is filled with trash and garbage, and rats and other vermin are often reported there. A clean-up of the vacant lot is expected to be triggered by the demonstration.

   b. An announcement was made by Rhoda Brown, secretary, of the resumption of operations by the Consumer's Lobby. The decision of the lobby to increase concentration on local issues was noted in the announcement. Enrollment of members is expected to be encouraged through the elimination of previous office locations at some distance from local neighborhoods. In dealing with future legislation, legal recognition of neighborhood rights will be the intention of the lobby, Ms. Brown asserted.

If You Would Like to Read More

If you would like to know more about editing for style and editing with a reader in mind, see:

Farb, Peter. *Word Play: What Happens When People Talk.* New York: Knopf, 1974. ■ This book provides a fascinating discussion of how people use language.

Gibson, Walker. *Tough, Sweet and Stuffy: An Essay on Modern Prose Styles.* Bloomington, Indiana: Indiana University Press, 1966. ■ This book shows the connection between a person's writing style and personal style: whether he or she appears tough, sweet, or stuffy.

chapter twelve
Editing for a Clear Organization

STEP 9

Edit for Connections and Coherence

Edit your paper to ensure that the relationships between ideas are clear and that the logic of your structure is evident to the reader.

STRATEGY 1: Transform listlike sentences

STRATEGY 2: Reveal the inner logic of your paragraphs

Everyone wants his or her writing to be well organized, to have a clear, logical structure. But what makes a structure clear to a reader, and how can you tell if yours will indeed be clear? In this section we will focus on one of the most important things you can do to organize and structure your writing: make connections between ideas explicit in the text.

STEP **Edit for Connections and Coherence**

One goal of a writer is to present his or her message so clearly that readers can build in their minds the same (or nearly the same) structure of ideas that the writer had in his or hers. However, writers often have important relationships in mind that they simply don't express in their words. Take, for example, this passage on how to take care of old pocket watches:

---

    (1)   (2)
Old pocket watches are delicate instruments. It's fun to look at the
                   (3)
mechanism working, but don't open the case very often.

For the writer the connection between the ideas I've numbered (1), (2), and (3) is absolutely clear. Is it to you? Could you explain it?

In the writer's mind there were meaningful connections between all of these ideas, but in her message there is only one important hook, the word "but." Here is how she revised it to clarify:

---

    (1)   (2)
Old pocket watches are delicate instruments. *Although* it's fun to *unscrew the back*
                   (3)
and watch the mechanism working, don't open the case

very often *because even fine dirt can damage or stop the moving parts.*

Notice how the revisions work. In the first draft there was indeed a connection between idea 2, "it's fun to look at the mechanism working," and idea 3, "don't open the case." However, the focus of the sentence was on the idea of "fun," whereas the passage was intended to be about watch care. By adding the word "although," the writer indicated that idea 2, having fun, was subordinate to her main point, the warning about not opening the case. Then by adding the "because . . ." clause at the end, she spelled out why that connection or recommendation was reasonable, since opening the case can damage the watch. Here she had to add information that was missing from the first draft.

Finally, the writer added the phrase "unscrew the back" when she realized that some readers might not make the connection between having a pocket watch and watching the mechanism unless they knew the back could be opened. So the revision made that information, which previously could only be inferred, explicit in the text.

Editing for clarity means making the hidden relationships in your own thinking clear in your prose. Major points should stand out as important or inclusive; subordinate ideas should be put in their place. When you don't make these relationships clear, you leave part of the work of writing up to your reader. He may find your material hard to follow and end up feeling confused (or, more likely, assume that it is you who are confused). Perhaps even worse, he may fail to see your point and build a very different structure from the one you had in mind. In either case you are asking the *reader* to draw inferences and make the right connections between your ideas. As can be seen from the pocket-watch revision, clear writing not only is more informative but is more persuasive because it often tells the reader the "hows" and "whys" behind your assertions.

Let us look now at techniques for testing your prose and making relationships explicit in both sentences and paragraphs.

STRATEGY 1: Transform listlike sentences

In editing sentences for clarity, look for two things. Does the sentence itself emphasize its main point? (Are powerful words in powerful places?) And are the underlying connections between sentences made explicit in the text?

One common irritant to readers is a sentence that reads like a list. For example: "The thing about a sentence with a listlike form is that there are a number of tiny points with independent bits of meaning that are set out in the sentence in a line so that the series of words and phrases read like so many pieces of popcorn strung out on a string." (Compare this to: "A listlike sentence, with its many independent points, lines up words and phrases like popcorn on a string.") Although easy to write, listlike sentences tend to be wordy and boring to read. Furthermore, like a list, they reduce all details to the same level of importance and make it hard for the writer to highlight what is significant.

Testing for a listlike style

To test your draft for a listlike style, look for an abundance of connective words (*that, which, and, plus,* etc.) and prepositions (*in, of, from, for, by, over, with,* etc.). Consider this sentence:

> The demand (on the part) (of students) (for a greater number of films), (in addition) (to increases) (in film, rental fees) (of most) (of the companies), has led us to request an increase (in the Film Society's allocation) (from the Funding Committee).

This sentence is weakened by two things. First, the grammatical subject of the sentence, "demand," is not the real actor (see Chapter 11). Second, the strings of prepositional phrases bog down the sentence. When you write a phrase such as "on the part," you create an independent little unit of meaning. A string of such independent units makes a weak sentence because it doesn't distinguish between major ideas and mere subordinate details, nor does it show their connections. A complex logical relationship is blurred into a simple list.

To transform listlike sentences, do three things:

1. Mark the prepositions (as was done in the preceding example), then promote key words to grammatically powerful places.

   > We request that the Funding Committee increase . . .

2. Put subordinate information into a subordinate clause.

   > Because students want more films . . .

3. Transform less important nouns into modifying words, and eliminate unnecessary prepositional phrases.

   > . . . in addition to *increases* in *film rental fees* of *most* of the *companies*

becomes

   > . . . and most companies' film rental fees have increased

Revised sentence:

> Because students want more films and most companies' film rental fees have increased, we request that the Funding Committee increase the Film Society's allocation.

Here is another way to combine elements of a sentence. Many sentences contain more than one "simple sentence," that is, more than one subject-and-verb unit. When you review your writing, ask yourself two questions: (1) Have I made the connections between my simple sentences or ideas explicit? (2) If not, how else can I combine them?

In English there are three major ways people combine simple sentences or ideas: by making them parallel or coordinate to one another, by making one subordinate to another, or by adding one to another as a modifier. Each way of combining simple sentences asserts a specific logical relationship between ideas. Furthermore, our language offers a number of devices (grammar, punctuation, and signal words) for indicating this relationship and making it more explicit. Here are some familiar patterns for combining simple sentences.

COORDINATE PATTERN

This pattern sets up two equal simple sentences in parallel or in contrast with one another. Like all sentence patterns, it has signals that tell you to look for a coordinate structure.

EXAMPLE: Mac is our accounts manager, *but* he works out of London.

SOME SIGNALS: *and, but, or, :, ;*

SUBORDINATE PATTERN

This pattern lets you show a subordinate relationship between two ideas by making one grammatically subordinate to the other.

EXAMPLE: *Although* he works out of London, Mac keeps a flat in Paris.

Since Mac does keep the books, he will know the answer — *if*, of course, anyone can find him.

SOME SIGNALS: *if, although, because, since, when, where, after*

MODIFYING PATTERN

This pattern lets you pack additional information into a sentence by turning one simple sentence into a modifying phrase or clause.

EXAMPLES: Mac, *who never did pass math methods*, manages our accounts.

(Simple sentence: Mac never did pass math methods.)

Managing our accounts from London, Mac drinks dark ale at the Stewed Horse.

(Simple sentence: Mac manages our accounts from London.)

Our accounts, *ineptly managed by Mac in London*, are going to pot.

(Simple sentence: Mac manages our London accounts ineptly.)

Relative pronouns (*who, which*)

Verb phrases that tie the expression to the main part of the sentence (in this example, *managing, managed by*)

Placement of subordinate or modifying material

As we have seen, an independent simple sentence can be reduced to a clause or phrase and inserted somewhere in another sentence. The next question is, how do you decide where to place it? For example, say you have the sentence "Doggy Odor-Eater powder is now on the market," and you want to add the idea, "It was developed in the last ten years." You have three major alternatives:

Left-branching sentence   *Developed in the last ten years,* Doggy Odor-Eater powder is now on the market.

Mid-branching sentence   Doggy Odor-Eater powder —*developed in the last ten years* —is now on the market.

Right-branching sentence   Doggy Odor-Eater powder is now on the market, *after being developed for ten years*.

Here are comments on the different types of placement.

LEFT-BRANCHING SENTENCE

This pattern places the modifying clause at the beginning. Setting up a reader's anticipation with background or qualifying information placed first, left-branching sentences rely on the strong clarifying effect the subject has when it comes. But the longer the reader has to wait without knowing your subject, the more he is likely to become confused. Reread the second sentence in this paragraph, which was a left-branching one. Did you become impatient waiting for the subject, "left-branching sentences"?

MID-BRANCHING SENTENCE

This pattern —inserting modifying material between the subject and the verb —tends to create suspense, even to the point of taxing the reader with perverse demands on his attention. (The sentence you just read was a mid-branching one.) If the interruption is too long, the reader is forced to hold major ideas in suspension until the sentence is completed. Used more discreetly, the mid-branching sentence begins with a grammatically powerful element, shepherds modification into the middle —often isolating it with dashes —then makes the mind accelerate toward a tie-up idea and closure. For example: "Clearly, multinational corporations —the giant conglomerates that have covered the globe and permeated many foreign economies —are often the source of a country's economic stability."

This type of sentence is developed by adding material: creating a structure that follows a natural pattern of the human mind just as this sentence does, with a series of qualifying phrases added one after another. Right-branching sentences are easy to write and easy to read—to a point. Their weakness is that the writer may tend to ramble on and create listlike sentences without sufficient force or emphasis.

The simple sentence test

In editing for connections, watch out for paragraphs made up of a list of simple sentences. Here is an easy diagnostic test you can use to see if your paragraph reads like a list of ideas and if you need to add more cues to help the reader see connections between your phrases and sentences. Consider the paragraph below:

> Rescue dogs are often specially trained. They work in areas where a bomb or earthquake has buried people in debris. Their job is to locate where the persons are buried. Rescuers can dig them out before they suffocate or die from other injuries. The dog must guide rescuers to the spot and be willing to sit and bark until help comes. Some dogs can be easily trained for rescue. Collies, shepherds, Airedales—in fact, most working breeds—will happily bark. Spaniels, setters, pointers, and some hounds refuse to bark once they have found their person. They will bark at home if someone comes to the door, but not while they are working. These breeds have been selectively bred not to bark while working and not to scare the game.

To test his first draft of the paragraph, we can look for three things:

1. How many sentences *begin* with the main subject and verb (such as "dogs are," "they work") rather than with a signal word or a subordinate or modifying clause? If all of your sentences start right out with the main subject and verb, your paragraph probably will read like a list of unrelated assertions. In Figure 12-1 the main subjects and verbs are shown in boldface; 10 out of 10 sentences have the initial pattern of main subject plus main verb. This helps explain why each sentence reads like one more item on a grocery list.

2. Next, count up all the additional simple sentences that are embedded within each sentence and that function as modifying or subordinate material. In Figure 12-1, all of the subordinate subject and verb combinations (or embedded simple sentences) are underscored. Add this number to the number of combinations you found in Step 1.

Now compare this total to the total number of sentences. How many simple sentences (including embedded simple sentences) did

189

FIGURE 12-1

FIGURE **12-1**   *An application of the simple sentence test*

1 main S/V	Rescue **dogs are** often specially **trained.**
1 main S/V, 1 subordinate S/V	**They work** in areas (where) a bomb or earthquake has buried people in debris.
1 main S/V, 1 subordinate S/V	Their **job is** to locate (where) the persons are buried.
1 main S/V, 1 subordinate S/V	**Rescuers can dig** them out (before) they suffocate or die from other injuries.
1 main S/V, 1 subordinate S/V	The **dog must guide** rescuers to the spot and **be** willing to sit and bark (until) help comes.
1 main S/V	Some **dogs can be** easily **trained** for rescue.
1 main S/V	**Collies, shepherds, Airedales**—in fact, most working breeds—**will** happily **bark.**
1 main S/V, 1 subordinate S/V	**Spaniels, setters, pointers,** and some **hounds refuse** to bark (once) they have found their person.
1 main S/V, 2 subordinate S/V's	**They will bark** at home (if) someone comes to the door, (but) not (while) they are working.
1 main S/V	These **breeds have been** selectively **bred** not to bark (while) working and not to scare the game.

you average per sentence? The example has a ratio of 17:10 —almost two simple sentences per sentence. This is not bad, but could be improved given the closely related ideas in the paragraph. As discussed before, combining simple sentences into more complex sentences is an effective way to make more explicit connections.

    3. Finally, count the number of signal words (they are circled in Figure 12-1) that tell the reader you are using a coordinate, subor-

chapter twelve / Editing for a Clear Organization

dinate, or modifying pattern. The example has 9 word or phrase signals and no punctuation signals.

Here is a revision in which the writer tried to vary the simple sentence beginnings, combine more ideas per sentence, and increase the number of signals to the reader. In the revised paragraph, only 3 of the 6 sentences have simple, main-subject-plus-verb beginnings. The ratio of simple sentences (including embedded sentences) to total sentences is now 17 to 6, or nearly three simple sentences per sentence. And the passage now contains 14 signals to the reader.

> Rescue **dogs are** often specially **trained** to work in areas where a bomb or earthquake has buried people in debris. Their **job is** to locate where the persons are buried so that rescuers can dig them out before they suffocate or die of other injuries. Since the dog must guide rescuers to the spot, **he must be** willing to sit and bark until help comes. As a result some **dogs,** including collies, shepherds, Airedales, and, in fact, most working breeds, **can be trained** for rescue; **others can't. Spaniels, setters,** and some **hounds,** for example, **refuse** to bark once they have found their person. Although they would bark at home if someone came to the door, these hunting **breeds have been** selectively **bred** not to bark while working because it would scare the game.

Remember that there are no set rules for how many sentences you should embed; simple sentences can be very effective. Nor will you always want to go to the trouble of counting up subjects and verbs. But this simple diagnostic test can help you focus attention on three common writing problems. It encourages you to make as many connections and give as many signals as seem reasonable in view of what you have to say. The final self-test in editing is always: does my style fit my purpose and reflect my underlying meaning?

STRATEGY 2: Reveal the inner logic of your paragraphs

A paragraph is a working unit or functional part of a paper designed to accomplish something for you and the reader. Before editing a paragraph, you need to know two things: what is the point you want this paragraph to make, and how are your ideas actually connected? Then, when actually editing the material, you apply the test: "Have

I indeed been able to make my point and connections clear in the text?"

Many people, however, rely on a weak editing test. They simply read the prose to see if it seems to "flow" or "sounds right." But what does that really mean, and how can a writer test effectively for these qualities?

Because "flow" is such a subjective concept, it is hard to test your own writing for flow as a reader would. What seems clear to you may not seem clear to a reader. The problem is that in re-reading your own prose, it is easy to unconsciously supply the missing verbal and logical connections and happily conclude that the paragraph is indeed clearly organized. Flow, it seems, is a quality that rests in the eye of the beholder. Your organization may be logical to you as writer, but it is only clear if the reader sees the connections that lead from one idea to the next. As editors, then, we need a more practical, operational definition of "flow" in order to test our writing from a reader's perspective, not our own.

Basic patterns readers expect

One of the simplest ways to test your paragraph organization is to see if it matches one of the basic patterns readers expect, such as topic sentence-restriction-illustration, problem-solution, cause-effect, or chronological order. Patterns such as these have a special claim to fame because they are general patterns readers have learned to expect in expository writing. They are not necessarily the best patterns for every purpose, or ones you *should* use, but they are patterns your readers will expect and therefore can easily follow.

THE TRI PATTERN

Probably the most familiar way of developing a paragraph is to present the topic in the first sentence, refine or restrict it in some way in the next sentence, and use the rest of the paragraph to develop or illustrate the point. A shorthand name for this pattern is the TRI pattern (topic-restriction-illustration). If the paragraph is long or complicated, writers will often return to the topic at the end with a concluding statement that sums up the discussion. The pattern becomes a TRIT.

The paragraph above that began with "Because 'flow' is such . . ." is a good example of a TRIT pattern. The first sentence sets up the topic, "flow is hard to test," and the next sentence refines or restricts the meaning of "flow" as clarity. The rest of the paragraph illustrates why the assertion in the topic sentence is true. Finally, the last sentence makes some restatement of the topic, while also reaching a new conclusion based on points made in the paragraph.

This pattern requires a topic sentence at the beginning. However, for dramatic effect, writers occasionally want to save their point and lead up to it at the end of a paragraph. Sometimes this can be done with great impact, especially in literary or dramatic writing where readers expect to be pleasurably surprised. However, whenever your paragraph begins without a topic sentence or a preview of your point, ask yourself these two questions. First, will my discussion be so interesting or dramatic that I can risk keeping the reader in the dark — violating the reader's topic sentence expectation —and still have him with me when I do make my point? Secondly, will the paragraph be so clearly developed that the reader will be building the same idea tree I am, even though I haven't given him the top-level idea at the beginning? Topic sentences are only a convention, it is true, but they are powerful ones with sound, practical reasons for their existence.

THE PROBLEM-SOLUTION PATTERN

A second familiar paragraph pattern has only two parts, a problem and a solution. Paragraphs that start with rhetorical questions such as, "How did earlier societies build such monuments as the pyramids?" often take the problem-solution pattern.

THE CAUSE AND EFFECT PATTERN

This pattern is equally familiar. When a paragraph starts out "If the university chose to raise tuition by 10 percent . . . ," the reader automatically expects a discussion of the possible effects.

CHRONOLOGICAL ORDER

If a paragraph starts out, "The first step in training a horse is . . . ," the reader is immediately primed for a chronological organization. He may expect a series of detailed steps for what to do first, second, and third, or he may anticipate a more general organization based on importance (for example, the first thing is to gain the horse's confidence, then worry about breaking it to lead).

The advantage of using one of these patterns is very simple: readers know and expect them. By building on your reader's expectations, you increase comprehension and make your prose easier to follow. By the same token, when you use another pattern because it would better fit your purpose, you should increase the cues that tell the reader how ideas are related. Phrases such as "for example," "on the other hand," and "a final point" let the reader see your plan.

The underlying logical structure

This second test is both more rigorous and more helpful since it lets you see if the paragraph is logically developed around its main point.

The test itself is merely an extension of the issue tree that can be used to organize ideas. In a hierarchically organized paragraph, there will be one top-level idea, which we can label level 1. (Generally speaking, this will be the first or topic sentence of the paragraph.) In the rest of the paragraph every sentence should be *related to* this level 1 sentence. It should also be either *parallel or subordinate to* the sentence above it.

There are two ways you could test your paragraph. One is to pull a key word or phrase out of each sentence and sketch an issue tree. The second, which we will discuss here, is the Francis Christensen method indenting each part of a sentence or paragraph to show its relationship to the elements around it. This can be demonstrated with the following paragraph on creativity. Notice how the level 2 sentences expand or develop the ideas in level 1, the level 3 sentences develop level 2, and so on.

1 The stage of preparation must be taken seriously if one expects to be creative.

  2 Having relevant knowledge does not guarantee creativity, but it is certainly one very important condition.

    3 Van Gogh, while a revolutionary artist, had extensive knowledge and appreciation of traditional artists.

      4 Further, he spent years practicing technical skills, especially drawing which he regarded as fundamental.

  2 Acquiring the knowledge needed for creativity may require a great deal of work.

    3 Indeed, the only trait Anne Roe found that was common to the leading artists and scientists she studied was the willingness to work extremely hard.

1 and 4 Those who plan to relax until their creative inspiration seizes them are likely to have a long, uninterrupted rest.*

Note that each idea in this paragraph is clearly and logically related to the ideas that went before it: it is either parallel or subordinate to the ideas above. For the reader this paragraph would "flow" because there are no gaps in the logic and no unrelated ideas to sidetrack the discussion.

A second thing to notice is that this paragraph follows the TRIT (topic-restriction-illustration-topic) pattern. And yet the final sentence is really serving two functions. From one perspective it is a level 4 idea that seems to develop the idea above it, that leading artists and scientists work hard. At the same time the final sentence

---

* John R. Hayes, *Cognitive Psychology: Thinking and Creating* (Homewood, Ill.: Dorsey Press, 1978).

offers us a more detailed statement of the topic introduced on level 1. It serves to recapitulate the main idea and tie the entire paragraph together.

Checking the structure of a paragraph can often help you detect any sentences that break the logical flow or depart from the paragraph's central focus. Such breaks in logic or focus are often very hard to identify by just reading, because the "unconnected" idea may be clearly connected to something in your own mind even if it does not fit into what you wrote on paper.

The paragraph below has just such a problem. The writer had let the topic and its train of associated ideas dictate what she said in the paragraph. Notice how the two italicized sentences are indeed *related* to the topic she is thinking about but are not clearly connected to the main *focus* of this paragraph, which is to describe, from the tenant's point of view, the possible results of protesting a rent hike. In the act of composing, the writer had simply been sidetracked from the point of the paragraph by her own knowledge.

> The primary objective of a rent hike protest is to have the increase reduced or, ideally, eliminated. In practice there is little chance of either of these occurring. Realtors tend to be unresponsive to complaints of
>
> (a) tenants about rent increases. *Some of the most frequent and unannounced rent hikes are found in the tight rental situations around urban universities.* But a protest can have positive results for tenants if it serves to limit future increases or influences the landlord to improve the building's upkeep. Ironically these benefits accrue only to those who remain in their apartments. For tenants who find the rent hike truly prohibitive, the only hope is to inform the realtor that they are moving out solely
>
> (b) because of rent. *Sometimes entire groups of tenants get angry enough to leave in protest.*

Clearly this is a time for the writer to turn editor and evaluate this paragraph as a functional unit. Is each sentence here pulling its weight and contributing to the purpose the writer had in mind? One of the quickest ways to test the fit of each idea is to sketch a small issue tree of the paragraph, using the key words from each sentence. As you will see in Figure 12-2, the top idea of this tree is not an exact phrase found in the first sentence but a key word "results," that captures the point of the paragraph.

One of the first things this tree tells us is that sentence (a) concerning rent hikes around universities does not develop the key idea above it (realtors are unresponsive) or the top-level idea (results of a protest). It is really connected only to the term "rent hikes." At the time of writing, the sentence had probably seemed to follow, since it does relate to the last words in the preceding sentence. But to the eye of an editor it is clearly irrelevant to the larger purpose of the paragraph and should be deleted.

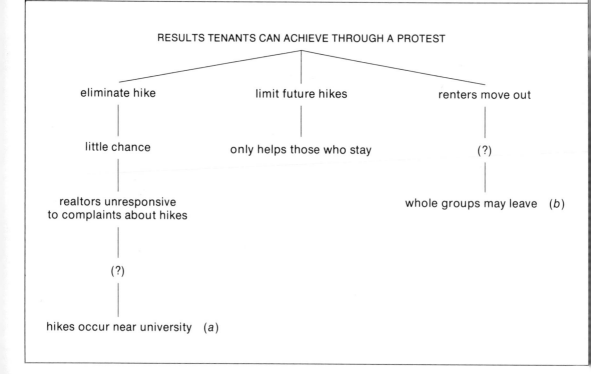

FIGURE **12-2** *Testing the logical structure of a paragraph*

RESULTS TENANTS CAN ACHIEVE THROUGH A PROTEST

eliminate hike   limit future hikes   renters move out

little chance   only helps those who stay   (?)

realtors unresponsive   whole groups may leave (b)
to complaints about hikes

(?)

hikes occur near university (a)

Sentence (b) presents a slightly different problem. Although it does seem related to the main point of the paragraph, that connection is not explicit enough. The sentence is focused on what groups do, not on the results that such a protest can bring. By seeing this on her tree, the writer realized that she had shifted focus. Sentence (b) is indeed developing a part of the sentence above it, but it is not connected to the top-level idea of "results tenants can achieve." So she rewrote the last sentence to make it fit her real focus on results: "If an entire group of tenants can decide to leave in a group, this last-ditch effort will sometimes get results."

To sum up, then, checking the hierarchical structure of a paragraph by using either the Christensen indentation method or an issue tree lets you test the logical flow of a paragraph in two ways. It helps you see if each idea is logically related (parallel or subordinate) to other ideas and if all the ideas are logically connected to the main focus of the paragraph.

Cues for the reader

Issue trees and the Christensen method let you see if the underlying organization, or skeleton, of your paragraph is logically constructed. But notice how both of these methods rely on your turning the paragraph into a *visual* pattern with numbers and levels in order to see its structure clearly. Unfortunately, as writers we are usually confined to writing lines of words on a page, which the reader must mentally construct into a hierarchy of ideas as he or she reads. This problem is a real one for the writer, because in the process of reading, people often misunderstand complex discussions and restructure the writer's ideas.

Fortunately, our language also provides us with a large repertory of cues, hooks, and signals that let us make our structure and connections explicit. Some of these devices have been touched on previously. They range from grammatical signals such as conjunctions, to punctuation signals such as colons, to visual cues such as paragraph indentation, to verbal cues such as pronouns and repeated words. Look at the paragraph in Figure 12-3 and notice how many hooking devices the author has used to tie the paragraph together.

Here are some types of devices used:

1. *Pronouns.* The "we" in sentence 4 hooks back not only to "higher animals" but to the readers themselves, referred to in the first sentence with "our."
2. *Summary nouns and pronouns.* The "this" in sentence 6 pulls together the entire paragraph by referring to "experiment" and "play" in sentence 5 and to the "process of learning" in sentence 1. Sometimes a summary noun will do this job. For example, sentence 6 might have read: "Perhaps the nature of a *trial run* is what gives. . . ."
3. *Repeated words.* "Scientist," "learning," and "errors" reappear.
4. *Repeated stems.* Bronowski used "an experiment" (the noun) followed by "experiments" (the verb).
5. *Rewording of the same idea.* A "harmless trial run" is later redefined as a "setting in which errors are not fatal."
6. *Punctuation.* Colons usually tell us that an example or a list follows. Semicolons connect two main clauses that generally are closely related.
7. *Parallel construction.* The grammatically parallel construction of "the scientist experiments and the cub plays" (sentence 5) emphasizes the parallel connection Bronowski wishes to make.

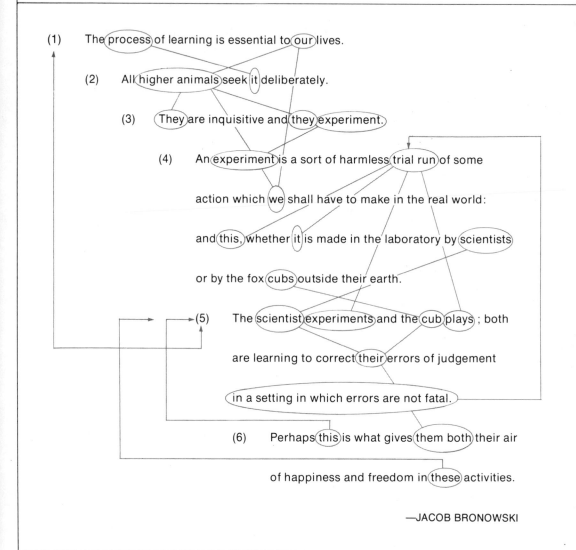

FIGURE **12-3**   *A passage with many word and phrase cues*

(1)   The process of learning is essential to our lives.

(2)   All higher animals seek it deliberately.

(3)   They are inquisitive and they experiment.

(4)   An experiment is a sort of harmless trial run of some

action which we shall have to make in the real world:

and this, whether it is made in the laboratory by scientists

or by the fox cubs outside their earth.

(5)   The scientist experiments and the cub plays ; both

are learning to correct their errors of judgement

in a setting in which errors are not fatal.

(6)   Perhaps this is what gives them both their air

of happiness and freedom in these activities.

—JACOB BRONOWSKI

Source: Jacob Bronowski, *The Common Sense of Science* (Cambridge: Harvard University Press, 1953).

The writer's judicious use of repetition is effective because it meets an important expectation readers bring to prose. Normally, readers expect sentences to begin with something they already know about or with a word or topic that was previously mentioned. We might call this the sentence's *old information*. Readers then expect the sentence to add something new, the sentence's *new information*. Notice how this pattern of old information leading to new information works in the following series of sentences.

Shopping for a Turkey

Old . . .   New . . .

The old information was stated in the title.
In buying a turkey, you get more meat for your money from a whole bird than from a boned, rolled turkey roast.

Old . . .   New . . .

The reference to "the whole bird" is old information from the preceding sentence.
And the bigger that whole bird is, the more meat you will have in proportion to bone.

Old . . .   New . . .

The reference to a turkey's weight is old information, but the fact of one-half waste is new.
A turkey weighing less than 12 pounds is one-half waste.

Old . . .   New . . .

"As a result" is old information, referring to the points made previously in the paragraph.
As a result, it is more economical to buy half of a large, 20 pounder than to buy a small, 10-pound turkey.

At times this pattern of moving from old information to new information is broken. For example:

Old . . .   New . . .
And the bigger that whole bird is, the more meat you will have in
New . . .   Old . . .
proportion to bone. One-half waste is what you'll get with a turkey

weighing less than 12 pounds.

Sometimes the sentence with new information at the beginning is confusing and needs rereading. However, by violating expectations, you can also create surprise and emphasis, as the sentence above did by surprising us with the phrase, "One-half waste . . ." To sum up, then, you can use various kinds of repetition, including the old information / new information pattern, to make clear connections between sentences.

In addition, you can make explicit connections by using some of the common words and phrases listed in Figure 12-4. These not only highlight the logical connection between your ideas, but often give the reader a preview of what is coming.

FIGURE **12-4**   *Common cues for the reader*

CUES THAT LEAD THE READER FORWARD

To show addition:		*To show time:*	
Again,	Moreover,	At length	Later,
And	Nor,	Immediately thereafter,	Previously,
And then,	Too,	Soon,	Formerly,
Besides	Next,	After a few hours,	First, second, etc.
Equally important,	First, second, etc.	Afterwards,	Next, etc.
Finally	Lastly,	Finally,	And then
Further,	What's more,	Then	
Furthermore,			

CUES THAT MAKE THE READER STOP AND COMPARE

But	Notwithstanding,	Although
Yet,	On the other hand,	Although this is true,
And yet,	On the contrary,	While this is true,
However,	After all,	Conversely,
Still	For all that,	Simultaneously,
Nevertheless,	In contrast,	Meanwhile
Nonetheless,	At the same time,	In the meantime,

CUES THAT DEVELOP AND SUMMARIZE

To give examples:	*To emphasize:*	*To repeat:*
For instance,	Obviously,	In brief,
For example,	In fact,	In short,
To demonstrate,	As a matter of fact,	As I have said,
To illustrate,	Indeed,	As I have noted,
As an illustration,	In any case,	In other words,
	In any event,	
	That is,	

To introduce conclusions:	*To summarize:*
Hence,	In brief,
Therefore,	On the whole,
Accordingly,	Summing up
Consequently,	To conclude,
Thus,	In conclusion,
As a result,	

Projects and Exercises

The following exercises will give you some straightforward practice in building a few basic kinds of sentence patterns. Many of the ideas about language mentioned here come from an interesting book called *Word Play* by Peter Farb, listed in the suggested readings at the end of Chapter 11.

1 *Making Details Modify.* In this exercise treat the top sentence as your basic, simple sentence. Go through the sentences beneath it and underline all of the key words or ideas. Then rewrite the basic sentence, using your underlined details to modify or replace part of the sentence. Here is an example:

> The Harbor Seal can't use its hind flippers on land.
>
> > This seal is thick-bodied.
> >
> > Its flippers are useless for walking.
>
> The thick-bodied Harbor Seal can't use its hind flippers for walking on land.

a. Much of our speech consists of pauses and hesitations.

> This occurs when speech is spontaneous.
>
> More than half of such speech may be so.

b. Listeners rarely pay attention to pauses.

> These pauses are by the speaker.
>
> Listeners don't notice pauses so long as the pauses are at certain places.
> Readers expect pauses in places that are significant grammatically.

c. When speaking in certain ways, people pause in the discourse.

> This happens when speech is careful and the speaker is self-conscious.
>
> Such pauses occur at the places made significant by grammar.

d. However, sometimes something else happens.

> This happens in situations in which speech is casual or spontaneous.
>
> The rate of pauses that are placed in a correct way drops significantly.

2 *Making Ideas Coordinate.* Treat the top sentence as your basic sentence. Transform the key points from each group into coordinate words or phrases that you can work into the basic sentence. That is, try to make them parallel to some other part of the basic sentence or parallel to the basic sentence itself. Naturally, you may have to reword some of the new elements. Here is an example:

The extinct Irish Elk was not exclusively Irish.

> It was not an elk.

> It was the largest deer that ever lived.

The extinct Irish Elk was <u>neither</u> exclusively Irish <u>nor</u> an elk, <u>but</u> was the largest deer that ever lived.

a. The human speaker is apparently born with a capacity for learning language.

> All people are able to use language with infinite creativity.

> Novel utterances can be constructed by humans even in unfamiliar speech situations.

b. The human speaker shares the globe with animals.

> Some animals shriek.

> Others squeek.

> Hoots, coos, howls, and calls are characteristic of some species.

c. Chimpanzees employ one kind of sound in social play.

> When a young chimp is lost, they make another sound.

> An attacked chimp makes a particular sound.

> Animals don't combine two or more kinds of sounds to send complicated messages.

3 *Making Ideas Subordinate and Modifying.* In the following exercise, the basic sentences, marked (B), are the core of a complete paragraph. The other sentences contain information that should be (S) subordinated to the basic sentence or (M) used to modify it. Figure out how the (S) and (M) sentences might be related to the basic sentence. Then express that relationship to the reader by using a grammatically subordinate structure or a modifying structure that adds information by modifying or expanding upon some other element of the basic sentence. Combine the information in the order presented, as in the following example:

> (S) Many advisors say that study habits affect success in college.
> (B) Something is true.
> (M) The thing is that relatively few teachers tell you how to study their subject.

> <u>Although</u> many advisors say that study habits affect success in college, it is true <u>that</u> relatively few teachers tell you how to study their subject.

a. (S) Children are not born with a tendency to speak baby talk.

   (B) What could explain its presence around the world?

(B)   Most adults claim something about it.

(M)   They claim that baby talk makes it easier for children to learn to speak.

(B)   Indeed, one thing is true.

(M)   The thing is that baby talk words have simpler consonants and fewer vowels than adult language.

(B)   But baby talk is actually a special language adults invent for talking to children.

(S)   An example of this would be "Is 'itsy-bitsy' easier to say than 'tiny'?"

(S)   Adults teach the language to children.

(S)   This only goes on for a few years.

(B)   Adults force children to stop using it.

b. (S)   The origins of language are lost in the past.

(B)   Sufficient documents exist for us to trace the early history of some modern languages.

(B)   The multiple origins of English are better known than the origins of many other languages.

(S)   A number of documents about English have survived.

(S)   The Roman occupation ended in A.D. 410.

(B)   Celtic was still the native tongue in Britain at that time.

(S)   Some Latin was spoken in the towns, but Celtic was the native tongue.

(B)   The Celts might have had a major influence on the English language.

(S)   The Celts as a people were subjugated first by the Romans, then by the Jutes, Angles, and Saxons.

(B)   Their effect was small.

(S)   Some Celtic place names do survive.

(M)   Examples of surviving names are Thames, Avon, and London.

(B)   Little more than a dozen Celtic words are used in today's vocabulary.

(M)   Words that are used include "curse," "cross," and "ass."

4   This editing problem is a test of your ingenuity. It asks you to take a given body of information (see the matrix below) and to combine ideas using a coordinate pattern, subordinate pattern, and additive (or modifying) pattern *all in one sentence.*

swimming	drown	requires water	builds stamina and health	necessary public safety skill
motorcycling	crash	requires bike, helmet	develops reflexes	conserves gasoline
tennis	bruises and strain	requires racquet and balls	builds reflexes, stamina, and health	supports a newly thriving national industry

a.   First, work *across* the matrix. Write one sentence for each sport using all the information in the row. In combining the ideas into a sentence, try to use all three patterns: coordination, subordination, and modification. Here is an example for the game of poker:

poker	insolvency	requires chips and a deck of cards	builds facial control and memory	keeps people off the streets

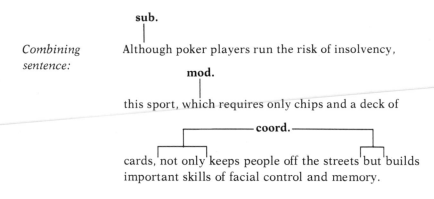

Combining sentence:

sub.

Although poker players run the risk of insolvency,

mod.

this sport, which requires only chips and a deck of

coord.

cards, not only keeps people off the streets but builds important skills of facial control and memory.

b. Now work *down* the matrix. Write one sentence for each column. To solve this problem you will have to generate a concept that ties all the facts together and then use whatever sentence patterns you need to fit all of the ideas into a sentence. The example below creates the new concept "equipment costs."

| Olympic pool |
| $5,000 Harley |
| $200 racquet |

Combining sentence: The equipment costs can be enormous for the swimmer
mod.
|

and motorcyclist who require an Olympic pool and $5,000
sub.
|

Harley, while the tennis player will, at most, pay only $200 for a racquet.

If You Would Like to Read More

If you would like to know more about editing with a reader in mind, see:

Becker, A. L. "A Tagmemic Approach to Paragraph Analysis." *College Composition and Communication,* 16 (Oct. 1965) 237–42. ▪ This study includes a discussion of basic paragraph patterns.

Christensen, Francis. "A Generative Rhetoric of the Paragraph." *College Composition and Communication,* 16 (Oct. 1965) 144–56. ▪ This article gives a detailed discussion of hierarchical paragraph organization.

Larson, Richard. "Toward a Linear Rhetoric of the Essay." *College Composition and Communication,* 22 (May 1971) 140–46. ▪ The author studies the function of paragraphs in a developing argument.

O'Hare, Frank. *Sentence-Combining: Improving Student Writing Without Formal Grammar Instruction.* Urbana, Ill.: *National Council of Teachers of English Bulletin,* 1973. ▪ This book gives a detailed discussion of ways of combining simple sentences, or kernels, into complex sentences.

Index

A 0
B 1
C 2
D 3
E 4
F 5
G 6
H 7
I 8
J 9

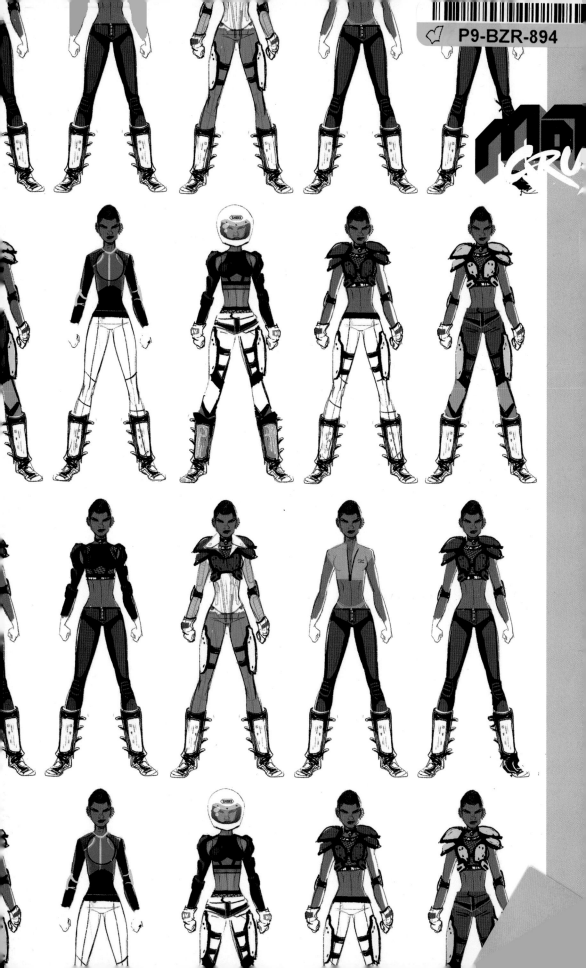

WORLD GRAND PRIX
WGP RECOMMENDS

CRUSH
CRUSH Vol.2
CRU

Creators
BABS TARR
BRENDEN FLETCHER
CAMERON STEWART

Original Cover Artists
**BABS TARR, CAMERON STEWART, KRIS ANKA,
JAKE WYATT, KEVIN WADA**

BREAKDOWNS
BABS TARR, JAKE WYATT, ROB HAYNES, PAUL REINWAND

Color Assistants
HEATHER DANFORTH, VICTORIA EVANS, ELLEN ALSOP

Lettering
ADITYA BIDIKAR

Logo, Publication Design, WGP In-World Captions
TOM MULLER

Editor
JENNIFER M. SMITH

MOTOR CRUSH Vol. 2 — Originally published as MOTOR CRUSH #6–11

ULTERION

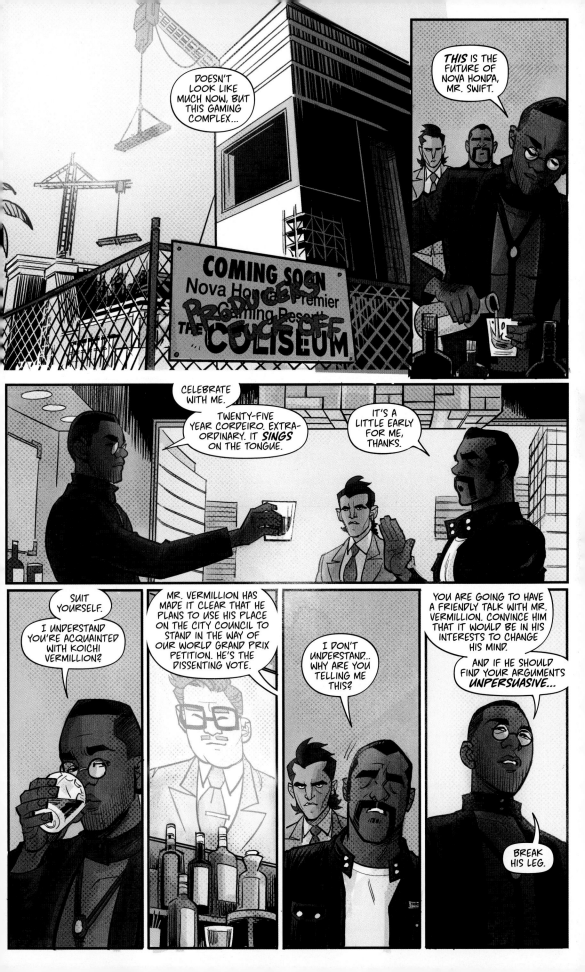

WHEN THE WGP ESTABLISHES ITSELF IN NOVA, YOU ARE IN A GOOD POSITION TO BECOME A STAR. YOU'VE BEEN A NATIONAL CHAMPION, WE CAN HELP MAKE YOU GO *GLOBAL.*

I'M SORRY, MR. YAGO--*SIR*--BUT... I'M GOING TO HAVE TO DECLINE.

THE *DRINK* WAS AN OFFER, SULLIVAN.

THIS IS NOT THAT.

LOOK, I KNOW I BORROWED SOME MONEY FROM YOU, BUT I'M GOOD FOR IT. THE SHOP IS DOING WELL AND AS YOU SAY, I'VE GOT SOME GOOD RACES COMING UP--

YOU MISUNDERSTAND THE TERMS OF OUR ARRANGEMENT. I'M NOT IN THE HABIT OF GIVING OUT LOANS.

I MADE AN *INVESTMENT.* AND I EXPECT A RETURN.

BUT...KOICHI IS MY FRIEND.

OUR *DAUGHTERS* ARE FRIENDS...

WELL THEN.

I EXPECT YOU'D WANT ONLY *ONE* OF THEM TO GET HURT.

AND DON'T THINK WE DON'T KNOW WHAT YOU SPENT THAT MONEY ON.

RRRMBLLE

BING BONG

DOM, FORGIVE ME...

...SULLY? WHAT ARE YOU DOING HERE SO LATE?

IS EVERYTHING OKAY?

I'M SORRY, KOICHI. I'M SORRY.

...W-WHAT IS THAT FOR?

JULI!

JULIANNE!

BAM

SULLY, WHAT'S WRONG?

DAD...?

I NEED TO TALK TO YOU. RIGHT NOW.

SULLY, WHAT--

RIGHT NOW!

EVERYTHING'S FINE. DON'T WORRY.

DAD, WHERE ARE YOU GOING?

JUST STAY RIGHT THERE AND EAT YOUR BREAKFAST, BABY. BACK IN A MINUTE, OKAY?

LET US BY, MINK.

YOU THOUGHT YOU COULD JUST *RUN*, SWIFT? YOU THOUGHT WE WOULDN'T COME FOR YOU?

WE KNOW WHERE YOU LIVE. WE KNOW WHERE *SHE* LIVES. YOU'RE NEVER OUT OF OUR SIGHT.

"I PUT A *TRACKER* ON YOUR BIKE, IDIOT."

BOSS ISN'T HAPPY.

I DIDN'T AGREE TO HURT PEOPLE. I WON'T DO IT. I'M NOT YOUR MUSCLE.

SULLY...I--I CAN'T EXPLAIN BUT...PUT THIS IN THE GAS TANK.

DOM'S *MEDICINE?* WHAT? WHY?

JUST... TRUST ME. PLEASE.

THIS IS BRONCOS.

HEY! WHAT IS THAT?

NOW *GO!* DRIVE!

DO IT!

BRM

BRM

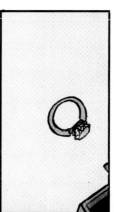
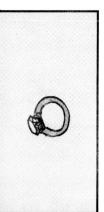

M-MY LEG...MY...

THAT'S THE ONE YOU OWED US.

YOU WERE NEVER GOING TO BE SAFE.

NONE OF US ARE.

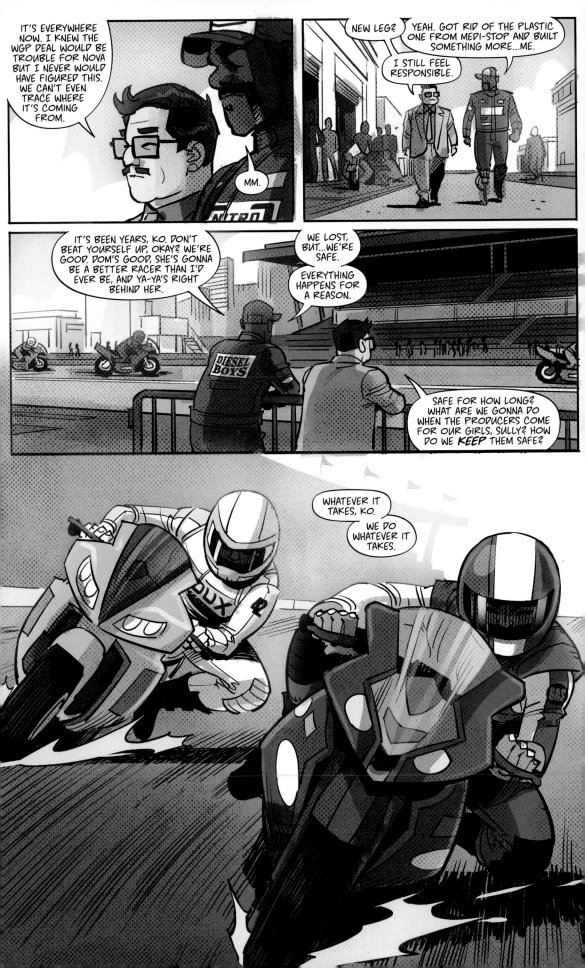

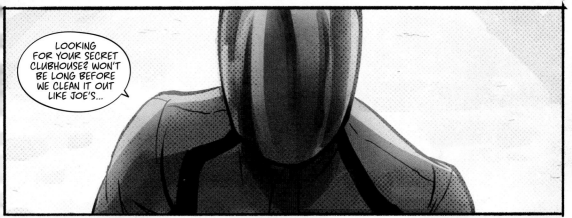

COME ON, LET'S GO THIS WAY...

EVERYTHING'S DIFFERENT NOW, DOM. THERE'S BEEN A REAL CRACKDOWN. CRUSH POSSESSION IS A SERIOUS CRIME. AND WHEN THE COPS DON'T SWEEP UP, THE PRODUCERS SEND IN THEIR ENFORCERS TO BREAK SOME LEGS.

YOU STILL HAVEN'T TOLD ME WHERE MY DAD IS...

WELL, THAT'S THE THING, DOM. HE'S ONE OF THE ENFORCERS.

WHAT?!

HE'S A BIG GUY, LOTS OF MUSCLE...

BUT...DAD WOULDN'T HURT ANYONE--

WELL, HE HAS. A LOT OF PEOPLE. I'VE SEEN HIM WORK OVER SOME OF THE BANGERS. IT'S... SCARY.

I THINK SOMETHING CHANGED IN HIM WHEN YOU DISAPPEARED.

WELL, NOW I'M BACK.

KNOCK KNOCK KNOCK

I DON'T WANT TO INTRUDE ON... **WHATEVER.** BEA AND I WERE JUST CONCERNED WHEN YOU DIDN'T COME HOME LAST NIGHT. THOUGHT I'D CHECK HERE.

GUESS I DIDN'T NEED TO WORRY...

NO, NO, LOLA, IT'S NOT LIKE THAT. CALAX WAS JUST--

WHO'S THIS? SOMEONE ELSE FOR OUR LITTLE MISSION?

MISSION?

AH, THIS IS LOLA. MY, UH, MY...FRIEND.

CALAX GOTHARD. CALL ME CAL.

I'M GONNA GO TO THE MARKET AND GET A BOX OF QRINKLE ROUNDS. THE SWEET BLUE KIND.

I'LL BRING ENOUGH FOR ALL OF US.

REALLY? A DIRTY CRUSH SCUDDER?! I DON'T EVEN--

WOW.

I REALLY THOUGHT YOU KNEW ME BETTER THAN THAT.

...SORRY.

SO...WHAT IS THIS ABOUT A MISSION?

TWENTY YEARS AGO, RISING SEAWATERS CUT OFF THE LAND WE NOW KNOW AS TURTLE ISLAND. A BRIDGE WAS BUILT TO CONNECT THEM, BUT PASSAGE IS TOTALLY CONTROLLED BY THE PRODUCERS, SO WE HAVE TO FIND ANOTHER WAY ACROSS.

WE CAN'T ARRIVE BY WATER, BECAUSE THERE ARE ARTILLERY TOWERS WATCHING FOR TRESPASSING BOATS. THEY'LL SINK US BEFORE WE CAN EVEN TAKE A BREATH.

SO WHAT ELSE IS THERE? WE CAN'T FLY...

WE GO UNDER-GROUND.

HERE. THIS PIPELINE CARRIED GARBAGE AND SOLID WASTE TO THE MAINLAND FOR PROCESSING BEFORE BEING PUMPED BACK OUT INTO THE OCEAN.

YOU WANT US TO GO THROUGH THE POOP PIPE?!

EXCUSE ME?! I DID NOT SIGN UP FOR THIS!

RELAX, IT'S NOT IN USE ANY LONGER. IT MAY NOT SMELL GREAT BUT IT SHOULD BE EMPTY, AND LARGE ENOUGH FOR US TO DRIVE THROUGH. IF WE BURN WE SHOULD ONLY BE IN THERE FOR A FEW MINUTES.

IT'S ALL WE'VE GOT.

I AM NOT LETTING YOU RIDE MY BABY THROUGH A SEWER, DOM.

I'LL GET MY DUDES TO MEET US WITH SOME CLANGERS WE WON'T SWEAT LEAVING BEHIND.

YOU GUYS GOT A PHONE I CAN USE?

LIFESTREAM
At the tone, enter number. Long distance charges may apply.
BEEP

HOW ABOUT 1-800-KISS-MY-ASS?

FWVVV FWVVV

FWVVV

I'M ACTUALLY SURPRISED THAT IT WOULD BE THIS--

--EASY...

I THOUGHT YOU SAID THIS TUNNEL WAS DISUSED?

I GUESS THE MACHINERY IS STILL POWERED UP...

UP THERE...

THAT LOOKS LIKE A RELEASE BUTTON. MAYBE IF IT'S PRESSED THE FAN WILL STOP LONG ENOUGH TO PASS THROUGH.

IT'S UP SO HIGH, THOUGH...

WE'D NEED SOMETHING THAT CAN GET UP THERE...

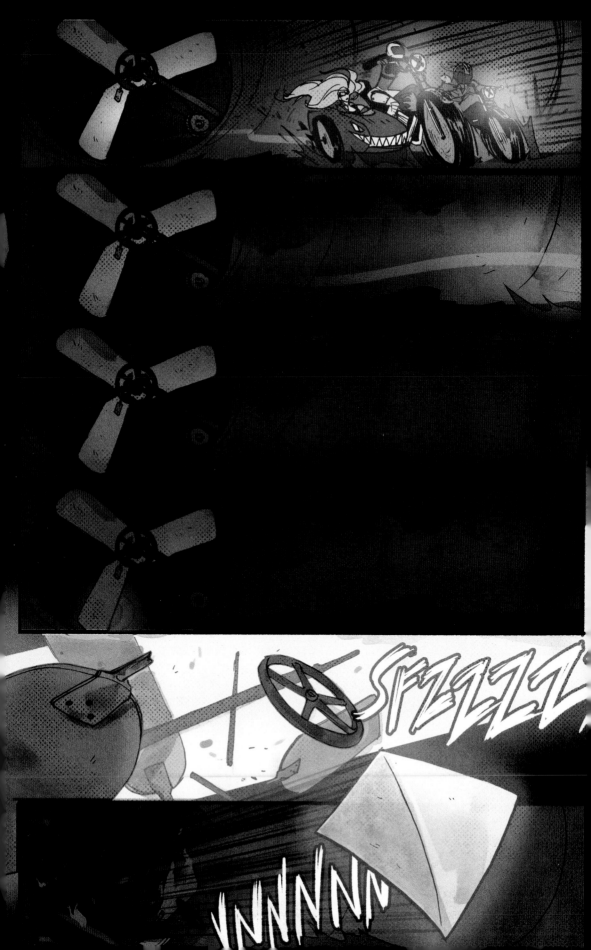

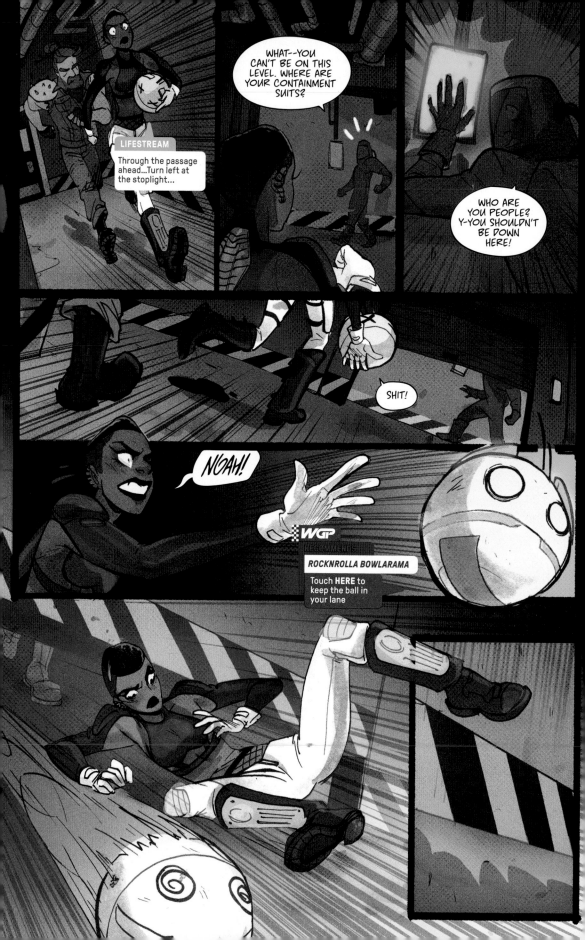

WORLD GRAND PRIX
WGP

WORLD GRAND PRIX
WGP

WORLD GRAND PRIX
WGP

WORLD GRAND PRIX
WGP

Every now and then, Dad would load up the van and drive us up the coast to the miro tree grove for a picnic.

Years before, there had been a chemical spill upstream, and now the sunshine that filtered through the leaves made everything in the grove look blue.

It felt like another world, where normal rules didn't apply.

KRANK!

AGH!

YOU'RE OKAY, HONEY. IT'S NOT BROKEN.

I'LL SORT YOU OUT BEFORE YOUR DAD GETS BACK WITH THE FIREWOOD.

Juli was a miracle worker. She could make any place feel safe. Like home.

I used to dream she'd move to Nova and live with us.

SEE? ALL BETTER. NO NEED FOR TEARS.

P-PLEASE DON'T TELL DAD I CRIED...

THIS IS BETWEEN YOU AND ME, BABE.

WE KNOW...

WHERE DID YOU GO? THE DAY OF DAD'S ACCIDENT, HE SAID YOU JUST DISAPPEARED! HE NEVER TALKED ABOUT IT, NEVER TOLD ME WHAT HAPPENED...I THOUGHT YOU MIGHT HAVE DIED!

I--I NEVER GOT TO SAY GOODBYE TO YOU...

IS THIS WHERE YOU'VE BEEN, ALL THIS TIME? ARE YOU A HOSTAGE OR PRISONER OR--

This gas is making me float...and giving me a rush. Wait, is this--

THIS IS CRUSH!

DRIP BY DRIP, ATOM BY ATOM...

PARTICLES RACING, JOINING AND DIVIDING, RESHAPING ME.

YOUR MEDICINE.

STRETCHING THROUGH TIME.

WE'VE GOT TO GET YOU OUT OF HERE!

HE'S GOING TO KILL SULLY, DOMINO.

WHAT? WHO?

KRAKOOM

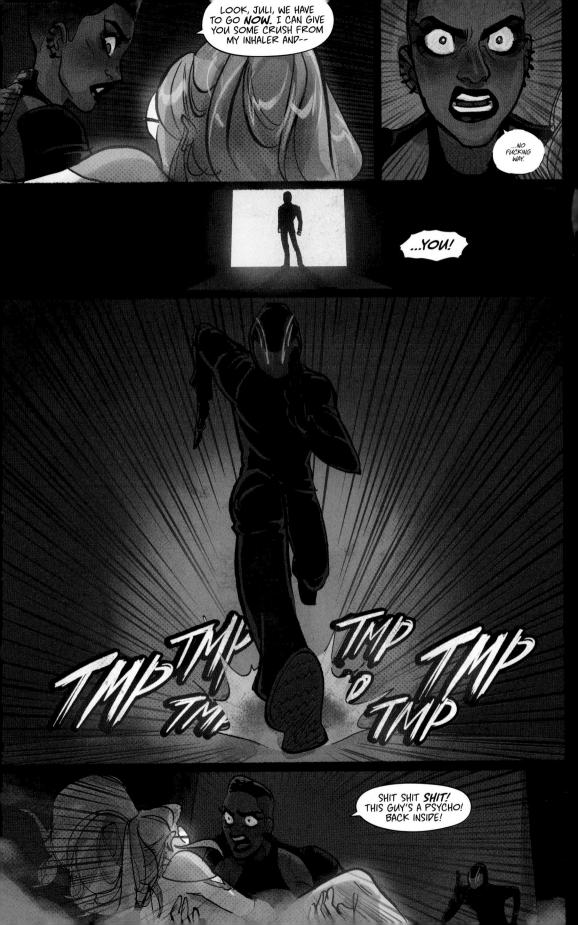

YOU KNOW HOW TO HANDLE ONE OF THESE THINGS?

IT'S GOT A FEW TOO MANY WHEELS FOR MY LIKING, IF I'M BEING HONEST.

CRAZY DAY, HUH? HAH! YOU TWO GOOD?

I AM NOW. THANKS, CAL.

TAKE CARE OF THE REST OF THE STASH.

DENIM FANG'LL TAKE GOOD CARE OF OUR CUT.

BUT DON'T WORRY, CRICKET, A LITTLE BIRDIE TOLD ME THIS ISN'T THE LAST SCORE YOU'RE GONNA LEAD US TO.

FANG-A-LANG!!

WHAT? WHAT'S THAT SUPPOSED TO--

I NEED TO GET INSIDE.

BUT WHAT'S HE TALKING ABOUT? WHAT LITTLE BIRDIE?

KEEP IT DOWN, OKAY? I HAVE NEIGHBORS.

DON'T LET BEATRIZ SEE THE CRUSH. I PROMISED HER I'D STAY OUT OF YOUR DRAMA. SHE'LL KILL ME.

I'LL JUST KEEP OUT OF HER WAY AS MUCH AS--

...BEA?

BEATRIZ!

WHAT HAPPENED? WHO DID THIS? ARE YOU HURT?

MY HEAD...

PRODUCERS. THEY KNOW I'M HERE.

YEAH, THEY SURE DO. AND THEY HAD A MESSAGE FOR YOU.

THEY SAID NEXT TIME THEY WON'T BE SO GENTLE.

THEY SAID YOU HAVE TO GIVE YOURSELF UP TO MINK MASTERS.

I'M SORRY, LO. SHE CAN'T STAY HERE.

I'M NOT GONNA LET HER RUIN US LIKE SHE DOES EVERYTHING ELSE.

BEA, SHE JUST LOST SOMEONE...LET'S JUST GIVE HER A FEW HOURS TO FIGURE SOMETHING OUT--

LO! LOOK AT OUR HOME! I WAS ATTACKED! BECAUSE OF HER!

SHE'S RIGHT.

I SHOULDN'T STAY HERE. IT'S BEST IF I GO.

THANKS FOR YOUR KINDNESS.

I'M REALLY SORRY.

Where the hell am I going? I don't even know where I am.

I don't know the rules anymore.

Once upon a time this guy and I raced head-to-head on every track in the circuit. He was always #1. But we both knew it was only a matter of time before I beat him.

Decimus quit the game to shit-talk me and I...

CRUSH KILLS!
DECIMUS SAID NO.
DO YOU?

A WGP Public Service Announcement

VERMILLION FOR THE WIN?
WGP Racer Sonoya Vermillion poised to unseat champ Clover Lazan in finals

Hot rockets...

VERMILLION FOR THE WIN
WGP Racer Sonoy

Please be home, please be home...

OKAY, OKAY, RELAX!

I'M ONLY FAST ON MY MOTOR--

...

WHAA-AAA--AAAY

YA-YA! YA-YA!

WHAT'S HAPPENING OUT HERE? ALWAYS A RUCKUS!

SHE'S OKAY. SHE JUST PASSED OUT.

I GUESS SHE HAD A SHOCK.

UM, HI, MR. VERMILLION...

MOJ BOŽE, DOMINO?! BOŽE!

I...I CAN HARDLY BELIEVE IT. IT'S REALLY YOU? YOU'RE NOT A GHOST?

HEH, YEAH, IT'S ME. LET'S GET YA-YA UP AND...

AND THEN I NEED TO ASK FOR YOUR HELP.

AH. WELL. I'M REALLY NOT SURE THAT IT'S WISE FOR YOU TO BE HERE RIGHT NOW...

...OH... OKAY?

WELL, CAN I COME BACK LATER? OR TOMORROW? I'M REALLY WORRIED ABOUT MY DAD--

I'M SORRY, IT'S A VERY BAD TIME. SONOYA IS QUITE BUSY WITH HER RACING COACH, THE FINALS ARE ONLY A FEW DAYS FROM NOW.

IF HE WERE TO SEE YOU, IT WOULD BE... COMPLICATED.

HOLD UP, I'VE GOT WAY BIGGER PROBLEMS THAN THE WGP LEARNING I'M ALIVE. I NEED TO--

AM I DREAMING? DOMINO IS BACK?!

EEEEEE!!

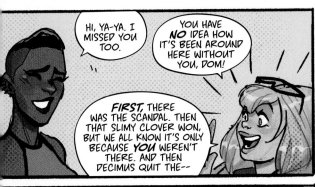

HI, YA-YA. I MISSED YOU TOO.

YOU HAVE **NO** IDEA HOW IT'S BEEN AROUND HERE WITHOUT YOU, DOM!

FIRST, THERE WAS THE SCANDAL. THEN THAT SLIMY CLOVER WON, BUT WE ALL KNOW IT'S ONLY BECAUSE **YOU** WEREN'T THERE. AND THEN DECIMUS QUIT THE--

OH! DOM! YOU'RE NEVER GONNA BELIEVE THE HOTNESS THAT'S HELPING ME BEAT THAT LITTLE SNOT CLOVER LAZAN THIS WEEK!

I HEARD A SCREAM.

IS THERE A PROBLEM?

DOM, MEET MY NEW TRAINER--

DECIMUS WEXLER.

WE WERE STRATEGIZING OVER LUNCH. DECIMUS SAYS THE WGP IS TOTALLY CORRUPT, BUT HE CAN HELP ME GET A CLEAN WIN! ISN'T THAT RIGHT, HOTROD?

YES, THAT IS CORRECT. AN EXAMPLE FOR ALL.

WE CAN PROVE THAT THERE'S NO ROOM FOR CHEATERS AND **ADDICTS** IN THE WGP.

Y-YOU WANT ME TO FIX YOU A PLATE, DOMINO? YOU MUST BE STARVING!

THAT'S OKAY, MR. VERMILLION. MAYBE I **SHOULD** COME BACK ANOTHER TIME.

DAD, THESE FALLATTIES ARE **SO** GOOD!

SPLRTT

BETTER EVEN THAN LAST TIME!

THERE'S MORE IF YOU WANT 'EM, YA!

IS EVERYTHING OKAY, DOMINO? YOU HAVEN'T TOUCHED YOUR FOOD.

SORRY, MR. VERMILLION.

I LOST MY APPETITE.

LIKE YOU LOSE EVERY-THING?

WOW... THAT'S KINDA MEAN, DECIMUS...

MAYBE MEAN IS WHAT SHE **NEEDS.** SOMEONE TO TOUGHEN HER UP AND KEEP HER FOCUSED ON WHAT'S **IMPORTANT.**

THERE IS A PATH FOR HER, IF SHE'LL TAKE IT.

...AREN'T YOU SUPPOSED TO BE TRAINING **ME**?

NOW, I THINK WE ALL WANT WHAT'S BEST FOR DOM, SHE'S MADE SOME MISTAKES BUT--

YOU KNOW WHAT'S IMPORTANT TO ME? MY **FAMILY.**

YOU REMEMBER MY DAD?

YEAH, YOU **DO.**

VERY **HIGH-STRUNG,** AS I RECALL.

YOU F--

OH MY GOD, **WHAT**?! NO!

Yeah, I'm sparked. I love Mr. Vermillion but...

I don't know if I'll *ever* understand how he could sit by and do nothing while my dad--his *friend*--is in trouble.

Taking care of *mine* means running a gauntlet through a million armed Enforcers into a heavily defended fortress, risking life and limb... *again.*

I know he's just trying to protect Ya-Ya. We all need to take care of our own.

Well, if I've gotta gamble, the city's biggest mega-casino is probably the right place for it...

WHAT EXACTLY ARE YOU DOING?

LO?

YEAH, IT'S ME. I FIXED UP THE CATBALL, REPLACED THE LEV-DRIVE. FIGURED I'D SEND HER OVER TO THE HOUSEBOAT, BUT SHE TRACKED YOU HERE INSTEAD--

GREAT! LISTEN, SONOYA'S GONNA NEED SOME EMERGENCY WORK ON HER BIKE FOR TOMORROW'S RACE...

UH...OKAY, SEND HER OVER HERE TO THE SHOP. BUT...*ALONE.* I DON'T WANT YOU TO COME.

...WHAT? WHY?

YOU **KNOW** WHY. WE'VE BEEN THROUGH THIS A MILLION TIMES.

LESS THAN A **DAY** AFTER YOU RAIDED AND DESTROYED THE PRODUCERS' STRONGHOLD I FIND YOU HERE, PROBABLY PLANNING SOME OTHER CRANKSHIT STUNT. YOU JUST CAN'T STOP YOURSELF. YOU MAY NEED CRUSH TO LIVE, BUT I DON'T THINK YOU *FEEL* ALIVE WITHOUT *DANGER.*

I'M OUT, DOM. FOR GOOD.

NO, WAIT, DON'T--

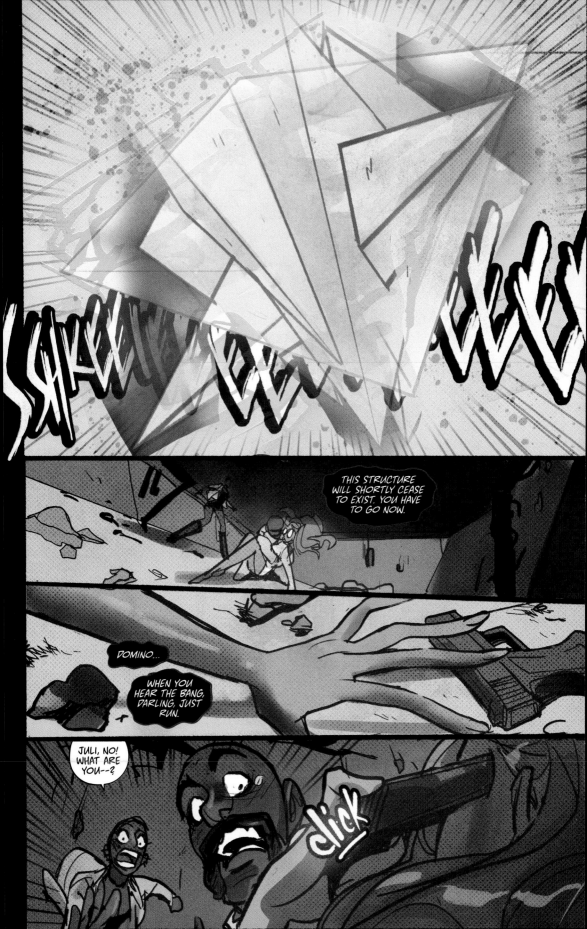

WGP
INFOPOP
IN MEMORIAM

"We call for a unit of silence to honor those lost in the tragic collapse of Nova Honda's Coliseum complex last night. May their spirits ride on to peace."

—Praveen de Blois, WGP Vice President, Sales and Marketing

CAN'T BELIEVE IT'S GONE...

JUST GET ON WITH THE RACE, GODDAMNIT!

SHUT UP, ASSHOLE!

ALL RIGHT, FELLAS, SETTLE DOWN.

INFOPOP
NEWSBULLETIN
WGP
World Grand Prix vows to rebuild Nova Honda Coliseum. Sponsors flood in from around the globe.
Click HERE to pledge support.

COLISEUM

FLASHBACK
The Coliseum was a cultural hub of Nova Honda.
Touch HERE to see more historical images.

FEELS WEIRD NOT BEING AT THE TRACK, BEA.

I KNOW THIS IS HARD FOR YOU, LO. THANKS FOR KEEPING ME COMPANY TODAY.

IT'S GOOD TO BE WITH THOSE YOU LOVE DURING TOUGH TIMES...

WHAT THE HELL IS THAT?!
...SHIT.
SWWEEEEE
SWWEEEE
RIDE HARD FOR THE EXITS!
NOW!
CRICKET!! GET YOUR ASS OUTTA--
WHAT IN THE HELL--?
"I COULDN'T COMPREHEND WHAT I SAW IN THERE, BUT I DIDN'T STICK AROUND TO FIGURE IT OUT..."

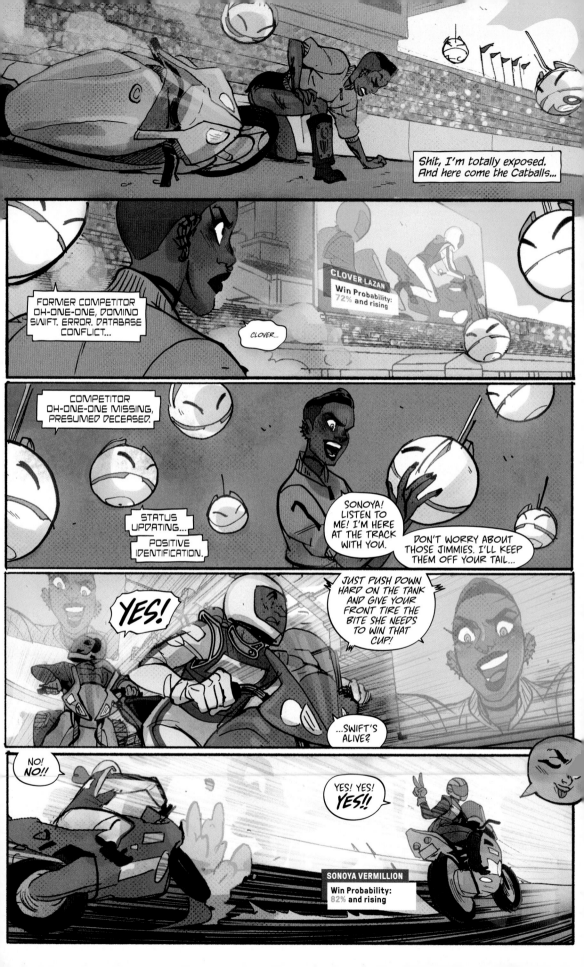

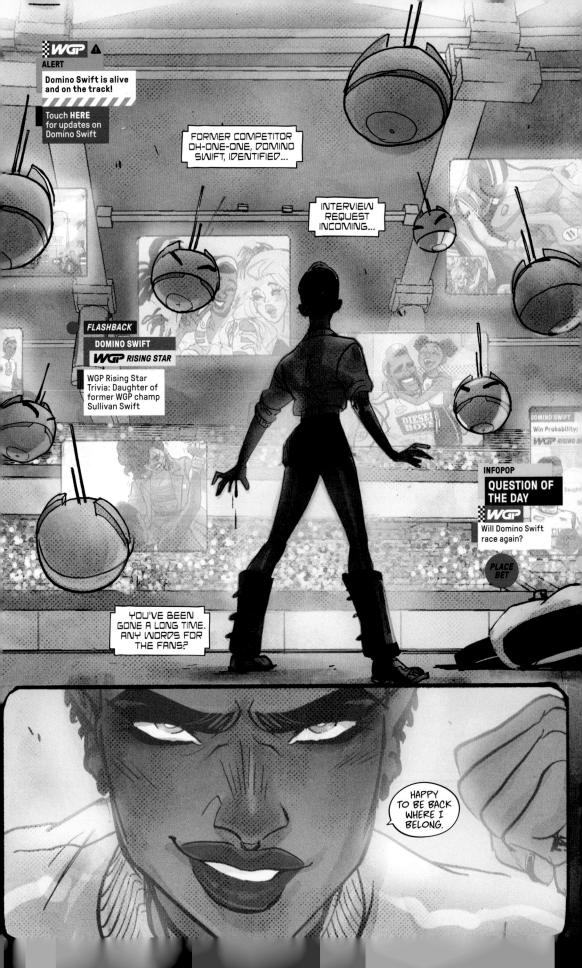

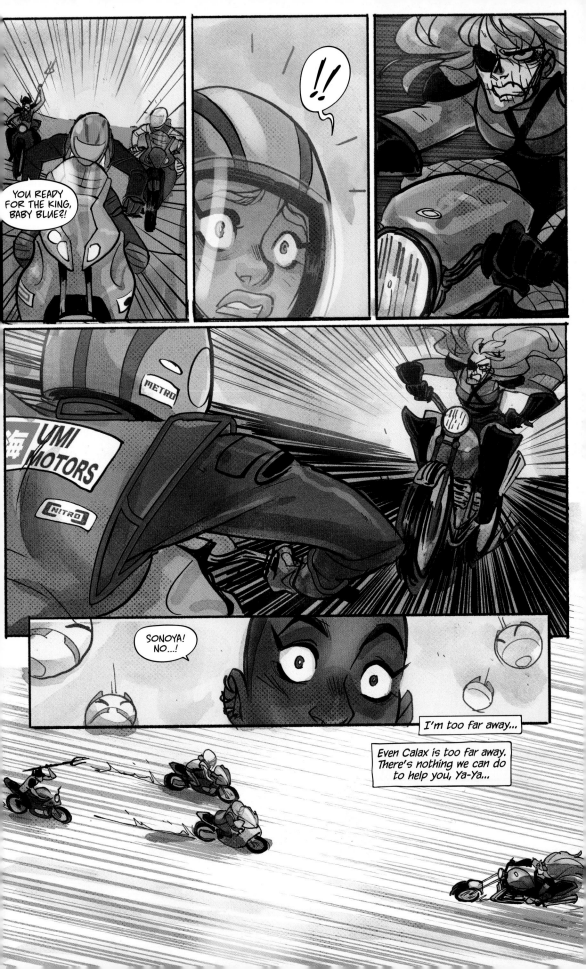

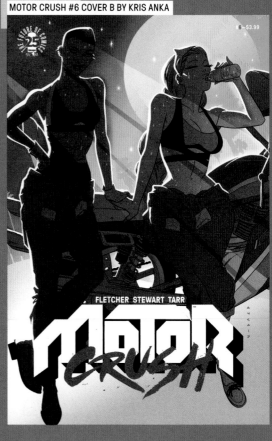

MOTOR CRUSH #7 COVER A BY BABS TARR

MOTOR CRUSH #7 COVER B BY CAMERON STEWART

MOTOR CRUSH #8 COVER A BY BABS TARR

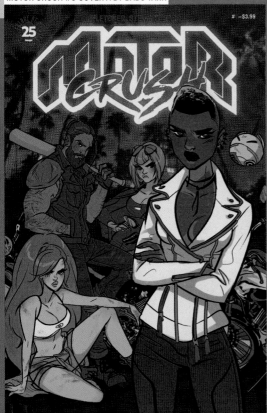

MOTOR CRUSH #8 COVER B BY CAMERON STEWART

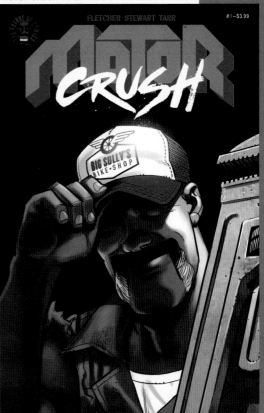

MOTOR CRUSH #9 COVER A BY BABS TARR

MOTOR CRUSH #9 COVER B BY CAMERON STEWART

MOTOR CRUSH #10 COVER A BY BABS TARR

MOTOR CRUSH #10 COVER B BY CAMERON STEWART

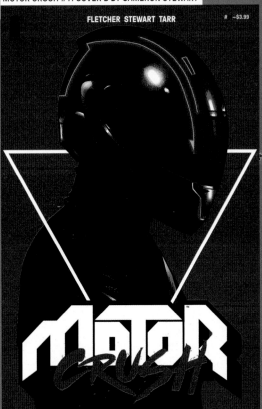

FLETCHER STEWART TARR

~$3.99

ORIGINAL MOTOR CRUSH #6–11
COVERS, ILLUSTRATED BY BABS
TARR AND CAMERON STEWART, KRIS
ANKA, JAKE WYATT, AND KEVIN WADA,
DESIGNED BY TOM MULLER.

First printing. May 2018. Published by Image Comics, Inc. Office of publication: 2701 NW Vaughn St., Suite 780, Portland, OR 97210. Copyright © 2018 Brenden Fletcher, Cameron Stewart, and Barbara Tarr. All rights reserved. Contains material originally published in single magazine form as MOTOR CRUSH #6-11. "Motor Crush," its logos, and the likenesses of all characters herein are trademarks of Brenden Fletcher, Cameron Stewart, and Barbara Tarr, unless otherwise noted. "Image" and the Image Comics logos are registered trademarks of Image Comics, Inc. No part of this publication may be reproduced or transmitted, in any form or by any means (except for short excerpts for journalistic or review purposes), without the express written permission of Brenden Fletcher, Cameron Stewart, and Barbara Tarr, or Image Comics, Inc. All names, characters, events, and locales in this publication are entirely fictional. Any resemblance to actual persons (living or dead), events, or places, without satirical intent, is coincidental. Printed in the USA. For information regarding the CPSIA on this printed material call: 203-595-3636 and provide reference #RICH-789145. Representation: Law Offices of Harris M. Miller II, P.C (rights.inquiries@gmail.com). ISBN: 978-1-5343-0551-9